THE HISTORY OF PAYROLL IN THE U.S.

THE EVOLUTION OF THE PROFESSION AND THE PROCESS FROM COLONIAL AMERICA THROUGH THE END OF THE 20TH CENTURY

Written by Leonard A. Haug, CPP

Edited by Michael P. O'Toole, Esq.

Published by the American Payroll Association

In the preparation of this text, every effort has been made to offer the most current, correct, and clearly understandable information possible. Nonetheless, inadvertent errors can occur, and tax rules and regulations are constantly changing.

This material is distributed with the understanding that the publisher and author are not engaged in rendering legal, accounting, or other professional services. If legal advice or other professional assistance is required, the service of your attorney or certified public accountant should be sought. Readers are encouraged to consult with appropriate professional advisors for advice concerning specific matters before making decisions affecting their individual operations.

Please visit our Web site at americanpayroll.org

ISBN: 1-930471-12-2

Printed in the United States

Dedication

This book is dedicated to payroll professionals of the past, present and future, and to the memory of Donald W. Sharper, founder of the American Payroll Association, who gave the profession both focus and energy and who taught us the power of a positive attitude.

Leonard A. Haug, CPP

Acknowledgments

The idea for this book was born out of a love of history and a passion for the subject of payroll. The absence of a book on the history of payroll was the driving force. The American Payroll Association provided the support and encouragement to take on the project and for close to three years these elements have kept me focused and committed to the effort.

While the concept for this book was conceived some three years earlier, it has taken many hours and miles of physical and electronic travel, over the last several years, to locate, collect, organize, and compile the material.

This book would not have been possible without the assistance and contributions of many organizations and people. Through this process, I have gained a whole new respect for researchers, archivists, historians, curators, and librarians, both in the private and public sectors. I have found them, with few exceptions, to be very knowledgeable and responsive to those in search of information. I would like to extend a special thanks to the Fitchburg Public Library and to the Fitchburg State College Library, both of Fitchburg Massachusetts, for their frequent assistance and guidance.

I would also like to acknowledge the support given to the author by many associations, companies, government agencies, historical societies, institutions, libraries, museums, and publishers for their willingness to share information and, of course, to grant permissions to use copyrighted text and images that appear throughout this book.

I would also like to thank the following members of the American Payroll Association staff for their efforts in bringing this project to completion: Michael P. O'Toole, Esq., Senior Director of Publications and Government Relations (editor); John J. Cervini, Jr., Multimedia Manager (layout and production); Donna Greenfield, Manager, Art Department (cover design and photo enhancement); and Jennifer Sanfilippo, Graphic Designer (photo enhancement).

This effort has been a wonderful journey, and I am grateful to all of those (living and deceased) who have made my "travels" on this book both educational and enjoyable and who have helped me to appreciate, first hand, the fact that few books, if any, are ever the work of just one individual.

Cover photos: Payroll Flow Chart courtesy of U.S. Rubber Co.; Pay Window courtesy of Westinghouse Electric Co.; Esso Oil Refinery Workers courtesy of National Archives

Inside front cover photos (clockwise from top left) courtesy of: Charles River Museum of Industry; J.L. Nichols & Company; American Textile History Museum; Lowell National Historical Park

Inside rear cover photos (clockwise from top left) courtesy of Porter-Cable Machine Co.; Worcester Historical Society; Richard Van Vleck; Unisys Corporation

Introduction

There are many fine books on payroll administration, accounting and tax compliance to aid the payroll professional to perform his or her job. These technical books are absolutely essential to train new payroll employees and to help more experienced payroll personnel keep pace with constantly changing laws and regulations.

However, there is no book on the history of the profession and the evolution of the process within the United States.

The history of payroll is a rich one and it is closely linked to the history of America. It is a story built largely on fact but supplemented by fiction and folklore, with much of it captured in images and literature. The paymaster (as the early practitioner was often referred to) and the pay process have literally touched the life of every American in some direct or indirect manner since the very earliest days of American history.

Americans love to talk about payday, the payroll, and the paycheck, and even though the process has changed dramatically over the years, the basic elements of the profession and the process especially as related to the human dynamics of the function have remained virtually unchanged.

This book was conceived on the notion that the evolution of the profession and the process would be of interest not only to those in the profession but also to a broader readership with a keen interest in anything pertaining to American history.

In order to fairly represent the perspectives of the various time periods covered in this book, the author has attempted to utilize as many artists, photographers and writers of each time period as possible.

Therefore, *The History of Payroll in the U.S.* to a large extent is an anthology – a collection of images and writings about paymasters and payrolls presented by those who have performed the work and by those close to them – the employer, the worker, and all others who have had important observations and commentary to offer.

At the same time, the evolution of the payroll discipline and the process have been molded and changed by the events of each decade. The story of the payroll function and process is in many ways a fragmented one. It is only with the ability to look back that the story of the function and the process can be presented in a manner that seems logically ordered to one living and working in the twenty-first century.

It is the hope of the author that this book will give pride to those in the profession and provide a sense of heritage and interest in payroll history while at the same time giving to all readers some greater appreciation of the many contributions that payroll professionals have made over the course of American history.

About the Author

Leonard A. Haug, CPP has always tried "to be on top of things" and has had a passion for payroll ever since he assumed his position as Payroll Manager for Digital Equipment Corporation back in the mid-1980s. Over the next 15 years he would build and lead his payroll team to recognized payroll best in class status in areas of quality, customer service, and cost.

For almost as long, Mr. Haug has been an active member of the American Payroll Association, serving as both a member and chairperson of many boards and committees. He has received numerous accolades for his contributions to the profession, including the 1994 American Payroll Association Payroll Man of the Year Award.

Mr. Haug has authored and co-authored articles, publications, and books and is a frequent speaker on payroll and related topics.

Mr. Haug is pictured in this mid 1990s photo (on the far right) with members of the Digital Equipment Corporation Payroll Team to whom he readily admits he owes much of his business success.

The author resides in Princeton, Massachusetts with his wife, Carole. They have one daughter, Laura.

Table of Contents

CHAPTER 1: Ancient Roots

The Beginning of Organized Governments and the Chaldean-Babylonian Empire 1

Business and Pay Practices Among Other Ancient Peoples 1

The Roman Army Paymaster and Pay Process 1

The Origins of Metallic and Paper Money 2

A Slow Evolutionary Process 3

Reference Sources 4

CHAPTER 2: European and British Heritage

European Heritage 5

British Heritage 5

    The Linkage Between "Pipe Roll" and "Payroll" 5

    The Origin of Key Payroll-Related Words 5

    The First British Army Paymasters and Paymaster Generals 5

    "Right Honorable" Richard Rigby, Paymaster General of the British Forces During the
        American Revolution 6

    Sir Edmund Burke, Paymaster General, Brings Reform 6

    The Structure of the Paymaster General's Office in 1775 6

    The Eighteenth Century British Military Pay Process 7

    Possible Origins of Gross and Net Pay 7

    Paying in Different Currencies – What Currency to Pay the Troops in? 7

    Padding the Payroll Through the Use of "Warrant Men" – An Early Ghost Employee? . . 8

    Advice to the British Military Paymaster – On the Lighter Side 8

    Britain and the Beginning of Its Industrial Revolution 8

    The Birth of the Corporation 9

    New Production Methods and the Birth of the Supervisor and Manager Role 9

    Poor Working Conditions Bring About Legislative and Social Change 9

    The Origin of the Minimum Wage 10

    The Origin of Welfare Programs 10

    The Origin of Termination Laws – Responsibilities of Employer and Rights
        of Employee 10

    The Origin and Evolution of British Employer and Employee Income Tax 10

    British Description of Mid-Nineteenth Century "Pay-Day at the Works" 11

    Reference Sources 12

CHAPTER 3: The Colonial and Pre-Revolutionary Period

The Virginia Company Arrives 13

The Barter Bookkeeping System 13

Workers and Pay Processes of the Early to Mid Colonial Period 13

Early Industries 14

Early Industry Pay Processes of the Colonial Period 14

Reference Sources 16

CHAPTER 4: The Revolutionary Period and the Paymasters of the Continental Army

Revolutionary War Bonds Issued for Raising a Company in the Continental Army 17

Continental Army Establishes Paymaster General Position 17

James Warren Appointed First Paymaster General 17

William Palfrey Becomes the Second Paymaster General 17

Continental Army Pay Process Organized and Improved 18

Continental Army Cash Flow Problems 18
"Red Tape" at Valley Forge 19
Attempted Robbery of Continental Army Paymaster 19
John Pierce, Paymaster General, Pays All Those Who Served in the Revolution 20
Reference Sources 21

CHAPTER 5: Expanding Territories and the Old West
Meriwether Lewis – A Paymaster First, an Explorer Second! 23
Senate Amends Army Paymaster Organizational Structure and Regulations 23
Nathan Towson – An Army Paymaster With Longlasting Impact 24
Purser Samuel Hambleton and Oliver H. Perry at the Battle of Lake Erie 24
The Importance of Early Frontier Army Paymasters 24
The Funding of Early Army Payroll Accounts 24
Early Frontier Army Payroll Processes 24
Examples of Frontier Pay Delivery Hazards 24
Military Escorts of Paymasters on the Santa Fe Trail 25
The Misfortunes of Paymaster Jeremiah Yellott Dashiell 25
Wells Fargo Used in California to Deliver the Payroll 26
Paymasters in the Arts, Science and Literature 26
    William Rich Hutton – Paymaster Clerk and Artist of Early California 26
    Paymaster Jose Estrada – Perhaps the First American to Get Smallpox Vaccination . . . 26
Reference Sources 28

CHAPTER 6: Pre-Civil War Industries and Pay Processes
The Manufacturing Environment 29
The Office Environment 29
The Whaling and Merchants Industries and Pay Processes 29
Early Textile Pay Processes 31
Military Influence on Industry 34
The Origin of "The Ghost Walks" 34
Reference Sources 35

CHAPTER 7: Civil War Paymasters and Pay Processes
The Union Army's Paymaster's Manual 37
Internal Revenue Stamps Used to Partially Offset Military Costs 37
Union Army Paymaster Generals 38
Scope of Effort to Pay Federal Troops 38
Scope of Effort to Pay Confederate Troops 38
U.S. Army Paymasters in the Trenches 38
U.S. Naval Paymasters and Pay Processes 39
Paymasters in the Arts, Science and Literature 39
    Walt Whitman, Copyist in the Washington, D.C. Paymaster's Office 39
    Winslow Homer's "Pay-Day in the Army of the Potomac" 40
    A. Waud's "Paying Off the Teamsters in the Army of the Potomac" 40
Profiles of Civil War Paymasters 40
    Assistant Paymaster Richard French Goodman, Aboard the USS Nightingale and
        USS Miami 40
    Paymaster's Clerk Ellsworth H. Hults Aboard the USS Galena 41
    Paymaster William F. Keeler Aboard the USS Monitor 42
    Assistant Paymaster Douglas French Forrest Aboard the CSS Rappahannock 44
    Paymaster George Foster Robinson Saves the Life of Secretary of State Seward 44
    Paymaster's Steward John Swift Aboard the Silver Cloud 45
Money During the Civil War 45
Pay Discrepancies and Disputes 45

African-American Soldier's Equal Pay Letter to Abraham Lincoln 46
Letters With References to Paymasters and Pay 46
Confederate Paymasters and Pay Processes 47
Women Hired by U.S. Treasury 47
Reference Sources 48

CHAPTER 8: The Post-Civil War Period
U.S. Army and Cavalry Paymasters and Pay Processes 49
    Elizabeth B. Custer, Wife of General Custer 49
    A Cavalryman Remembers Life With the Sixth and Paymasters and Paydays 50
    Paymaster as Historic Figure of the Old West 50
    Paymaster as "Angel" 51
    Paymaster as "Collection Agent" 51
    Description of Paymaster's Office, Paymaster's Arrival and Pay Clerks 51
    Stories and Folklore of Army and Cavalry Paymaster Escorts and Robberies 51
    Paymasters in the Arts, Science and Literature 52
        Rufus F. Zogbaum, Painter of Military Life 52
        Frederic S. Remington, Painter of the American West 52
        Additional Paymaster Samuel C. Staples and His "Random Sketches" 53
    Congress Authorizes U.S. Mail and Express Services to Deliver the Payroll 53
Early Railroad Paymasters and Pay Processes 53
    Paymasters and Pay Processes of the Central Pacific Railroad 53
    Paymasters and Pay Processes of the Union Pacific Railroad 54
    The Paymaster's Car at Promontory 54
    Pay Tickets 55
    "The Day the Eagle Screams" – Better Known as Payday 55
    Railroad Paymasters With Towns Named After Them 55
        David L. Gallup 55
        James Madison Hanford 55
Paymasters and Pay Processes of the Early Industrial Era 55
    Overview of the Period 55
    Establishment of the Factory System 56
    Small Firms Give Way to Giant Corporations 56
    Seeds for New Organizational Structures and Processes Are Planted 56
    Rise of the "Welfare Company" 57
    Beginning of Progressive Government 57
        Payment of Wages 57
        Work by Women and Children 57
        Maximum Work Days and Work Weeks 57
        Health and Safety 58
    Time Keeping Methods of the Mid and Late Nineteenth Century 58
    Factories Change Time Record Keeping From Units of Days to Hours 59
    Wage Calculation Tables and Aids 59
    Birth of the Time Recording Industry and the "Time Clock" 59
    Typewriters and Carbon Paper Come of Age 61
    Women Become a Major Part of the Workforce 61
    Banking and Its Contributions to the Transition 61
    Origins of American Accounting Association 61
Spanish-American War Army Paymasters 61
    Brigadier-General Francis S. Dodge, Paymaster General in the U.S. Army 62
    Major John R. Lynch, Politician, Author and Paymaster in the Regular Army 62
    Major Richard R. Wright, Educator, Banker and Paymaster in the
        Spanish-American War 63
Reference Sources 64

CHAPTER 9: The Twentieth Century: The Pre-World War I Years

United States Manufacturers in 1900 67

Images of the Office Environment and Office Worker of the Day 67

Arrival of Office Technology 68

Scientific Management Picks Up Momentum 70

    Scovill Manufacturing – An Early Leader in Scientific Management and Timekeeping . 70

    Scientific Management Applied to Payroll 70

        "Saving Time in Paying Men" 71

        Advice on How to Avoid Mistakes in Paying Workers 72

        Employee Badge Numbers Assigned 72

        Providing Change for the Payroll 72

        To Get the Payroll Through on Time 73

More and More Companies Develop "Welfare Consciousness" 73

The Nation Recognizes the Need for New Approaches to Unemployment 73

The Personnel Department Emerges as a Distinct Function and Science 74

The Textile Industry and the Strikes of 1912 75

Paymasters in the Arts, Science and Literature 75

    Painting ("Pay-Day") by J.C. Leyendecker 77

    Extract From "The Jungle" by Upton Sinclair 77

    Extract From "The Long Day" by Dorothy Richardson 78

    Extract From "The Pay-Roll Clerk" by Adelaide Lund 78

    Extract From "The Passing of the Pay-Car" by C.F. Carter 78

Form 1040 Is Introduced in 1913 79

Reference Sources 80

CHAPTER 10: World War I Paymasters and Pay Processes

Paymasters and Pay Processes in War-Related Industries – Payday at the Du Pont
    Smokeless Powder Plant 81

Army Pay Call 81

Purchase of Liberty Bonds Through Payroll Deduction Plans 82

More Soldiers and Fewer Workers Create Workforce Shortage 82

Automation and Technology to the Rescue With Labor Saving Devices 82

Wartime Tax Reporting – Vendors Design and Market Year-End Wage Reporting
    Tools 83

Images of Paymasters and Pay Processes of the Day 84

Company Newsletters – an Early Vehicle for Communicating Payroll Information 84

American Cities Take Leadership Role in Improving the Payroll Process 85

    "Municipality Payrolls – Their Preparation, Certification, Audit and Payment,"
      by G.M. MacAdam 87

    New York City Payroll – "These Plans Saved $65,000 a Year" 87

Less Work on Pay Day 89

Large Cash Payrolls Create Growing Security Threat 89

Concerns Over Fraud Increase With Larger Check Volumes 90

Reference Sources 91

CHAPTER 11: The Post-World War I Years

Contemporary Company Organizational Structures 93

Scientific Management Taken Very Seriously 93

Vendor Products Emphasize Time, Labor, and Cost Control Advantages 95

Putting the Payroll on an Automatic Basis 95

Pay Envelope Begins to Evolve Into Pay Statement With New Purpose 97

Henry Ford Speaks to the Value of Multiple Pay Days 97

Paymasters in the Arts, Science and Literature 98

    "Where Every Day Is Pay Day" by James H. Collins 98

Payday at the Factory Shop 98
The Ghost Has Become an Auditor 98
Every Day Is Payday 98
Importance of Punctuality 98
Machinery Is Essential for Large Payrolls 99
Overview of the Payroll Process 99
The Origin of Payroll Deduction Savings Plans 100
Early Forms of Payroll Employee Stock Purchase Plans 100
Description of Federal and State Income Tax Withholding Procedures 100
Auditor Routines for Confirming Payroll Accuracy 101
The Birth of Armed Security Services for Payroll Deliveries 101
Early Arguments for and Against Payment by Check 102
The Power of the Paymaster 103
Personnel Departments and Directors Are Added to Company Rosters 103
On the Lighter Side – Company Uses "Pay-Pan" to Shorten Payday Rush 104
Reference Sources 105

CHAPTER 12: The Great Depression
Over Fifteen Million American Workers Lose Their Jobs 107
Jobs Were Scarce and Workers Often Went Payless 107
The Thirty-Hour Workweek and the Debate Over a Minimum Hourly Wage 107
The Payroll Office Environment of the Late Twenties and Early Thirties 108
Payroll Banditry Reaches Record Proportions 109
In Memory of a Shoe Factory Paymaster – Frederick A. Parmenter 109
Armored Cars – A Partial Solution 110
Profile of the Brink's Express Company 110
Early Initiatives on Check Versus Cash Payments 112
The American Bankers Association and Their Payroll Check Plan (1927) 112
The American Electric Railway Association (1928) 113
The Monthly Labor Review (1929) 113
The Illinois Chamber of Commerce Conducts Survey 113
The National Crime Commission Report Triggers Country-wide Debate (1930) 113
Payroll Disbursement Processes Begin to Change 114
Origin of On-Site Company Check Cashing Services 114
First Evidence of Partial Outsourcing of Payrolls 114
Reference Sources 115

CHAPTER 13: The Franklin Delano Roosevelt Era
The "New Deals" 117
The Social Security Act 117
An Early Debate Over Pay Envelope Messages 120
The Fair Labor Standards Act 121
Laws on Pay Frequency 122
World War II 122
Time Clocks and Workers Go on Overtime 122
"Girl" Paymasters Step Forward 123
Soldier's Individual Pay Record 123
Funding the War Efforts – The Sale of Defense Bonds via Payroll Deductions 124
The Birth of the Federal "Pay-as-You-Go" Income Tax Program 126
Paymasters in the Arts, Science and Literature 127
Norman Rockwell Captures the Mood of the New Taxpayer 128
Making It All Work – The Technology of the Period 128
Growing Importance of Forms and Forms Processing Equipment – Moore Business
Forms 130

Examples of Employer Pay Processes of the Period 132
   The City of Rochester, New York and Growing Numbers of Deductions 132
   The City of Austin, Texas and Centralizing Payroll Operations 133
   The City of Bridgeport, Connecticut and the Use of Tabulating Robots to Lower Cost . 133
   The Ford Motor Company and Pay Disbursement Practices 134
   Held Electric Accounting Company – Early Payroll Service Provider 135
Reference Sources 136

CHAPTER 14: The Post-World War II Years Through the Fifties
The Entrance of African-American Women Into the Office Environment 137
The Late Forties and Early Fifties Payroll Environment 137
The Growing Impact of Fringe Benefits 138
The Beginning of Local Income Tax Withholding by Payroll 138
State Revenue Departments Follow Suit – Slowly 139
Professions in "Pay-Offs" Take Off! 139
   Paymasters, Inc. Opens Its Doors for Business in 1947 139
   Automatic Payrolls Incorporated – The Future ADP, Inc. – Begins Operations
     in 1949 139
Continued Movement Toward Payment by Check 140
A Railway Payroll Captured in Photos 141
The Mid-Fifties Payroll Environment 142
   Electric Machines Are "In" 142
   Teletype Machines and Early Piloting of Remote Check Printing 143
The Late Fifties Payroll Environment 144
   The Transition of the Computer From Science to Business 144
   Signs of the Times 145
   Tactics to Promote Payment by Check and Early Forms of Payroll Direct Deposit . . . 146
   Computers and State Income Taxes 147
Paymasters in the Arts, Science and Literature 148
Reference Sources 150

CHAPTER 15: The Sixties – The Advancement of Computer Technology
The Advancement of Computer Technology 151
Seeing the Possibilities 151
Getting Potential Users Comfortable With Video Screens and Keyboards 151
Leveraging the Computer 153
The Growing Power of the Data Processing Department 153
Movement From FORTRAN to COBOL to Lessen the Communication Problem 153
Computer-Like Equipment Starts to Move Into the Office 153
Functions Like Payroll Served as Proving Grounds for Other Applications 154
Many Employers Migrated in Phases Using Service Bureaus 154
A New Profession and a Shortage of Computer Programmers 154
Birth of Software Development Companies 155
Other Office Tools of the Period 155
Traditional Solutions Continued to Provide Advantages 155
Changes in Federal Tax Withholding Methods and the Implementation of Medicare 156
Reference Sources 157

CHAPTER 16: The Seventies – The Arrival of Mini and Microcomputers
Computers and Banking 159
The Establishment of NACHA and Electronic Payroll Direct Deposit 159
Smaller Computers Bring Computing Power to More Users More Cheaply 160
Intel Introduces "the Computer on a Chip" and Microcomputer Processing 161
New Computers Offer Stiff Competition 162

The Beginning of the Shift From Data Center to Office and Hardware to Software 163
Contingency Planning and the Impact of Weather on Payrolls 164
Computers Couldn't Beat the Holiday Payroll Blues 165
Reference Sources 167

CHAPTER 17: The Eighties – Payroll Comes of Age
The Payroll Environment of the Early Eighties 169
The American Payroll Association Is Created 169
Fred O'Boyle and the Rest of the Story – History Leading Up to the Birth of APA 170
Payroll Survey of the Early Eighties 170
Technology Enables Centralization of Payroll Operations 173
Social Security and FLSA Celebrate Their 50th Anniversaries 173
Social, Regulatory, and Tax Changes Push Payroll Forward 173
    The Tax Reform Act of 1986 173
    Flexible Compensation and Benefit Programs Take Root 174
    Child Support Enforcement Through Mandatory Payroll Withholding 174
    Sick Pay Taxation Rules Change 175
    Use of Federal Supplemental Flat Tax Rate Allowed 175
    The Beginning of Magnetic Media Reporting 175
Year-End Reporting Can Be a Full-Time Job 175
The IRS "Audit" 176
Banking Update 176
Ending the "100 Years War" With Human Resources 177
Vendors Begin to Offer Integrated Payroll and Human Resources Software 177
Growth of the Service Bureau Industry 179
The Birth of the Modern Time and Attendance Industry 179
Views and Perspectives on Payrolls of the Eighties 180
    Greater Emphasis on Information Impacts the Work of Payroll 180
    New Payroll Project-Related Roles Created 181
    Payroll Roles Become More Technical 181
    Payroll Managers Speak Out on the Challenges of the Eighties 182
On the Lighter Side – Through the Eyes of Payroll Managers With a Sense of Humor . . . 182
    Sam McLaughlin and "A Computer With a Mind of Its Own" 182
    Howard Freedman and "The Many Hats a Payroll Professional Wears in a Day" 182
End of a Decade – and Payroll Comes of Age 183
Reference Sources 185

CHAPTER 18: The Nineties – Leaping Toward the New Millennium
The Payroll Environment of the Nineties 187
Major Trends and Issues of the 1990s 187
    Focus on Total Quality Management 187
    Businesses Begin to Look at End-to-End Processes 187
    Downsizing and Its Cousin "Rightsizing" 187
    Shared Service Centers Seen by Many as THE Solution 188
    Haunted by the Past – the Y2K Problem 188
    A Continuous Stream of Acquisitions and Mergers 188
    Movement Away From Paper 188
        Government Lends Support for Electronic Filing and Reporting 188
        Employers and Employees Embrace Direct Deposit 189
        Electronic Pay Statements Begin to Replace Paper 189
    Expanding Beyond Domestic Boundaries 189
        Banking Community Moves to Support Cross-Border Payments 189
        Employers Begin to Adopt Global Payroll Models 190
    Professional Employer Organizations (PEOs) Arrive 190

Technological Wonders to Behold! 190
An Avalanche of Vendor Payroll-Related Products and Services 191
  Payroll Software Advances to a New Level 191
  Specialized Payroll Software Products Assist the Payroll Professional 191
  Time and Attendance Solutions Characterize Technology of the Nineties 192
  Partnerships and Alliances Abound 192
Focus on Employee Self-Service (ESS) Tools 192
Using IVR Technology to Reduce Labor and Costs and Improve Customer
  Service 192
Tapping the Internet and the Intranet 193
Competition Between In-house and Service Bureau Solutions Increases 193
New Management Approaches – Self-Directed Teams 201
The Arrival of the Payroll Telecommuter 201
Profile of a Typical Payroll Organization of the Nineties 201
American Payroll Association Contributes to Payroll Progress 202
  First President-Elect – Carol Franket 202
  Emphasis on Education and Training 202
  Influencing Legislative Outcomes 203
  In the National Limelight 204
    In-flight Video Tells Public About Payroll 204
    Using Television to Educate Taxpayers on W-2s 205
    APA's Dan Maddux Founds Annual National Payroll Week 205
At the End of the Millennium 205
Reference Sources 207

CHAPTER 19: Looking Back With Pride and Moving Ahead With Confidence
Looking Back With Pride 209
Moving Ahead With Confidence 210

INDEX 211

CHAPTER 1:
Ancient Roots

The Beginning of Organized Governments and the Chaldean-Babylonian Empire

Historians tell us that the roots of modern business, finance, accounting, and yes, disbursement methods, extend back to between 4500 and 7000 B.C. and the days of the Chaldean-Babylonian Empire, which is believed to be the seat of the first organized government. However, the "art of numeration" or counting goes back even further to the very beginning of intelligent human life. (1)

It was from the need of early governments to form and manage their state infrastructures and to levy taxes that the science of accounting was born. (1)

A.C. Littleton lists in his book *Accounting Evolution to 1900* seven preconditions for the birth of systematic bookkeeping including: 1) the art of writing; 2) arithmetic; 3) private property; 4) money; 5) credit; 6) commerce; and 7) capital. (2)

Some or all of these conditions were in place in the Chaldean-Babylonian Empire, and baked clay tablets prepared by scribes that have been preserved provide evidence today of such business activities going back to the year 2600 B.C. Such records included how long laborers worked and what wages they received. (1)

Business and Pay Practices Among Other Ancient Peoples

By 415 B.C., Grecian society had developed an even more sophisticated system to manage business activities within the public economy. The highest ranking position was that of the Treasurer or Manager of the Public Revenue, a position once held by Aristides. In addition, there were many subordinate treasurers and checking-clerks including clerks with the highest authority for disbursements. Checking-clerks maintained records on stone as illustrated in this Account of Disbursements of the Athenian State for the period 418 B.C. to 415 B.C. (Exhibit 1-1) (1)

In the case of the Israelites, the Bible furnishes us with a number of references to matters of accounting and elaborate reckonings under the Mosaic Law including the receipt of temple offerings and the various disbursements made by the king's scribe and high priest. (1)

The Roman Army Paymaster and Pay Process

Organized payrolls were first required to sustain large military forces. A Greek, Polybius, makes reference to "paymaster" in his translation of *The Military Institution of the Roman Army* by Flavius Vegetius Renatus as follows:

"About the same time, likewise, the consuls send notice to the magistrates of the allied cities of Italy, from which they design to draw any forces, what number of troops are wanted, and cities, having raised their levies in the same manner that has now been mentioned, and administered to them the same oath, send them away attended by a paymaster and a general." (3)

Exhibit 1-1: Account of Disbursements of the Athenian State (418 B.C. – 415 B.C.) carved on stone tablet; Courtesy of British Museum; Greek and Roman Antiquities; Greek Inscription No. 23

Polybius also noted that Roman soldiers were obliged to purchase their staples, clothes, and arms at a set price and to have these amounts deducted by the quaestor (a Roman official with responsibilities for financial administration) from their pay. (3)

Origin of the English Word "Salary"

Salary comes from the Latin word salarium meaning literally 'salt-money', that is, money paid to Roman soldiers for their allowance of salt.

A Comprehensive Etymological Dictionary of the English Language by
Dr. Ernest Klein; Elsevier Publishing Company; 1967

As reflected in a more recent translation of *The Military Institutions of the Romans,* there are not only further references to the pay function and process but also to characteristics deemed desirable in those who perform the function (such as emphasis on exactness) and to early forms of payroll record keeping and savings deduction programs:

On Records and Accounts: "…the superintendents of the levies should select recruits for their skill in writing and accounts…..for the whole detail of the legion, including the lists of the soldiers exempted from duty on special detail, the rosters for their tour of military duties and their pay lists is daily entered in the legionary books and kept….with greater exactness than the regulations of provisions or other civil matters in the registers of the police. The daily guards in time of peace, the advance guards and outposts in time of war, which are mounted regularly by centuries and messes ….are likewise punctually kept in rolls for that purpose, with the name of each soldier whose tour is past, that no one may have injustices done him or be excused from his duty by favor. They are also exact in entering the time and limitation of furloughs…..." (4)

On Soldiers' Pay Deposits: "The institution of the ancients which obliged the soldiers to deposit half of every donative they received at the colors was wise and judicious; the intent was to preserve it for their use so that they might not squander it in extravagance or idle expense. A reserve of this kind therefore is evidently of the greatest service to the soldiers themselves; since…… their stock of savings by

this method is continually increasing. The soldier who knows that all this fortune is deposited with his colors, entertains no thoughts of desertion, conceives a greater affection for them and fights with greater intrepidity in their defense. He is also prompted thereto by interest, the most prevailing consideration among men. This money was contained in ten bags, one for each cohort. There was an eleventh bag also for a small contribution from the whole legion as a common fund to defray the expense of burial of any of their deceased comrades. These collections were kept in baskets in the custody of ensigns chosen for their integrity and capacity answerable for the trust and obliged to account to every man for his own proportion." (4)

The Origins of Metallic and Paper Money

In the early years of the ancient world, the use of money was unknown and payments (including those for wages) were paid "in kind" (i.e., grain, salt, etc.). (1)

"The exact date when metallic coins of a precise weight were adopted as a method of completing transactions has been lost in the obscurity of antiquity. However surviving records indicate that during the First Dynasty of Babel, 2225 –1926 B.C., a monetary system using metallic money was well established. However, it remained for the Greeks and the Romans to further refine the use of metallic coins. During the reign of Caesar, the Roman coin was well established throughout the known world." (5)

The first documented use of paper money was the Kwan, a Chinese note issued during the Ming Dynasty between 1360 and 1399 A.D. As trade between regions increased during the Middle Ages, there was a need to develop a more portable payment system. Receipts and negotiable notes initially issued against coins on deposit with goldsmiths, merchants, and money lenders began to replace metallic money, especially for large amounts, and eventually these methods evolved into paper money. (5)

A Slow Evolutionary Process

As is evident from this brief history, the origins of payroll along with those of accounting, bookkeeping, and coin and paper currencies can be traced back to the beginning of many ancient civilizations and have evolved to their present day forms over a very long period of time.

Reference Sources

1. A History of Accounting and Accountants; Editor/Partial Author: Brown, Richard; Verlag Sauer & Auvermann; Frankfurt, Germany; 1968 (original issue date 1905); pp. 16-26

2. A History of Accounting Thought; Chatfield, Michael; Robert E. Krieger Publishing Company; Huntington, NY; 1977; pp. 15-17

3. The Military Institution of the Romans; Polybius; Oliver J. Thatcher, ed.; University Extension Company; Milwaukee; 1901; pp. 172-186

4. De Re Militari; Flavius Vegetius Renatus; Clark, John, translator; Stackpole Books; Harrisburg, PA; 1965; pp. 54-55

5. Money - Its Origin, Development and Modern Use; Moore, Carl H.; Russell, Alvin E.; McFarland & Company, Inc.; Jefferson, NC and London; 1987; pp. 8-9

CHAPTER 2:
European and British Heritage

European Heritage

While many of our contemporary financial, accounting and disbursement practices have evolved from ancient roots, our European and British heritage has played a significant role in how U.S. business practices are performed today.

For example, the Italians, specifically a Venetian named Pacioli, is credited in 1494 with perfecting if not inventing double entry book-keeping. By the mid fifteenth century, Italians had already been using a method called "cross-entries" for a hundred years or so, but it was not until double entry bookkeeping was introduced that businesses really began to apply the power of balancing and of proving the equality of debits and credits. From an accounting perspective, the entire history of the human race can be divided into the thousands of years leading up to Pacioli's "Method of Venice" and the little more than 500 years that have followed since his revolutionary accounting concept was introduced. Pacioli captured his accounting theories in what may be the oldest accounting book in existence, *Summa de Arithmetica, Geometira, Proportioni and Proportionalita*, dated 1494. (1)

These accounting principles would later become the tools used by business and financial personnel, including payroll practitioners, throughout the modern world.

It is not surprising then, that the first professional accountants, then referred to as mathematicians, were also Italians, a role that may have had its Italian origins in the Vatican, where a high ranking official with the title of "logotheta" or accountant had been a part of the papal staff since the year 1001. (2)

British Heritage

British pay methods, both in the military and the private sector, significantly influenced American payroll practices, especially in the eighteenth and early nineteenth centuries.

The Linkage between "Pipe Roll" And "Payroll"

Records, initially maintained on clay or stone tablets, eventually were captured on parchment. The earliest accounting records in the English language date around 1130. The English "Pipe Roll," or the "Great Roll of the Exchequer" as the crown's record was referred to, was prepared by the crown's treasurer annually to reflect all of the debts owed the crown. Supporting "Pipe Rolls," maintained by individual sheriffdoms within the crown, included not only monies due the crown but also all the payments made on behalf of the crown. (2) These early "rolls" may have served as pay registers for employees of the crown. It is highly probable that today's "payroll" has its origin in the "pipe rolls" of the early days of the last millennium.

The Origin of Key Payroll-Related Words

According to the Oxford English Dictionary, the word "pay-day" first appeared in English print around 1529, the word "paymaster" around 1550, and the word "pay-roll" around 1740. (3) By the end of the first half of the twentieth century, the use of the connecting hyphen was phased out and the terms "pay-day" and "pay-roll" gradually became "pay day" and "pay roll" and then simply "payday" and "payroll." The term "paymaster" was replaced with "payroll manager" as cash payrolls gave way to check payrolls and the function of the paymaster was extended beyond the disbursement of funds, although references to the term are seen even today.

The First British Army Paymasters and Paymaster Generals

"Even before the English Civil War of 1642 - 1651 there were army officers called 'paymasters' whose duty was to defray the expenses of specific military campaigns. There being then no permanent British army there was no post or office with overall responsibility for the paymasters. However, in 1649 Cromwell created two posts of Treasurer at War to pay the expenses of his newly-formed parliamentary army, and although these disappeared when that army was disbanded at the Restoration they were replaced in 1660 by the overall paymaster in the first standing army of Charles II." (4) The first Paymaster General, Sir Stephen Fox, served for more than 19 years from 1660 to 1679.

"Initially the post was entitled Receiver and Paymaster of the Guards, but soon it became Paymaster General of the Guards and Garrisons, then Paymaster General of the Guards, Garrisons and Land Forces and by 1743, simply Paymaster General of the Forces. This officer, always a leading member of the government of the day, employed a small staff of clerks and other personnel to carry out the day-to-day administration on his behalf." Henry Fox (Lord Holland), the youngest son of Sir Stephen Fox, served as Paymaster General of the Forces from 1757 to 1765. These early paymaster generals were the predecessors of the British Paymaster General Office (PGO). (4)

Exhibit 2-1: Right Honorable Richard Rigby; Etching by James Sayers; 1782; (RN51560); Archives Engravings Collection; Courtesy of National Portrait Gallery, London

---

Quotation:

"Both good and evil are sure paymasters at the last"

1615 – PP. Hall Contempl., O.T. x. iv.

"Right Honorable" Richard Rigby, Paymaster General of the British Forces During the American Revolution

Paymaster Generals of this period in British history were political appointees and were often notorious for the abuse of funds under their control. For example, Right Honorable Richard Rigby, the Paymaster General of the British Army (Exhibit 2-1) during the American Revolution, barely escaped impeachment for his "peculations." "In 1781 the department was investigated by a parliamentary commission. It was found that the paymaster was accustomed to submit to the Treasury an estimate of sums

required of the service of the army, and that the Treasury without scrutinizing the necessity or accuracy of the demands was accustomed to pay the money to him. In this way he was able to accumulate large balances from which he calmly pocketed the interest." (4).

Sir Edmund Burke, Paymaster General, Brings Reform

It should be noted that reform came in 1782 under the leadership of the next Paymaster General, Sir Edmund Burke. (Exhibit 2-2) Burke set new standards for the office and implemented controls to prevent profiting from public funds, thereby ending what some critics of the day had called "that opulent subordinate office." (5)

The Structure of the Paymaster General's Office in 1775

During the American Revolution, the British Paymaster General's Office was staffed with five officers including a Deputy Paymaster General,

an Accountant, a Computer of Off-reckonings, a Cashier of Half Pay, and a Keeper of the Stores. Eight clerks supported the officers. There were also eight subordinate paymasters abroad including one stationed in Boston. (5)

The Eighteenth Century British Military Pay Process

"The method of paying the army was, generally speaking, as follows: Each regiment possessed a civil agent, appointed by the colonel, with power of attorney to transact its financial affairs and under bond. At the time of the Revolution, there were no regimental paymasters in the strict sense of the word. The colonel was accustomed to appoint one of the officers to act in that capacity in addition to his other duties. In the payment of the regiment, therefore, the money passed from the paymaster general to the agent, from the agent to the regimental paymaster, then to the captains, who in turn disbursed it to the men." (5) Up until the years preceding the American Revolution, a wealthy Massachusetts merchant, Charles Apthorp, acted as the North American Agent in behalf of Thomlinson & Trecothick, the banking house and agent of the Crown. (6)

Possible Origins of Gross and Net Pay

The process of calculating a soldier's pay was a complicated one, with lots of deductions (or stoppages as they were called). "The pay of the private soldier at the time of the American Revolution was eight pence a day. Of this he got little in food and drink and probably nothing in coin." His pay was divided into two parts, one known as "gross off-reckonings" and the other as "subsistence." Stoppages were taken from gross off-reckonings to cover fees imposed by the Paymaster General, the Army Hospital (Chelsea), and the Agent. Expenses withheld from subsistence included everything from the cost of food to the cost of clothing and arms repairs. Any remaining pay left after all stoppages from gross off-reckonings and subsistence had been taken was referred to as "net off-reckonings." The process of off-reckoning was so complicated that the paymaster general appointed an "Off-reckoning" officer to oversee the process. (5)

Exhibit 2-2: Sir Edmund Burke; Studio of Sir Joshua Reynolds; 1771; (Reg. No. 655); Courtesy of Picture Library, National Portrait Gallery, London

Paying in Different Currencies – What Currency to Pay the Troops In?

During the years preceding the American Revolution, His Majesty's Treasury was faced with many monetary problems. The Treasury, for example, was always trying to control the issuance of specie (coin money) in such a way as to equalize the value of the various currencies and to prevent paymasters and agents from capitalizing on fluctuating differences. (7)

In a letter dated March 20, 1755, Major General Edward Braddock, Commander of the North American British Troops, writes to Newcastle, Williamsburgh "that small coined Silver will be greatly wanted for the payment of the Troops, and as no considerable Quantity of it can be got in this Province; I must beg of your Grace to direct the Contractors, Mr. Hanbury & Mr Thomlinson, to send over as soon as possible, if they have not already done it, four or five thousand pounds, in Piastrines and Half Piastrines: which is the more necessary, as all the Money already brought over by the Regimental Paymasters is in Spanish Gold and dollars." (7)

By paying some troops in one form and other troops, stationed nearby in another form, it was hard for regimental officers to convince soldiers that they were not being cheated. (7)

Padding the Payroll Through the Use of "Warrant Men" – An Early Ghost Employee?

One of the unique characteristics of regimental finance was the warrant man. This fictitious man was put on the payroll to meet a variety of expenses at each level. The colonel covered the cost of lost clothing from deserters by adding a warrant man to the payroll; the captain did the same to cover the cost of recruitment; and each regimental officer added warrant men to cover the cost of unanticipated expenses. Could this have been an early form of the ghost employee? (5)

Advice to the British Military Paymaster – On the Lighter Side

The following (unedited) satirical work printed in 1867 (although originating from the late eighteenth century) reflects British humor (and spelling) at the expense of the military paymaster and is presented in the form of advice:

"To the Paymaster: Yours is as snug an office as any; particularly when the regiment is upon foreign service; but if you have to give security, or have a commission to answer for your miscarriages, you must take care to go on fair and softly. Make your accounts as intricate as you can, and, if possible, unintelligible to every one but yourself; lest, in case you should be taken prisoner, your papers might give information to the enemy. Always grumble and make difficulties, when officers go to you for money that is due to them; when you are obliged to pay them, endeavour to make it appear granting them a favour, and tell them they are lucky dogs to get it. I dare say, they would be of the same way of thinking, if you had it in your power to withhold it. Be careful to keep up a right understanding with the agent. You must also keep upon good terms with the commanding officer; which will be no difficult matter, if he is extravagant and needy. Just before muster-day get leave, or take it, to be absent from the regiment, and pretend that it is upon the business of your

office, as to receive money, and the more to your credit: for shewing people that they cannot do without you, will give them a high idea of your importance; and you will be sure of a hearty welcome on your return. Always close your accounts with errors excepted; and, as you give people this caution, it is but fair that the mistakes should be all in your own favour. I know not whence they call your monthly pay-rolls abstracts; unless it be considering them as *abstracted from all found* arithmetick, and just calculation. When you pay any allowance to officers and soldiers beyond the usual subsistence, be sure to deduct six-pence in the pound for your friend the agent; who certainly deserves that perquisite, for his great trouble and risk in taking care of the money for you so long: especially, as you may swear he has not put it out to interest." (8)

Britain and the Beginning of Its Industrial Revolution

In 1700, the total population of the United Kingdom was 6.5 million people. More than 3 out of 5 people were employed in agriculture or rural occupations. "Most lived in villages which were mainly self-supporting. Villages grew their own food, brewed their own beer, made their own clothing, and manufactured their own farm implements. Apart from salt and iron they required little else from the outside World." (9)

Prior to the British Industrial Revolution, ninety percent of all children were brought up in a rural environment. However, from very early on, the majority of people in the 18th century depended upon a wage as well as the land. (10)

As the years passed, areas in Britain that for generations had been used for farmland became untended and villages became populated towns. Roads were constructed and the invention of steam brought automation and the first railroad. The number of people significantly increased and the proportion of children and young people rose. The labor force moved from farms to factories and the work grew to be specialized. Workers became increasingly mobile and achieved progressively higher standards of living. A formal banking system was created. (10)

In this context an outright industrial revolution took shape during the latter part of the 18th century, led by Britain, which retained its position of leadership in industrialization well past the middle of the 19th century. Woolen manufacturers, iron masters, and hat makers were among some of the largest and earliest industries. Government supported their growth through special legislation and grants. (10)

The Birth of the Corporation

Perhaps one of Great Britain's most important contributions to American business was the "corporation." Long before America had ever been settled, the corporation had become an integral part of the social structure of England and the use of joint stock and shares of common capital to fund business enterprises had been fine-tuned. The institution further matured during the American colonial period as migrating British subjects brought this knowledge to the new land. The first English settlements on American soil as well as the first truly private corporations for religious, educational and business purposes were made possible through the efforts and through the expense of such corporations. Much of the legal definition of today's corporation has its origin in English law. (11)

New Production Methods and The Creation of the Supervisor And Manager Role

The new machines introduced in the 18th century required a structured organization of job functions that was very different from the old home-based handicraft tradition. Adam Smith in *The Wealth of Nations* (1776) provided the classic description of the new production system as exemplified by a pin factory: "One man draws out the wire; another straights it; a third cuts it; a fourth points it; a fifth grinds it, etc. with the important business of making a pin divided into about eighteen distinct operations." According to Smith, a single worker "could scarce, perhaps, with utmost industry, make one pin in a day, and certainly could not make twenty." The new methods enabled a pin factory of "middling size" with ten workers to turn out as many as 48,000 pins a day. (12)

"Because machines could justify their high cost only if a heavy and continuous demand existed for their output, their presence led to a division of labor between the entrepreneur who owned them and his employees. The owner

supervised his workers, compelling them to work at the pace of the machine. Even in enterprises that were not yet fully mechanized, the advantages of factory discipline were apparent at an early stage of the Industrial Revolution. Josiah Wedgwood designed his pottery works 'with a view to the strictest economy of labor.' His plant was laid out so that the pots were first formed and then passed through the paint room, the kiln room, the account room, in which an inventory of production was made, and finally to storage. In potteries before this time, the workers could wander from one task to another; in Wedgwood's factory, the employees were assigned a particular post and worked at one task only. Out of the 278 men, women and children employed by Wedgwood in 1790, only five had no assigned post; the rest were specialists. It is interesting to note that Wedgwood's chief difficulty was not so much in training his workers as it was in introducing them to a novel form of discipline that ran contrary to centuries of independence. It was a constant test of Wedgwood's ingenuity to enforce six hours of punctual and constant attendance upon these workers, to get them to avoid waste, and to keep them from drinking on the job and taking unauthorized "holidays." Because he was a busy man involved in all the tasks of running an enterprise and could not stand over his workers and control their movements, he had to develop a hierarchy of supervisors and managers." (13)

Poor Working Conditions Bring About Legislative and Social Change

Workers of the period were paid in cash as well as truck (in goods). Deductions were used to reduce the level of wages in many factories and workshops, and often included the cost of space and tools provided by employers. (10)

"There can be little doubt that the condition of the workers, especially the women and children, in the early textile factories was miserable: 14 to 16 hours every day spent performing repetitive tasks in noisy, smelly, and unsanitary surroundings; and the workers' slum homes were equally unhealthy. It was at this period that the 'social question' arose: why should poverty continue to exist in a nation that had the capacity to produce enormous quantities of goods?" (13)

The debate over this question would lead to many social changes that ultimately would improve worker conditions and pay.

Many of today's social, business and payroll practices, including those related to labor and taxation, can be traced to British origins, from both the public and private sectors, as illustrated in the following paragraphs.

The Origin of the Minimum Wage

The concept of a minimum wage may have had its origins in the 1760s. County magistrates at the time controlled what wages people should be paid. At a court hearing held in the County of Berkshire, "they came to the conclusion that wages locally were no longer sufficient to support an industrious man and his family and they summoned a meeting of Justices of the Peace and other discreet persons to work out a wage policy. They decided to recommend to farmers and other employers throughout the county to increase the pay of their laborers in proportion to the present price of provisions. Where a farmer failed to do so, his laborers were to be entitled to claim an allowance to the size of their families, on a sliding scale calculated with reference to the cost of bread. Where the standard loaf cost a shilling, every laborer was to have a guaranteed minimum of three shillings a week, plus one shilling and sixpence for his wife and for each additional member of his family." (14)

Some 35 years later in 1795, Samuel Whitbread introduced the first bill in Parliament to give magistrates the power to enforce a minimum wage. (15)

The Origin of Welfare Programs

Prior to the Industrial Revolution, counties (known as parishes) imposed a "poor tax" on employers and owners of large houses to offset the cost of parish relief (possibly an early form of welfare). Under the "Poor Law," recipients of parish relief were forced to work or be subject to stern penalties, including whipping and/or imprisonment in workhouses. As harsh as these programs were, they were early attempts at preventing and responding to problems of poverty and unemployment. (15)

The Origin of Termination Laws - Responsibilities of Employer and Rights of Employee

Under the poor tax rules, employers were responsible for paying the tax to the local parish when their employees had resided in the parish for one year. To avoid payment of the poor tax, some British employers discharged their workers during week 51. In 1760, laws were passed to prevent such tactics. Under the new laws, no person or employer could terminate his or her servant or employee before the end of his or her term without reasonable and sufficient cause and only then with advance notice and compensation. Modern day termination laws may have been conceived during this period. (15)

The Origin and Evolution of British Employer and Employee Income Tax

Quotation:

" War involves in its progress such a train of unforeseen and unsupposed circumstances that no human wisdom can calculate the end. It has but one thing certain, and that is to increase taxes."

- Thomas Paine

The lack of any attempt by the state to influence by taxation or other means the distribution of incomes was an important element in building up the new economic system during the British Industrial Revolution. In fact, there was no tax before the income tax was introduced as a war measure by William Pitt in 1799. It was discontinued in 1802 after the end of the war and then renewed when peace was again broken. So strong was the opposition against the tax, especially in the City of London, that as soon as the war was over Parliament repealed the law and in 1816 ordered the destruction of tax records. It would be many years into the future before a permanent employer/employee income tax structure would be institutionalized. (10)

British Description of Mid-Nineteenth Century "Pay-Day at the Works"

The following excerpt from an 1862 *Chambers' Journal of Popular Literature, Science and Arts* provides some insight into payday at an English Iron Works, around the mid-nineteenth century: "In the annals of the poor, payday is the greatest of periodical events. Coming, as it generally does on a Saturday, it is a pleasant winding-up of their week's or fortnight's labour to go to the cashier's office and receive the equivalent of the work they have been performing. It is interesting to stand at the office-door, or inside, where the pay-clerk is surrounded with books and papers, and rolls of banknotes, and multitudinous piles of gold, silver, and copper counted out ready to hand, and watch the various characters who come to be paid. There has been during all pay-time a sound of money chinking near the outer door of the office......If we were to look round the works soon after pay time, we should find many a workman, struggling hard, perhaps, by the aid of his 'glasses' to make an equitable division of the cash among the several men he has been reckoning. Here and there, a foreman has got a little band of artisans round him, whom he pays one by one, and checks off the amount in his memorandum-book, with the air of one who has been used to it, and who knows to the fraction of an hour what each of his hands has done for him in daily labour since last pay-day. These foremen are rather apt to grind the men down to the lowest penny, and consequently the 'hands' in general would much rather be employed by the master direct than be placed under a foreman; but the system can hardly be dispensed with in large undertakings, where an extended supervision indeed would be required, if foremen were not allowed to contract for the work. How soon will the paper and metal currency paid away by the cashier early to-day be distributed all over the neighbourhood! It will radiate from the office to town and country; and the cottager from the distant village, away from the smoke, will take some of it back in return for the basket of fruit or vegetables she finds a good market for in the black [coal mining] country. .... Big loaves from the baker, and heavy joints from the butcher, bring down the working-man's exchequer considerably, and by the time the huxter's score is wiped off, the funds are really getting low. It is well if the old dame can get her good-man to turn towards home without entering the 'public,' for she wants, badly enough the rent and liquidating that long standing doctor's bill." (16)

11

Reference Sources

1. A History of Accounting Thought; Chatfield, Michael; Robert E. Krieger Publishing Company; Huntington, NY; 1977; p. 4

2. A History of Accounting and Accountants; Brown, Richard; Verlag Sauer & Auvermann; Frankfurt, Germany; 1968 (original issue date 1905); pp. 39 & 41-45

3. Oxford English Dictionary; Simpson, J. A. & Weiner, E.S.C.; Clarenden Press; Oxford; 1989; Volume XI; pp. 379-381

4. 150 Not Out; Ulph, Colin; HM Paymaster General's Office; Crawley, West Sussex, England; 1985; pp. 1, 9-10, 38

5. The Organization of the British Army in the American Revolution; Curtis, Edward E.; Scholarly Press, Inc.; St. Claire Shores, MI; 1972 (reprint of original edition of 1926); pp. 22-23, 37-39

6. Apthorp House 1760 –1960: Garrett, Wendell D.; Adams House, Harvard University; Cambridge, MA; 1960; p. 6

7. Military Affairs in North America 1748 – 1765; Editor: Pargellis, Stanley; Archon Books; 1969 (Reprinted from 1936 American Historical Association); pp. 81, 240 & 270

8. Advice to the Officers of the British Army; Credited to Grose, Francis; Townsend, Lord George; Williamson, John; Agathynian Club Publications; Bradstreet Press; Edition No 1 (120 copies); New York; 1867; pp. 71-73

9. British Economic and Social History; Hill, C.P.; Edward Arnold (Publishers) Ltd.; London; 1957; pp. 13-14

10. A Concise Economic History of Britain from 1750 to Recent Times; Court, WHB; University Press; Cambridge; 1958; pp. 131, 147

11. History of American Corporations; Davis, Joseph S.; Harvard University Press; Cambridge; MA; 1917

12. An Inquiry into the Nature and Causes of the Wealth of Nations; Smith, Adam; P. F. Collier & Son Company; New York; 1909; p. 10

13. History of the Organization of Work; Encyclopedia Britannica; Internet Version (www.eb.com)

14. Poverty and the Industrial Revolution; Inglis, Brian; Panther Books; London; 1972

15. The Industrial Revolution in the 18th Century; Mantoux, Paul; University Press; London; 1966; pp. 432, 436, 458

16. "Pay-Day at the Works"; *Chambers' Journal*; William and Robert Chambers; Volume 38; July – December 1862; pp. 300-303

Contributions (from sources 9, 10 and 12 through 15) to this chapter have been made by Moira H. Dickson, Vice President, HRIS, Merrill Lynch, London, UK.

CHAPTER 3:
The Colonial and Pre-Revolutionary Period

The Virginia Company Arrives

In 1609 the Virginia Company arrived with a shipload of new settlers in Jamestown. By 1700 the Saugus Iron Works had long been producing a ton of cast iron every day, the first union for shoemakers had already been granted a charter, regular mail service was already in place between Boston and New York, the population of the colonies was approaching 300,000, and the English Parliament, already feeling threatened by its own colonies, had passed the Wool Act forbidding the export of wool from the colonies.

The Barter Bookkeeping System

In the earliest years following the arrival of the first settlers, Colonial America was more backwards in many respects than many ancient societies with the economy localized, the inland transportation system yet to be developed, and agricultural methods only slightly ahead of those of past civilizations. Because the colonies were not permitted to issue currency, trade was carried on largely through a system of bartering. The barter system only required the seller and the buyer to agree on equivalent values for their exchanges. A simple method of bookkeeping called the "barter bookkeeping system" enabled both parties to keep track of who owed whom what. Under this system, a farmer might deliver milk to the cobbler on credit until the farmer needed a pair of shoes, at which time he would be "paid" in shoes. Ledgers at this time were comprised mainly of charges to men's names. Financial status and success were measured in asset growth rather than income and double entry bookkeeping was rarely applied. But all this was about to change rapidly. (1)

Workers and Pay Processes of The Early to Mid Colonial Period

Initially, workers did not specialize in one particular type of work. Rather, farmers supplemented their livelihoods by performing a variety of jobs, sometimes on a cyclical basis. Over time, such workers developed skills in a particular discipline and became "country" artisans. The blacksmith, the cooper, and the tinker are examples of such artisans. (2)

As business increased, the part-time and home-based artisan became a full-time craftsman and moved his business to town. Over time, the craftsman became a master of his trade. In the process, apprentices and journeymen were hired to learn the trade and assist the master. (2)

The sale of merchandise was initially based on a negotiated versus fixed price and every sale became a competition of wits. Due to a shortage of cash and the fact that nine out of every ten colonists were farmers, masters were often forced to advertise their willingness to take "country pay," (i.e., farm produce). (2)

The master (assisted by his wife who often acted as the salesperson) performed all aspects of the business including those related to the payment of wages. Apprentices received training in the "mysteries" of the trade in addition to "meat, drink, washing and lodging" for their services and were normally indentured (Exhibit 3-1) for a period of 3 to 5 years. Journeymen, in addition to board and lodging, were paid a wage. The average wage of a journeyman throughout the eighteenth century was about fifteen shillings a week. (2)

Some shopowners in the larger towns became highly specialized craftsmen. They began to produce customized products (known as "bespoke" work) and to sell their products to customers beyond their immediate area. This often necessitated the hiring of additional laborers. (2)

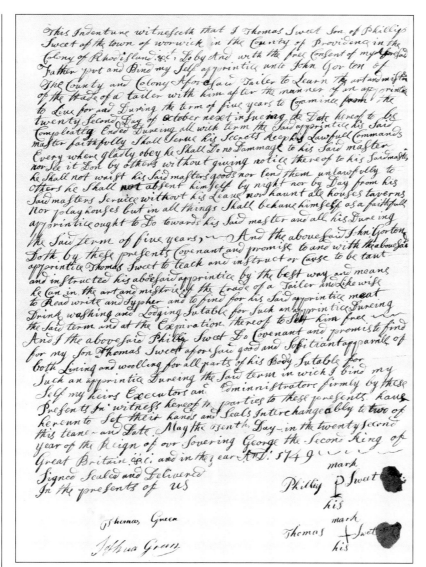

Some shops began to produce "group" products that required artisans from many trades, such as shipwrights (shipbuilders). (2)

Businesses known as "manufactories" were the among the earliest forms of the factory and included papermakers, glass blowers, braziers, clockmakers, and ironmasters. (2)

Early Industries

Until the mid-eighteenth century, America existed on the fringe of the world economy. However, by the end of the colonial period, it had advanced considerably. Beyond the production of staples such as wheat, rice, indigo, and tobacco, colonial manufacturers were beginning to match Great Britain in terms of sheer output in some industries. (3)

Much of the early industry focused on what is sometimes referred to as "naval stores," providing Great Britain with raw materials such as pitch, turpentine and resin. Soon exports were

expanded to include many processed lumber products, and ultimately the building of ships, which in turn created many other associated industries to produce sails, anchors, rope, etc. (4)

Iron making also became an important industry very early on, beginning with the basic components such as mining and smelting, and then the production of iron bars. (4)

Added to the above were the fishing and fur trading industries, and on a smaller scale tanneries, leatherworking, mills (of various kinds), printing shops, rum distilleries, and so forth. (4)

While Colonial America was still an agrarian and artisan society, Philadelphia by 1750 was one of the great urban centers of the English-speaking world. New York was catching up. Baltimore was beginning to expand, and all the towns along the Atlantic from Charleston to Boston were developing a myriad of businesses based on importing goods and producing a variety of products to meet the growing demands of a rapidly expanding population. (3)

However, the lack of skilled laborers, capital, and transportation, the dominant position of agriculture, and the export restrictions of the mercantile system imposed by Great Britain delayed the growth of industries in the colonies. Manufacturing (including the production of textiles) would remain at the household industry phase well past the day when George Washington would be inaugurated as the first president of the United States. (4)

Early Industry Pay Processes of The Colonial Period

Laborers in this period of American history were mainly individuals working for themselves as farmers or artisans, free laborers, indentured servants, and slaves.

The pay processes for free laborers, regardless of the industry, were similar during this period. Workers at an iron foundry, a ship builder, or a small manufacturer producing items for export were paid in a similar fashion. Workers were often hired to perform specific tasks for specific periods of time and few were hired as "permanent" employees. For smaller concerns the payment of wages to workers was often recorded along with other types of expenses in journals as illustrated in this 1757 Account Book of the Spermaceti Manufactury (Exhibit 3-2). In this exhibit, two entries have been made related to workers; one January 8 notation reads "Paid John Armington for work" and another on January 25 reads "Paid Amos Brock for 3 Weeks work of his Wife."

This more informal multi-purpose method of recording worker employment agreements, time, business expenses, payments, and receipts of all types would survive until the beginning of the industrial age in the coming century as reflected in this October 1809 Day Book used at one of Paul Revere and Sons' businesses in Canton, Massachusetts (Exhibit 3-3). Here the top entries capture the absences of workers Perkins and Bosworth.

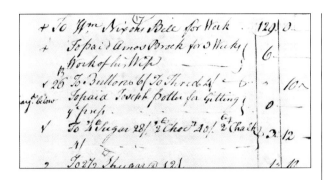

Exhibit 3-2: Spermaceti Manufactury Account Book, January 4 – February 12, 1757; Obadiah Brown Papers; MSS 315; Box 2; Folder 27; Courtesy of the Rhode Island Historical Society, Providence, RI

Canton October 1809

Perkins absent 3 days

Bosworth absent half day

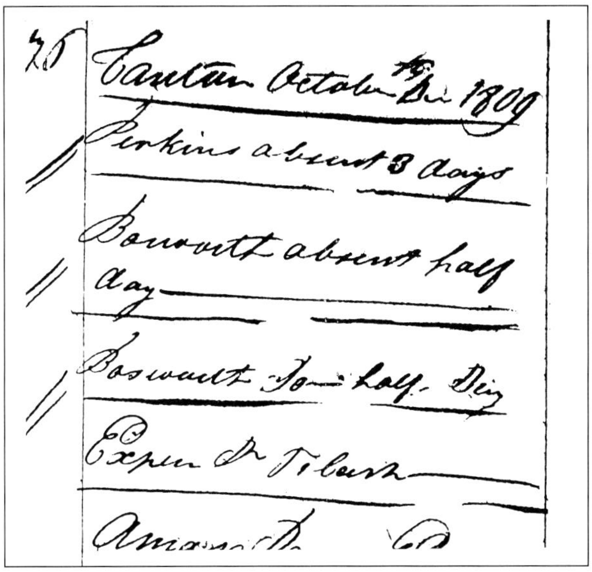

Exhibit 3-3: Revere Family Papers; Business Accounts and Letterbooks; 1805-1812; Volume 20; Microfilm; Roll 8; Courtesy of Massachusetts Historical Society, Boston, Massachusetts

Reference Sources

1. A History of Accounting Thought; Chatfield, Michael; Robert E. Krieger Publishing Company; Huntington, NY; 1977; p. 7

2. Colonial Craftsmen and the Beginnings of American Industry; Tunis, Edwin; The World Publishing Company; Cleveland, OH and New York.; 1965

3. The Workplace Before the Factory: Artisans and Proletarians; Safley, Thomas Max; Rosenband, Leonard N.; Editors; Cornell University Press; Ithaca; 1993; pp. 13-14

4. Dictionary of American History; Adams, James Truslow, Chief Editor; Charles Scribner's Sons; New York; Volumes II & III; 1940; pp. 119-120 & 336

CHAPTER 4:
The Revolutionary Period and the Paymasters of the Continental Army

Revolutionary War Bonds Issued For Raising a Company in the Continental Army

Paymasters were entrusted with funds to pay bounties for raising new military units and for disbursing funds to soldiers. Individuals signed documents called War Bonds to bind them to the Governor and State and ensure their performance of duties. Such individuals were often appointed captains and paymasters.

Continental Army Establishes Paymaster General Position

On June 16th, 1775, the Continental Congress resolved "that there be one Paymaster General, and a Deputy under him, for the army, in a separate department; that the pay for the Paymaster General be one hundred dollars per month, and for the Deputy Paymaster under him, fifty dollars per month." (1)

James Warren Appointed First Paymaster General

James Warren, of Plymouth, Massachusetts, was elected the first Paymaster General of the Army and assumed his post on June 27, 1775 (1). Prior to this appointment, James Warren had held a seat in the lower house of the Massachusetts Court and Provincial Congress, and later served as Speaker of the House of Representatives in the new General Court. During his tenure as Paymaster General, the army was stationed in Cambridge and Boston (2). While General Warren was the first Paymaster General and in fact the first soldier of the Finance Corps, he served for only a short time and was reassigned to other posts in service of his country.

The greatest of American painters of the pre-

Revolutionary period, John Singleton Copley, completed this portrait (Exhibit 4-1) of James Warren around 1762.

William Palfrey Becomes the Second Paymaster General

James Warren was replaced by William Palfrey of Boston, Massachusetts on July 9th, 1776. Palfrey was a gifted businessman who had entered into the shipping trade at the age of 18 under the guidance of one of the great merchants of the time, Nathaniel Wheelwright. Palfrey later became business advisor and correspondent for a number of wealthy and famous individuals of the day, including John Hancock. He also had become politically active and served unofficially as the secretary to the Sons of Liberty and as a communications medium between various British and American political figures, traveling often back and forth between the two continents. (3)

At the time of his appointment, at age 35, William Palfrey was serving as aide-de-camp to

General Washington. William Palfrey assumed his position in the Continental Army as Paymaster General at the rank of Lieutenant-Colonel. At the same time, the Continental Congress also created regimental paymaster positions for each regiment. (1)

Continental Army Pay Process Organized and Improved

"Down to the time of the appointment of Colonel Palfrey, there had scarcely been an army, except in the vicinity of Boston. From this period, operations were much extended, and with them the business of the pay-office, as well as of other departments of the general staff. During the summer, while the main army at

New York remained unmolested by the enemy, the department appears to have been thoroughly organized, and the system to have been arranged, upon which, with some amendments at a later period, it continued to be administered through the war. (Exhibit 4-2) At first, remittances of money for its use were made by the President of Congress; after the organization of the Board of War they came from the Secretary, and subsequently from the Paymaster, of that Board. They were sent to the Paymaster-General, and by him to his deputies, or directly by the Board to the latter, under an escort of horse; and receipts were returned as soon as the money could be counted. Very rarely, for particular purposes, and commonly then to a small

amount, it consisted of hard coin. Generally, it was bundles of sheets of continental paper money." (3)

Paymaster General Palfrey is credited with a number of improvements to the pay process including the appointment of special auditors to ensure a more complete accountability of all personnel entrusted with military funds and the replacement of mobile payroll operations (i.e., one that moves with the troops) with stationary headquarters. On this latter recommendation, he argued successfully that "It has been the opinion of all the sensible men I have conversed with on the subject, that the grand military chest, and the records belonging to it, should by no means accompany the army; that the Paymaster-General should reside in some central place, and keep his deputies with the army, who should be supplied by him with cash just sufficient to answer their present demands; and that all accounts and vouchers relative to the pay of the army should be transmitted to him at proper periods, to be arranged and filed in this office."

Palfrey argued that "Whenever a final settlement of public accounts becomes necessary (and the day will, sooner or later, most assuredly arrive), you will find we shall be entangled in a labyrinth of confusion, from whence it will be very difficult to extricate ourselves, and all for want of method, and a little attention at the beginning. The sooner, therefore, the reformation is begun, the easier the task will be." Congress approved his proposal and the Paymaster General's Office was permanently established in Philadelphia. (3)

William Palfrey was an outstanding American who contributed much to his country and to the payroll profession.

Continental Army Cash Flow Problems

"The Continental soldier had real reason to feel that his government, such as it was, did not appreciate his efforts. Irregularly paid, and then only in Continental currency – backed only by the ink of its paper and so depreciated as to give rise to that expression of complete worthlessness 'not worth a Continental (Exhibit 4-3)'." Soldiers often had to fend for themselves, and during the bitter period of 1780-1781 when soldiers had not been paid for five months and were on half rations, there were several mutinies. (4)

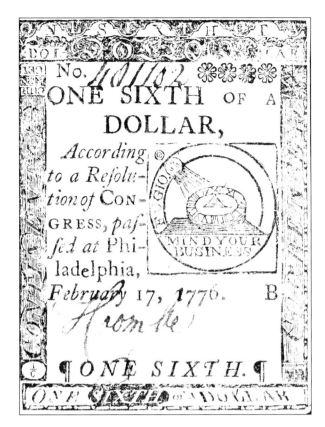

Exhibit 4-3: $1/6th Continental Congress Note (Front and Back); Courtesy of Boston Public Library, Print Department

"Red Tape" at Valley Forge

Keeping in mind the state of record keeping at the time, there were indeed many pay disputes and claims. William Palfrey and even George Washington were personally involved in reviewing and settling many of them including one involving General David Wooster of Connecticut. Resolution of the claim, carried forward by his son after his father was killed defending Ridgefield, Connecticut against British raids in 1777, ultimately required, at the recommendation of Paymaster General Palfrey, a Certificate from the Paymaster General of the Northern Department to substantiate the claim. Resolution of this one claim took over two years to resolve. (5)

Attempted Robbery of Continental Army Paymaster

Even though Continental dollars were not worth much, they were still the target of thieves. This story, captured in the personal papers of Josiah Bartlett, one of signers of the Declaration of Independence, tells of an ingenious paymaster who is delivering money to General Washington and is about to pass through an area infested with desperados and how the paymaster outsmarts the would-be thieves.

"A paymaster of the army, with a large quantity of paper money, designed for General Washington, had attempted the passage of the wood, a few weeks before. On arriving at the skirts of the wood, he was apprised of his danger, but as it was necessary for him to proceed, he laid aside his military garb, purchased a worn out horse, and a saddle and bridle, and a farmer's saddlebags of corresponding appearance: in the latter, he deposited his money, and with a careless manner proceeded on his way. At some distance from the skirt of the wood, he was met by two of the gang, who demanded his money. Others were skulking at no great distance in the wood, and waiting the issue of the interview. To the demand for money, he replied, that he had a small sum, which they were at liberty to take, if they believed they had a better right to it than himself and family; taking from this pocket a few small pieces of money, he offered them to them; at the same time, in the style and simplicity of a Quaker, he spoke to them of the duties of religion. Deceived by the air of honesty which he assumed, they suffered him to pass, without further molestation, the one observing to the other, that so poor a Quaker was not worth the robbing. Without any further interruption, the poor Quaker reached the other side of the wood, and at length delivered the contents of his saddlebags to General Washington." (6)

19

John Pierce, Paymaster General, Pays All Those Who Served in The Revolution

John Pierce of Connecticut succeeded Paymaster General Palfrey and is remembered best for his work, *Pierce's Register*, related to the payment of compensation due to soldiers who served during the Revolution. The Register of the Certificates issued by John Pierce, Esquire, Paymaster General and Commissioner of Army Accounts for the U.S., to officers and soldiers of the Continental Army under the Act of July 4, 1783 includes funding of the revolutionary debt under the act of August 4, 1790.

"As is well known, during the Revolutionary War, the Government was often in extremities on account of the lack of necessary funds, and especially the pay of the Army was at times greatly in arrears. To remedy, as far as possible, this unfortunate situation, the Continental Congress on 7/4/1783 when the War was approaching the end, passed the following resolution: 'Resolved, That the Paymaster General be, and he is hereby, fully authorized and empowered to settle and finally adjust all accounts whatsoever between the United States and the officers and soldiers of the American Army, so as to include all and every demand which they or either of them may have by virtue of the several resolutions and acts of Congress relating thereto: and that the said paymaster do give certificates of the sums which may appear due on such settlements in the form and manner which the superintendent of the finances of the United States may direct: 'Provided always, that the certificates to the officers shall be delayed for a reasonable time to obtain returns of payments or advances to them by the States or public departments, where in the opinion of the Paymaster General such delay shall be necessary. It should be noted that these settlements cover only the sums which remained unpaid at the end of the war."(7)

The process of issuing 93,000 certificates totaling more than 10 million dollars began on July 11, 1783 and was almost fully completed by September 15, 1785, just two years after signing the Definitive Treaty of Peace in Paris. (7)

John Pierce shares some of the frustration he was feeling from the pressures of the Paymaster General's position during this critical time in history in a letter to General Oliver Wolcott, Jr. in 1782 when he writes "I have flattered myself that my business would have permitted me to visit my friends, and for a moment get away from the thorny and perplexed paths of a public life, but I cannot, and indeed, advantage might be taken of my absence to ruin me…whim and injustice have induced some and perhaps my own unworthiness, others to write it. I thought that when I did justice to all and followed the strict line of integrity that then 'full sure my greatness would be ripening' – but such characters they oft must meet with disappointment and trouble – if I survive this war with reputation; joyfully in deed I will retire to my friends and domestic peace, and I bid a final adieu to ambition, and to the craft deceit and false friendships of a court." (8)

Paymaster General Pierce held the position of Paymaster General until the time of his death in 1788 and will long be remembered for the work that he did in paying all those who were owed monies from services performed during the Revolutionary War.

Reference Sources

1. A Sketch of the Organization of the Pay Department, U.S. Army, from 1775-1876; Carey, Major A.B., Paymaster, U.S. Army and the United States Army Paymaster General's Office; Washington, D.C.; 1876; pp. 5-6

2. Dictionary of American Biography; Malone, Dumas, Editor; Volume XIX; Scribner's Sons; N.Y.; p 478

3. Life of William Palfrey; Palfrey, John Gorham (grandson and noted historian); Sparks' Library of American Biography; Sparks, Jared; Volume XVII; Charles C. Little and James Brown; Boston; 1845; pp. 340-348, 410-411 & 431-435

4. The Compact History of the United States Army; Dupuy, Colonel USA Ret. R. Ernest; Hawthorne Books, Inc; N.Y.; 1956; pp. 31-33

5. "Red Tape at Valley Forge"; Reed, John F.; Manuscripts; Spring 1968; Volume 20 (2); pp. 20-27

6. Colonial Hall: Biography of Josiah Barlett; http://wecom.com/bba/ch/bartlett/jbartlettbio.html

7. Pierce's Register; Report of Daughters of the American Revolution; Genealogical Publishing Company, Inc.; Baltimore, MD; 1976; Original: Senate Document Volume 9 No 988; 63rd Congress; 3rd Session; Washington, D.C.; 1915

8. Manuscript Letter from Paymaster General John Pierce to Oliver Wolcott, Jr.; August 23, 1782; Courtesy of Connecticut Historical Society, Hartford, CT

CHAPTER 5:
Expanding Territories and the Old West

In the years following the American Revolution, the United States explored and significantly expanded its territories westward; acquired Florida from Spain; added many states to the Union; and fought two wars, the War of 1812 with England and the Mexican War of 1846. Paymasters, especially those in the military, played an important role throughout this period. The following material describes some of the more famous (and not so famous) army and navy paymasters of the times and provides some sense of the generic role of the paymaster and the pay process for this period in American history.

Meriwether Lewis – A Paymaster First, an Explorer Second!

Meriwether Lewis (Exhibit 5-1) was born on August 18, 1774 near Charlottesville, Virginia. In 1794, Lewis was called on by George Washington to serve in the Whiskey Rebellion. He went on to become first a lieutenant and at age 23 a captain. "Attracting the first attention where punctuality and fidelity were requisite, he was appointed paymaster to his regiment." (1)

Senate Amends Army Paymaster Organizational Structure and Regulations

At the beginning of the nineteenth century, the aggregate strength of the regular U.S. Army was slightly over 4,000. By the second half of the century the total had reached 16,000, with the distribution of garrisoned troops shifting from east to west as Texas and then rest of the southwestern territory was acquired by the United States and the need for an army presence increased. (2).

Throughout early American history, Congress frequently changed the structure of the Army's Paymaster Organization. While the office of the paymaster general was established in 1775, "it was the Act of 3 March, 1799 that first gave

Exhibit 5-1: Meriwether Lewis (c.1807); oil on canvas by artist Charles Willson Peale; Courtesy of Independence National Historical Park; Philadelphia, PA

shape to a regular system of deputy and regimental paymasters." A subsequent act in 1802 "provided for a paymaster of the army, seven paymasters, and two assistants, thereby abolishing the posts of regimental and battalion paymasters. These positions were restored in 1808. With the War of 1812, civilians were appointed as regimental paymasters and all paymasters and assistant paymasters were bonded in the performance of their duties." (3)

On April 6th, 1814, the United States Senate approved the following amendments: "Section 2. That the president of the United States be authorized by and with the advice and consent of the senate, to appoint to each military district so many assistant district paymasters, not exceeding thirty, as the public service may, in his opinion, require. Section 3. And be it further enacted, That it shall be the duty of the paymaster of the army, under the direction of the war department, to make all disbursements of money within that department to the district paymasters, and to adjust, state, and exhibit their several accounts, according to such forms, and with such periods as shall be prescribed for that purpose by the treasury department. Section 4. And be it further enacted, That to secure the regular and punctual payment of the troops, the district paymasters shall examine and transmit to their paymaster of the army the accounts and vouchers for all disbursements which have been made by them to the troops of the army or district where they shall be stationed, as soon as the first payment shall have been made, and accompany the same with an estimate for the next payment; which account and estimates shall be regularly transmitted, that settlements may be made and competent funds remitted." (4)

Nathan Towson – An Army Paymaster General With Longlasting Impact

In total, Nathan Towson of Maryland served as Paymaster General for over 34 years, from 1819 to 1854. Due in part to his many years of service, "Colonel Towson instituted regulations and procedures which remained in effect for almost 100 years. His programs lowered the cost of paying the troops from 4.3% of the amount paid to 1.3% and losses were virtually eliminated." (5) Oklahoma Fort Towson was named in his honor.

Purser Samuel Hambleton and Oliver H. Perry at the Battle of Lake Erie

Samuel Hambleton joined the U.S. Navy in 1806, during Jefferson's term when the Navy was in its infancy. He was commissioned a Purser. The title of Purser was changed to Paymaster by an Act of Congress on June 22, 1860 although the duties remained basically identical. Hambleton first served on a gunboat in New Orleans. In 1812, he transferred to Oliver Hazard Perry's fleet at Newport, Rhode Island and went with Perry in 1813 aboard the flagship, Lawrence. Hambleton, like many Navy pursers and other military paymasters before and after him, maintained a personal diary. His diary included observations of the War of 1812. Diaries of paymasters often provide valuable insights into the actual events of the day and have in many cases been published. (6)

The Importance of Early Frontier Army Paymasters

"The military paymaster, like the military agent, was an important personage on the frontier. Through his hands passed thousands of dollars each year, money which in 1805 was in truth, the only source of cash to the country." The significance to the local economy was great, especially during times of war. (3)

The Funding of Early Army Payroll Accounts

Paymasters during the early part of this period drew their funds directly from general headquarters. Beginning in 1810 and following the opening of ports of entry and the creation of land offices in the western territories, the military paymaster secured payroll funds directly from the Treasury Department or through private banks. It was often difficult to secure the exact denominations needed and army soldiers were often paid in bank notes versus actual currency. (3)

Early Frontier Army Pay Processes

Early frontier soldiers were normally paid every six months, although delays beyond six months were common. Prior to the War of 1812, when regular pay cycles were interrupted, for whatever reason, authority was often given to advance monies to soldiers (especially officers). Officers were also provided with special pay services. For example, officers could have a portion or all of their pay disbursed directly to their wives or other dependents back east. (3)

Examples of Frontier Pay Delivery Hazards

Early frontier forts were often located around "fur factories" which served as collection and processing points for the Indian fur trade. Troops stationed at such posts were mainly concerned with the control of traders and the confiscation of liquor within Indian

Territory. In such forts, the government-appointed civilian overseer would often use soldiers to perform fur processing work, a practice that was discontinued in 1822 at which point duty was limited to river traffic control. One such factory was Fort Osage on the Missouri River. In 1820, an Army paymaster, on route to pay soldiers at the fort, overturned his canoe and the soldiers' pay was lost. The factory had to use its own cash profits to pay the soldiers and submit a voucher for reimbursement from the government. (7)

Another example of the hazards faced routinely by paymasters of the day involved Major Asher Phillips of the paymaster corps who was on the first historic steamboat (The Robert Thompson) ever to travel any length up the Missouri. One hundred miles south of Louisville it collided with the steamer Tennessee. However, it was able to complete the trip and Major Phillips was able to deliver the long awaited pay to troops at Ft. Smith. (8)

Military Escorts of Paymasters On the Santa Fe Trail

Commercial trade began along the Santa Fe Trail in 1804. By 1824 trade moving over the Trail was reaching vast proportions just as the fur trade was at its peak. When war with Mexico was declared in 1846, movement westward along the Trail increased. The U.S. Congress authorized 50,000 volunteers be sent west. "Additional" paymasters were sent west to support the increased military presence. The Santa Fe and other trails such as the Oregon became major "highways" to the west. Military escorts were often assigned to accompany paymasters and their shipments of payroll funds destined for western forts against bandits and Indians. (9)

One example of the Indian threat on the Trail from Fort Leavenworth, Missouri to Santa Fe, New Mexico in 1847 is captured in an unnamed captain's report published in 1847. Under the command of Lieutenant John Love, 80 dragoons (early name for army frontier soldiers) were charged with the escort of over $300,000 for the troops at Santa Fe. Traders and travelers heading west would often attach themselves to these escorts for protection. While on route, the caravan was attacked by Indians and a number of military and civilian members of the party were killed and hundreds of heads of cattle driven off. Love was able to save the payroll and later completed the rest of the journey safely. (10)

The Misfortunes of Paymaster Jeremiah Yellott Dashiell

Jeremiah Yellott Dashiell was an accomplished M.D. and founder of the Louisville Medical College when he was appointed a paymaster in the United States Army by President Polk at the beginning of the Mexican War in 1846. He served as paymaster on the staff of General William Jenkins Worth in San Antonio, Texas and was dismissed in 1858. He subsequently was appointed colonel, assistant adjutant general, and inspector general of state troops on the staff of Governor Francis R. Lubbock. (11)

After the Civil War, he went on to become the editor of the San Antonio *Herald.* (11)

Paymaster Dashiell was the victim of two payroll-related disasters. In 1857, Paymaster Dashiell withdrew over $23,000 in gold and silver coins from the Charleston, S.C. Treasury for payroll to be delivered to the federal troops in Fort Pierce on the east coast of Florida during the Seminole Indian War period. Travel to the district was first by schooner and subsequently via a small boat. After the payroll had been transferred to the small boat and was entering an inlet, the boat capsized in heavy waves. While all on board were saved, the coins were lost. (12)

After the loss, Paymaster Dashiell withdrew an additional $28,000 in gold to replace the lost funds and continued on route. One evening, while waiting to board a steamship the following morning, Paymaster Dashiell and his escort left the payroll unattended in his room momentarily. During this time period, thieves took some of the payroll. The theft went undetected until the following day on the steamship, when Paymaster Dashiell decided to count the payroll. Paymaster Dashiell borrowed the deficit from sutlers (civilians who were under contract to the government to provide commissary and other services to soldiers at military posts) and others to pay the troops. Later, some of the thieves were apprehended and some of the coins were recovered. In regards to the earlier incident of the capsized boat and lost coins totaling $23,000, two young men found many of the 2600 gold coins while fishing off the Atlantic coast near the original site of the mishap over 100 years later (in 1963). (12)

Wells Fargo Used in California to Deliver the Payroll

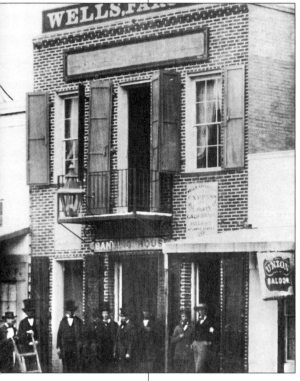

Exhibit 5-2: Wells Fargo's First Office, San Francisco; 1852; Courtesy of Wells Fargo Bank; Wells Fargo Bank History Room

The Army headquarters for California was located in San Francisco. Beginning in 1859, Wells Fargo was used to transport the payroll to the troops in Southern California by way of steamship traveling down the coast. The Wells Fargo Agent would pack up the payroll (often upwards of $30,000), board a steamship, and then disembark at the military posts along the coast including Fort Tejon, San Bernardino, Fort Mojave, and Fort Yuma. It was a joyful day when the *Los Angeles Star* reported that Mr. Rogers, clerk to the Paymaster (of the U.S. Army), had received the payroll from Wells Fargo and was in the district during the week for the purpose of paying off the troops. Wells Fargo (Exhibit 5-2) opened their first brick office building in San Francisco in 1852. (13)

Paymasters in the Arts, Science And Literature

William Rich Hutton — Paymaster Clerk and Artist of Early California

Exhibit 5-3: William Rich Hutton, photo of; (c.1850?); Permission of The Huntington Library, San Marino, California

William Rich Hutton (Exhibit 5-3) became a paymaster clerk and joined his uncle, William Rich, when he was appointed paymaster to the United States volunteer force in California. William Rich Hutton was trained in drawing, surveying, and mathematics and was only 21 when he traveled west with his uncle. His

appointment as paymaster clerk extended from 1847 to 1849. During this period, his position as paymaster clerk took him from San Francisco to Los Angeles and to early forts and settlements between these two locations.

William Rich Hutton is remembered for some 95 early drawings of California, Lower Mexico and other locations in the southwest. His drawings (Exhibit 5-4) demonstrate sound artistic talent but are more important from their historic perspective as they provide some of the earliest pre-camera images of early California scenes. The collection is now housed at The Henry E. Huntington Library and Art Gallery in San Marino, California. (14)

Paymaster Jose Estrada — Perhaps the First American to Get Smallpox Vaccination

Jose Estrada, paymaster of a mining company in Alta, California may have been the first American to receive the smallpox vaccination. On August 28, 1821, Estrada of Monterey wrote a letter to a friend in Santa Barbara stating that "a Russian surgeon has brought vaccine and today has vaccinated 54 persons, I being the first." The source of the vaccine might have been Spanish in origin and might have been purchased by the Russians in Lima, Peru and delivered to Alta, California for purposes of immunizing the population in Russian America where they had considerable interest in the control of smallpox, a dreaded disease of the time. (15)

Exhibit 5-4: Mission of San Carlos de Monterey, Carmel (1848?); sketch by William Rich Hutton; Permission of The Huntington Library, San Marino, California

Reference Sources

1. Lewis & Clark; Lighton, William R.; Riverside Press, Cambridge; Houghton, Mifflin and Company; Boston and New York.; 1901; pp. 5-7

2. A Guide to the Military Posts of the United States 1789 – 1895; Prucha, Francis Paul; The State Historical Society of Wisconsin; Madison, WI; 1964; pp. 143-144

3. "The Frontier Army Officer, 1794 – 1814;" Caldwell, Norman W.; Mid-Atlantic: An Historical Review; 1955; Volume 37 (2); pp. 117-119

4. "Mr. Worthington, From the Committee on Military Affairs"; United States Congress; Washington; 1814; Microfilm; Loc # Shoemaker 33389; American Antiquarian Society

5. "Finance Branch at USMA"; http://www.dmi.usma.edu/Branch/FI/Fi.htm; 1/27/1999

6. "Two Marylanders in the Early Navy: The Hambleton Family Papers"; M.S. 2021; Cox, Richard J.; Maryland Historical Magazine 1974; Volume 69 (3); pp. 317-32

7. "Expansion Westward"; http://bliss-usasma.army.mil/museum/7.html; 2/14/1998

8. The Fort Smith Story; http://www.fortsmith.com/fort/book.html

9. The Old Santa Fe Trail: The Story of a Great Highway; Inman, Colonel Henry; Corner House Publishers; Williamstown, MA; 1977 (Reprint)

10. Soldiers on the Santa Fe Trail; Oliva, Leo E.; University of Oklahoma Press; Norman, OK; 1967; pp. 81-84

11. "Dashiell, Jeremiah Yellott (1804 –1888); Handbook of Texas Online: Dashiell,Jeremiah Yellott; http:/www.tsha.utexas.edu/handbook/online/DD/fdal7.html

12. "The Fort Pierce American Gold Find"; Clausen, Carl J.; Florida Historical Quarterly; 1968; Volume 47(1); pp. 51-58

13. "Since 1852 – Wells Fargo;" Wells Fargo & Company; San Francisco; 1996; p. 6; & Wells Fargo Homepage www.wellsfargo.com

14. California 1847 – 1852: Drawings by William Rich Hutton; The Henry E. Huntington Library and Art Gallery; San Marino, CA; 1956

15. "Smallpox Immunization in Alta, California: A Story Based on Jose Estrada's 1821 Postcript"; Moes, Robert J.; Southern California Quarterly; 1979; Volume 61 (2); pp. 125-145

CHAPTER 6:
Pre-Civil War Industries and Pay Processes

The Manufacturing Environment

"In 1800 the typical American manufacturer was a master craftsman or mill proprietor, the typical employee was a handicraft worker, and the typical plant a room or series of rooms in the craftsman's home or in a small building adjacent to a stream which supplied the power for more complicated manufacturing operations." (1)

ARNOLD'S
READY RECKONER,
CALCULATED EXPRESSLY FOR THE USE OF
MANUFACTURERS AND MECHANICS,
IN CALCULATING THE VARIOUS PRICES OF
FACTORY AND MECHANICAL LABOR.
TO WHICH IS ADDED,
A TABLE SHOWING THE PRICE OF ANY QUANTITY OF WOOD,
FROM TWO FEET TO TWO CORDS, AT PRICES FROM
THREE TO SIX DOLLARS PER CORD.
ALSO,
A TABLE, EXPRESSING THE DIFFERENT PRICES OF BOARD
FOR DAYS AND MEALS.

BY ALFRED ARNOLD.

PROVIDENCE:
PRINTED BY KNOWLES AND VOSE.
1842.

An early tool used by such small manufacturers or mechanics as they were called was *Arnold's Ready Reckoner*. This tool (Exhibit 6-1) was designed to help small businesses calculate everything from the price of any quantity of wood to the amount of wages due a day laborer.

The Office Environment

"The main clerical work done in …. a lawyer's office, where documents often had to be reproduced in triplicate or more, was copying. The work in other offices of the day may have been more heavily concentrated on other tasks, such as bookkeeping, depending on the firm in question. But their small scale was a characteristic common to all pre-Civil War offices, reflecting the political economy of the time." Some enterprises operated on a national scale, i.e., insurance companies were in place to protect the commerce and shipping that flourished on the east coast seaports and factories located in New England. (2)

"Unlike the twentieth century clerical worker, a bookkeeper in a pre-Civil War business was acquainted with all of its financial dealings and records, rather than being restricted to a single specialized department that paid bills, or sent bills, or credited accounts, and so on. Antebellum firms were simply not large enough to necessitate breaking their office of operations down into different sections. Thus a bookkeeper understood the entire scope of a business's operations and his books disclosed a complete picture of its finances (to the extent, of course, that complete books were kept)." (2). The bookkeeper probably performed all duties related to the payment of wages, as this task would have been considered just one of the various bookkeeping functions performed by the clerical staff. Clerks prior to the Civil War were always male.

Unlike today, clerks during this time were often promoted to positions of management and ownership at the end of their indenture and many of them came from families who were already part of the merchant or propertied class. (2).

The Whaling and Merchants Industries and Pay Processes

Responsibilities and rights of owners, agents, and whalers were written out in long hand on large sheets (approximately 2' X 3') of parchment paper known as "Shipping Papers" (Exhibit 6-2), which contained all of the signatures (or marks) of every participant signing up for the voyage. This document served as a sort of early employment agreement and bound crew members, officers, and owners to a common set of objectives.

"The method of wage payment in the whaling industry was a singular one. The whaleman was not paid by the day, week, month, nor was

Exhibit 6-1: Arnold's Ready Reckoner; 1842; cover page; Courtesy of American Textile History Museum, Lowell, MA

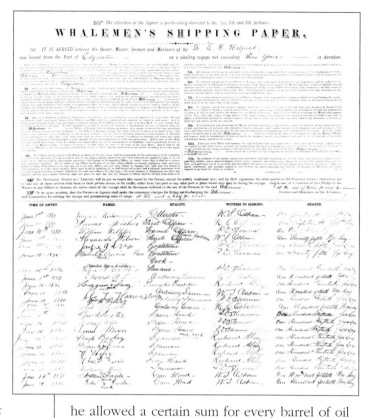

Quotation

"There's many a slip twixt the gross and the net."

A smart agent could easily adjust expenses to reduce the amount paid a whaleman since crewmembers were paid a percentage of the net value of the voyage after expenses.

In Pursuit of Leviathan; Davis, Gallman, & Gleiter; University or Chicago Press; Chicago; 1997

Lays for crewmembers were based not on a percentage of the gross profits but rather on a percentage of net value of the voyage after expenses. "Even if a large cargo was safely landed and sold at a satisfactory price, the number of dollars due to the crew was often shamefully cut down by the extortionate prices of "slops" (on board supply stores) and outfit and by the over-generous rates of interest charged upon advances." (3)

Net earnings were paid in one of several ways at the conclusion of each journey, which often lasted over 24 months. The whaler could be paid cash (if the amount was small) or even in the form of barrels of oil at the time of discharge. If the amount was large, the whaler would more likely be paid by means of an order (bill of exchange) on the owners, which the whaler would present to the agent on shore for payment. (3) At the point of payment, the whaler would sign (or place his mark on) a receipt and release form similar to the one shown here (Exhibit 6-3). Please note that Knowles & Company was one of the whaling agents in New Bedford, Massachusetts during the peak of the whaling industry and represented a number of owners.

he allowed a certain sum for every barrel of oil or for every pound of bone captured. Instead, his earnings consisted of a specified fractional share, known as a lay, of the total net process of a voyage. This system of lays … was employed to the virtual exclusion of other types of remuneration; and throughout the middle decades of the nineteenth century, the golden era of American whaling, the assigned fraction ranged from 1/8 in the case of a few favored captains to 1/250 for a young and inexperienced cabin boy. Between these two extremes there was a given time and approximation toward a going rate for each of the different ranks on board a whaler. The captains, mates, boatsteerers, and coopers received "short lays" ranging from 1/8 to 1/100 of the net proceeds; the able and ordinary seamen, stewards, cooks, and blacksmiths were entitled to shares which varied from 1/100 to 1/160; the green hands and boys had to be content with 'long lays' which fluctuated from 1/160 to 1/200; and instances of fractions as small as 1/250, or even 1/350, were not unknown." (3)

Approximately 70% of the net proceeds went to owners and agents with the remaining balance being distributed among the captain and the crew. (3)

$99.86

New Bedford April 17 1848

Received of Thomas Knowles & Co ninety nine 86/100 Dollars in full for my voyage in the Ship Minerva & against owners & officers to date

Francisco X Andrade
his Mark

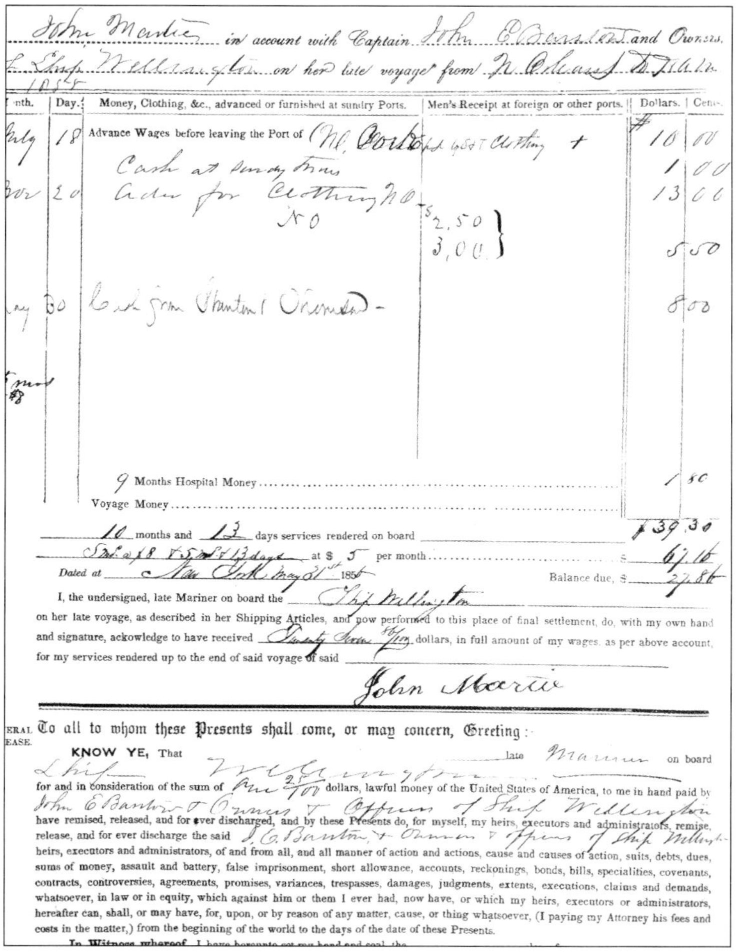

[Exhibit 6-4 pay record document with handwritten entries]

other mills of the time) and was a predecessor of the even larger mill-town corporations that would later be built in Lowell and Lawrence, Massachusetts and elsewhere.

The factory bell established a new discipline on workers who were called to the workplace. The sound of the mill bell was foreign to the agricultural worker or artisan who was accustomed to a more informal order. The factory bell regulated every facet of work life. Much of what is payroll today was born with the clang, clang, clang, of the mill bell.

But life was changed not by a bell, but by this new factory system with its large complex equipment in which factory management controlled what the workers made. The workers did not define the work process nor did they own the product they produced when it was completed. Instead they were paid wages for their labor.

Much of what is known about early New England textile factory payrolls, when many young women left their family farms for the factories, comes directly from the workers, especially as in this case from letters written to family members by female operatives:

Exhibit 6-4: Pay Record for Mariner John Marties; John E. Barstow Shipping Collection (1854-1861); MSS 0.104; Courtesy of Peabody Essex Museum, Salem, MA

Most mariners on merchant ships, on the other hand, were not paid via the lay system but through a fixed rate. The ship-master or land-based agent representing the owners acted as the paymaster. The ship-master would maintain an account (Exhibit 6-4) of all monies and provisions extended to a mariner during the voyage and would settle up (assuming the mariner had not deserted ship or died during the course of the voyage) back at the home port.

Early Textile Pay Processes

It was the clang of the mill bell that rang at the beginning of the industrial revolution in America. Pictured here is the 1852 Hooper Bell (Exhibit 6-5), the bell that replaced the original Revere Bell installed in 1814 at the first U.S. powered cotton mills at the Boston Manufacturing Company on the Charles River in Waltham, Massachusetts. These were also the first mills to employ a work force of young women who lived in company-owned houses. The Boston Manufacturing Company was a large well-financed mill operation (unlike many of the

Exhibit 6-5: The Henry N. Hooper Bell (1858); Photographer Jack Andersson, 1999; Permission of Charles River Museum of Industry, Waltham, MA

"April 12th, 1846
Lowell, Massachusetts

Dear Father; I was paid nine shillings a week last payment and am to have more this one though we have been out considerable for backwater which take off a good deal. The Agent promises to pay us nearly as much as we should have made but I do not think that he will. The payment was up last night and we are to be paid this week.

Editorial Note: Mary quoted her wages in English currency, though she was undoubtedly paid American money, nine shillings was equal to $1.50. Mary is referring to her wages exclusive of room and board charges. 'Backwater,' was a common problem in the spring, when heavy run-off due to rains and melting snow led to high water levels, causing water to back up and block the watershed. Mills often had to cease operations for several days at a time. The April payroll at the Lawrence Company indicates that Mary worked only fifteen of the normal twenty-four days in the payroll period. It was standard practice to post on a blackboard in each room of the mills the production and the earnings of each worker several days before the monthly payday, to enable operatives to see what they would be paid and to complain if the posted production figures did not agree with their own records of the work." (4)

Female mill workers of the first half of the nineteenth century "were subject to no extortion, and if they did extra work they were always paid in full. Their own account of labor done by the piece was always accepted. They kept the figures, and were paid accordingly." Treatment of mill workers was to change in the second half of the century. (5)

In addition to the mill bell, the factory gate (Exhibit 6-6) also acted as an early form of a timekeeping device. To encourage promptness, the gatekeepers were instructed to begin closing the gates exactly at the start of the workday or a few minutes earlier than the designated start of the workday. Those who were late were then forced to pass by the counting room to the side of the gate, where such workers would be docked for their late arrivals.

Within the mill itself, activities were primarily limited to production. The business aspects of the operation, including the keeping of the records and the payment of workers, were conducted elsewhere, normally in a small separate building or counting house adjacent to the mill

Exhibit 6-6: Gates at Boott Cotton Mills; Photographer Jack Andersson, 1999; Courtesy of Lowell National Historical Park

factory. Here, records such as "day-books" (or journals) and various ledgers were maintained (Exhibit 6-7). Daybooks consisted of bound blank paper and were used by the manufacturer himself or his clerk to informally record transactions including those related to worker wage payments and events of the business in chronological order along with accounting instructions. Information in the daybook would later be entered into ledger books that, in turn, would be summarized into annual financial statements. (6)

The mill office served as a place for workers to obtain small advances against future wages in order to buy groceries and other necessities. Those workers who were being dismissed or who were leaving the employment of the mill between pay periods were also paid off at the mill office.

Payday was normally every fourth week. The primary need for cash by the mill office was for payment of workers. The mill would normally draw hundreds of dollars from a local bank for this purpose. It is interesting to note that the primary "unit of production" during this period was the "household unit" and not the individual worker. A household unit normally consisted of a husband, a wife, and children but could also include other relatives and members as well. On payday, wages were paid to the head of the household as opposed to individual workers or "hands" as they were called. Each "household

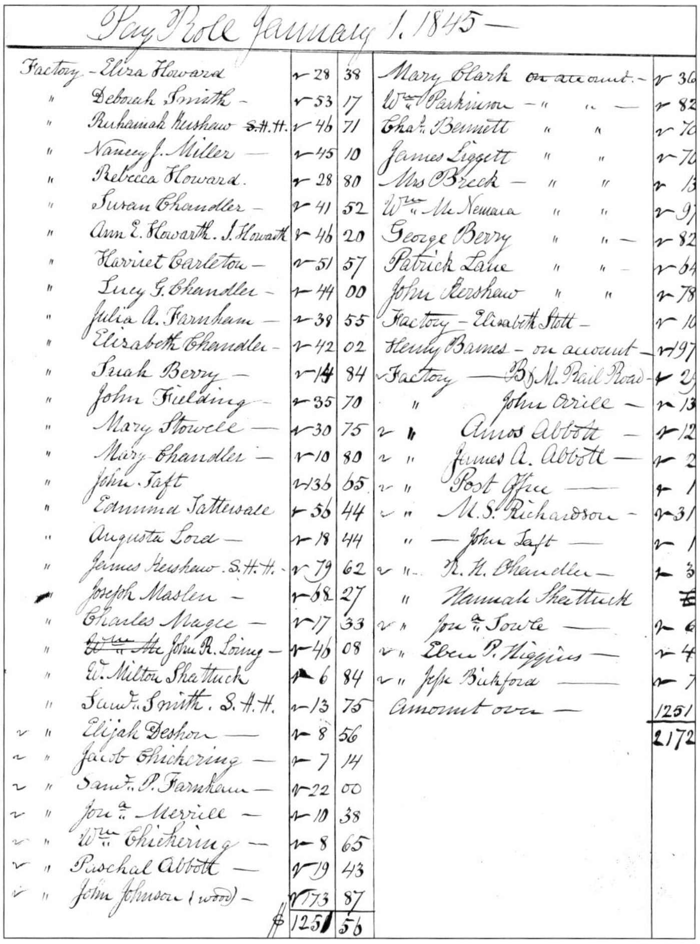

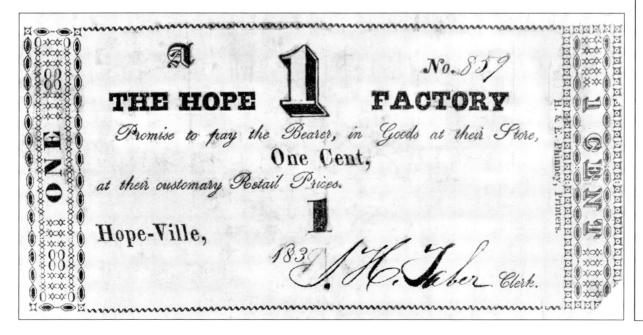

Exhibit 6-7: Factory (unnamed) Pay Roll Register; January 1, 1845; Courtesy of American Textile History Museum, Lowell, Massachusetts

unit" was assigned a separate ledger number and wage entries and records were captured accordingly. Some wages were paid in scrip or credits at local or company-owned stores in lieu of cash (Exhibit 6-8). A lesser number of mill manufacturers paid in check form against local banks. Some "household units" lived in mill owned houses and between rent and company store charges were often indebted to the mill.

Exhibit 6-8: Hope Factory Scrip Document (c. 1839); ink on paper; MSS Currency Collection; Courtesy of Rhode Island Historical Society, Providence, RI

Those paid in cash often preferred to carry uncollected wages on company books until such time as they needed the money or left the employ of the mill. (6)

Military Influence on Industry

The military has had a strong influence over the organization of the pay process in the private sector as illustrated in an excerpt from this 1859 letter in which a retiring military officer, Francis H. Smith, is giving requested advice to a friend who is establishing a business:

"Your letter of the 6th was only received yesterday – and I avail myself of the earliest moment to reply to it. You ask my advice about the management of the White Sulfur Springs Co. I would have a thoroughly military organization in the various departments of the establishment, similar to that which obtains in an army, and which we have in operation here. You need a Subsistence Department, under the control of a Commissary of Subsistence, to whom should be entrusted all the management connected with the supply, and issue of provisions. Then a Quartermaster General, to whom should be conferred the management of the beds, rooms, houses, stages, etc. and public grounds, and then a Paymaster's Department, under the control of a competent Cashier or Paymaster General. Over these departments should be placed a General superintendent whom you call President and to whom should be conferred the

general control of the whole, from A to Z, as a General does the barracks of his army." (7)

The Origin of "The Ghost Walks"

Quotation

"The paymaster is in town and the boys are anxious to see the 'ghost' walk."

1899; Gatewood; *Smoked Yankees*; p. 155

The use of the term "The Ghost Walks" first appeared in theatre in 1833 in R. Dyer's *Nine Years of an Actor's Life* with the line "If I played with applause, it was a matter of indifference whether 'the ghost' walked on Saturday or not." (8) By 1853 it appeared in the Fourth Edition of the Hotten Slang Dictionary as "Ghost, 'the ghost doesn't walk,' a theatrical term which implies that there is no money about, and that there will be no 'treasury'." By 1889, the Barrere & Leland Dictionary of Slang included a commercial utilization of the term "Ghost walking… in large firms, when the clerk whose duty it is goes round the various departments paying wages, it is common to say the ghost walks."

By the end of the nineteenth and into the early twentieth century this American slang term was in wide usage in both the military and private sector to mean paymaster and payday.

Reference Sources

1. Managers and Workers; Nelson, Daniel; The University of Wisconsin Press, Madison, WI; 1975; pp. 3-4

2. Woman's Place Is at the Typewriter; Davies, Margery W.; Temple University Press; Philadelphia; 1982; pp. 10-11; 16; 23-25

3. The American Whaleman – A Study of Life and Labor in the Whaling Industry; Hohman, Elmo Paul; Longmans, Green and Co.; New York; 1928; pp. 217, 223, 226, 234-235

4. Farm to Factory; Dublin, Thomas; Editor; Columbia University Press; New York; 1981 (Extract from Letter from textile operative, Mary Paul); p. 105

5. Early Factory Labor in New England; Robinson, Harriet H.; Wright & Potter Printing Company; State Printers; Boston; 1889 (Reprint)

6. Rockdale; Wallace, Anthony F.C.; Alfred A. Knopf; New York, NY; 1978; pp. 158-159, 163, 172, 360

7. Letters of "Francis H. Smith, August 11, 1859 Outgoing Correspondence;" Virginia Military Institute Archives; 1859

8. A Dictionary of Americanisms on Historical Principles; Mathews, Mitford M., Editor; University of Chicago Press; Chicago, IL; 1966; p. 887

CHAPTER 7:
Civil War Paymasters and Pay Processes

The Civil War period was particularly rich in information regarding paymasters and pay processes especially as they relate to the Union Army and both the Union and Confederate Navies, thanks in large part to the letters, diaries and journals maintained by paymasters. Paymasters tended to be well educated and many of them captured their observations in writing. At the same time, paymasters, especially in the Navy, normally served in other capacities in addition to their pay related duties. Some, like William F. Keeler of the USS Monitor, played key roles in highly publicized battles during the War.

The following collection of information provides insights not only into the role of the paymaster and pay process but also important observations of the Civil War and some of the key events and public figures of the day.

The Union Army's Paymaster's Manual

Thanks to J.H. Eaton, Additional Paymaster of the U.S. Army, the pay policies and procedures in effect during the Civil War have been captured in a manual (dated 1864) titled *The Army's Paymaster's Manual or Collection of Official Rules for the Information and Guidance of Officers of the Pay Department.* (1)

Considering the manual record keeping environment of the period, the following extracts from the Manual would indicate that the job of the paymaster must have been both complicated and time-consuming:

Clerks and Paymasters: "Paymasters are authorized to employ clerks by and with the appropriation of the Secretary of War Section." (1)

Muster Payrolls: "Before computing muster pay-rolls, the paymaster should examine them very critically, first the caption, then that the rolls are signed by the officer commanding the Company or Detachment, and countersigned by the inspecting and mustering officer; then to see if station and date are stated; then if the legal complement of officers and men is not exceeded; then that there are no discrepancies between the date of enlistment and date of last payment; and finally; to scrutinize closely the dates and remarks opposite each name, to make sure that there is nothing in violation of law, regulations, and particulars." (1)

Re-Enlistment for One, Two or Three Years: "All men re-enlisting will be entitled to the bounty provided by the Act of Congress July 4, 1864, and promulgated in General Orders, No. 224 …for one year: $100; for two years: $200; and for three years: $300." The law provides that one-third of the bounty "shall be paid to the soldier at the time of his being mustered (re-mustered) into the service; one-third at the expiration of one-half his term of service; and one third at the expiration of his term of service." (1)

Sutlers: "In case of a soldier's death, desertion, or discharge without pay, or the forfeiture of his pay by sentence of court-martial, the amounts due to the laundress and sutler will be noted on the muster-roll." Note: Sutlers were individuals who provided on-site commissary services to troops under government contract. (1)

Tax on Salaries: "Paymasters are to deduct and withhold the sum of three percent from all salaries and payments of every kind made in money to persons in the Civil, Military, Naval, or other employment in the service of the U.S. upon the excess of such salaries or payments over the rate of $600 per annum." NOTE: This was the first time in the history of the U.S. that taxes were withheld from earnings at the time of payment. The practice was discontinued shortly after the end of the War. (1)

Internal Revenue Stamps Used To Partially Offset Military Costs

During and for a number of years following the Civil War, private employers were also held accountable for paying taxes to the government on wages paid to employees. Taxes were paid

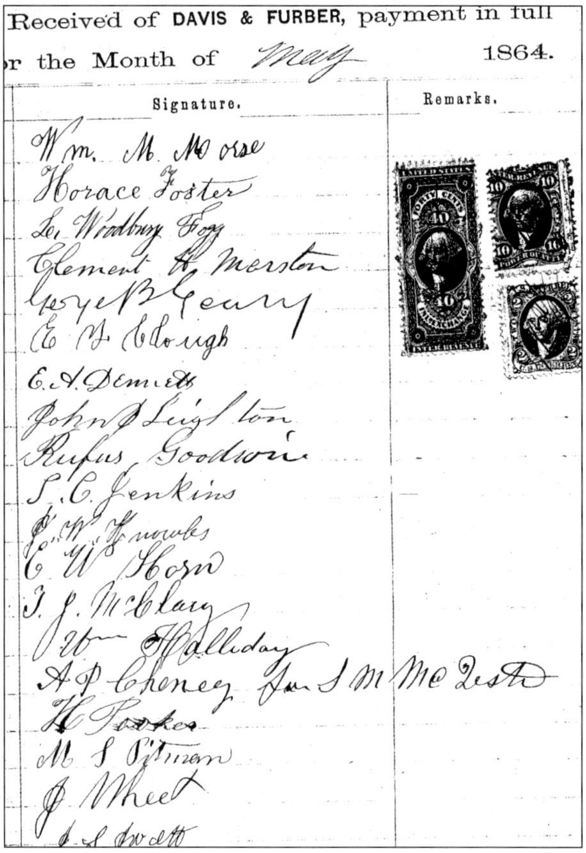
Received of DAVIS & FURBER, payment in full
r the Month of May 1864.

Signature.	Remarks.

Exhibit 7-1: Davis & Furber Pay Receipt Register; May 1864; MS 286; Courtesy of American Textile History Museum; Lowell, MA

in the form of Federal Revenue Stamps purchased and then placed on company pay registers (Exhibit 7-1) to verify the payment of such taxes.

Union Army Paymaster Generals

There were three U.S. Paymaster Generals who served during the Civil War, beginning with Benjamin F. Larned of Massachusetts (from 1854 – 1862), followed by Timothy P. Andrews of the District of Columbia (from 1862 – 1864), and ending with Benjamin W. Brice of Virginia (from 1864 – 1872). (2)

Scope of Effort to Pay Federal Troops

"During the Civil War, there was a marked increase in the scope of operations and activities. Paying the Federal Army of nearly a million men required the services of 447 paymasters." During the entire course of the War, the Pay Department of the U.S. Army disbursed over $1.1 billion. The loss from defalcations and accidents was less than $1 million. The total expense of paying the army was $6 million, representing less than 0.75%. This was a marked improvement over the War of 1812, which cost 4.36% of the total dollars disbursed. (3)

Scope of Effort to Pay Confederate Troops

"According to the most careful estimates made from the Confederate official returns, there were then at least five hundred thousand men on the army rolls, and more than three hundred thousand 'present and fit for duty.' Fully one-half of the white men of the Confederacy eligible to military duty were then enrolled for active service, while a large proportion of the other half were in civil and military service in other capacities." (4)

U.S. Army Paymasters in the Trenches

"Field soldiers in the American Civil War experienced less of the emotional chaos of combat than they did of interminable training or frequent boredom. Paymasters lived generally outside either extreme – their war was one of late-night lamplight and seven-day workweeks. Financially, of course, they were always on the spot: as long as they served the public trust, paymasters were fully and solely accountable for funds in their keeping. A man who made $2,000 a year and signed for a $3,000,000 payroll was accountable for three million dollars." (5)

"To pay their assigned army, paymasters first estimated weeks ahead the amount of cash needed from Washington. Upon receiving it, they took the funds out to the soldiers in the field. For the first couple of years, army encampments afforded paymasters a relatively safe and even simple environment in which to pay the troops. Commanders mustered and inspected their companies, and then sat with paymaster and clerk verifying data and vouching for faces. Using the unit records, paymasters calculated and disbursed the funds. However, as both sides began seeking the cover of trenches in the last two years of the war, the danger and the complexity of paying the solider increased." (5)

"Moving a payroll from a depository to the field, paymasters were usually well guarded, but guards could not help a man in the trenches with an armful of records, a box full of money, and sidearm useless for anything but close work. Yet, despite continual bombardment, paymasters spent long days in Civil War trenches paying the troops because it was their duty to do so, fulfilling the promise the U.S. Government had made to its soldiers, and the promise they had made to the U.S. Government. In the first 14 months of the war, paymasters disbursed more than $100 million and, during the entire war, a full billion. Pay a thousand soldiers a month (and keep copies of the records), calculating when they lost a gun or destroyed a saddle, deducting soldier deposits, giving receipts for money and effects of deceased soldiers, working with gold, silver, and wartime paper money under artillery bombardment – the paymasters paid the Army wherever they found it. Hardly a perfect system, yet amazing in the circumstances, and unheard of in the world of warfare to that time." (5)

U.S. Naval Paymasters and Pay Processes

Like the U.S. Army, the Navy and Marine Corps also maintained pay related documentation. One such document, *The Laws of the United States Navy and Marine Corps*, dated 1866, provides additional understanding of the paymaster's role and the pay process:

"Nor shall any commanding officer receive on board any petty officers or men, turned over from any other vessel to him, unless each of such officers and men produce to him an account signed by the captain and purser of the vessel from which they came, specifying the date of such officer's or man's entry, the period and terms of service, the sums paid and the balance due him, and the quality in which he was rated on board such ship." (6)

"That every such agent as may be appointed by virtue of the next preceding section, and every purser of the navy, shall give bond with one or more sufficient sureties, in such sums as the President of the United States may direct, for the faithful discharge of the trust reposed in him; and the paymaster of the army, the military agents, the purveyor of public suppliers, the pursers of the navy, and the agents appointed by virtue of the preceding section, shall whenever practicable, keep the public moneys in their hands, in some incorporated bank, to be designated for the purpose by the President of

the United States, and shall make monthly returns in such form as may be prescribed by the treasury department, of the moneys received and expended during the preceding month, and of the unexpected balance in their hands." (6)

Paymasters in the Arts, Science And Literature

Walt Whitman, Copyist in the Washington, D.C. Paymaster's Office

During 1862, in response to the news that his brother was wounded at the Battle of Fredericksburg, Walt Whitman (Exhibit 7-2), a Civil War nurse at the time, moved to Washington, D.C. and secured a position as a copyist in the Army's Paymaster's office while also performing volunteer work at the Army Hospital.

Exhibit 7-2: Walt Whitman (c. 1867); photograph albumen silver print by Mathew Brady; NPG.76.96; Courtesy of National Portrait Gallery, Smithsonian Institution; Gift of Mr. and Mrs. Charles Feinberg

In 1875, after his *Leaves of Grass* had already been published, *Memoranda During the War*, based on his Civil War diary and commentary, was published. In it, he captures the excitement of pay-day in the Army:

"Paying the Bounties – One of the things to note here now is the arrival of the paymaster with his strong box, and the payment of bounties to veterans re-enlisting. Major H. is here today, with a small mountain of greenbacks, rejoicing the hearts of the 2nd division of the 1st Corps. In the midst of a rickety shanty, behind a little table, sit the Major and Clerk Elridge, with the rolls before them, and much moneys. A re-enlisted man gets in cash about $200 down (and heavy installments following, as the pay-days arrive, one after another). The show of the men crowding around is quite exhilarating. I like well to stand and look. They feel elated, their pockets full, and the ensuring furlough, the visit home. It is a scene of sparkling eyes and flush'd cheeks. The soldier has many gloomy and harsh experiences, and this makes up for some of them. Major H. is order'd to pay first all the re-enlisted men of the 1st Corps their bounties and back pay, and then the rest. You hear the peculiar sound of the rustling of the new and crisp greenbacks by the hour, through the nimble fingers of the Major and my friend Clerk E." (7)

Winslow Homer's "Pay-Day in The Army of the Potomac"

Before Winslow Homer ever picked up a brush and began to paint his beautiful oil and watercolor paintings, he was a pencil and ink illustrator. In 1861 he was hired by Harper's and assigned to the Army of the Potomac. The Army had just recently been defeated at the Battle of Bull Run and was stationed in camps outside of Washington while being reorganized under McClellan. (8)

Exhibit 7-3: "Pay-Day in the Army of the Potomac;" Drawing by Winslow Homer; Harper's Weekly; February 28, 1863; Courtesy of Boston Public Library, Print Department

"His war illustrations, at this time and later, seldom pictured actual fighting. They were mostly of the everyday life in camp that made up nine-tenths of a soldier's existence, with its primitiveness, rough humor and simple recreations – soldiers gathered around a bivouac fire at night, …..a few restless souls playing cards and quarrelling; soldiers on payday descending on a sutler's tent and gorging themselves on pie, salt herring and cider." (Exhibit 7-3) (8)

A. Waud's "Paying Off the Teamsters In the Army of the Potomac"

During the Civil War, there were 8,000 – 10,000 African-American civilians employed as teamsters. "A teamster's life is a very hard one……It does not matter how much it storms, or how deep the mud, subsistence must be hauled to the camps, and day and night, toiling along with the tired horses and mules, the creaking wagons are kept busy carrying to and from commissary, quarter-master, and ordnance stores, in addition to keeping the camps supplied with fire-wood." In this sketch by Waud (Exhibit 7-4), teamsters are receiving their pay. (9)

Profiles of Civil War Paymasters

Assistant Paymaster Richard French Goodman, Aboard the USS Nightingale and USS Miami

Richard French Goodman (at age 24) served as an assistant paymaster in the U.S. Navy during the last year of the Civil War and made copious notes in his daily journal. He served in Florida aboard the Nightingale, a sailing vessel, and in Virginia aboard the steamer, Miami. His notes show how a junior officer saw the last year of the War in Northern Virginia and provide his reactions to the Confederate surrender, the death of President Lincoln, and the final days before his ship was decommissioned. (10)

Goodman, a graduate of Trinity College and son of a Hartford attorney, received his appointment from Gideon Welles, Secretary and Paymaster General of the Navy. Goodman wrote in his journal "I have been appointed an Acting Assistant Paymaster in the U.S. Navy for temporary service. I must procure sureties for twenty thousand dollars, take an oath that has been

Exhibit 7-4: "Paying Off the Teamsters in the Army of the Potomac;" Sketch by A.R. Waud; Harper's Weekly; March 7, 1863

sent to me and send in my Letter of Acceptance after which I will hold myself in readiness for immediate service. The order came upon me rather unexpectedly and I must go to Hartford for my sureties. My pay, $1300 per annum, commences when I am ordered on duty." (10)

In an April 10, 1865 notation, Goodman writes "most of our officers have been to Richmond and Petersburg but I have been compelled to remain on board to fix up my quarterly returns. General Lee has surrendered near Lynchburg in honor of which all gunboats in the river fired a national salute of thirty-five guns. The army boats which had no guns kept up a constant blowing of whistles and ringing of bells and seemed determined to make as much noise as possible." On April 15, Goodman records the following "President Lincoln was shot while sitting in his box at Ford's Theater but the assassin has not been caught although J.W. Booth the actor is supposed to be the one who did the deed." (10)

While Assistant Paymaster Goodman was offered a regular assistant paymaster position and promised rapid promotion, he chose to enter civil life. After acquiring his law degree from Albany Law University, he joined his father's firm as an attorney. He later went on to become the owner, editor and publisher of the Newton, New Jersey *Sussex Register*. In addition

he became a major in Company G of the Seventh New Jersey Regiment of the National Guard. Goodman also ran as a Republican for Congress but was not elected in 1890. He died at age 74 in 1915 and was called by the *Sussex Register*, "Our Finest Gentleman." (10)

Paymaster's Clerk Ellsworth H. Hults Aboard the USS Galena

Paymaster's Clerk Ellsworth H. Hults served aboard the ironclad "Galena" and is seen here in uniform. The Galena saw a lot of action as part of Farragut's Fleet at Mobile during an eight month cruise in 1864. Paymaster's Clerk Hults writes on Monday, July 4th off Mobile, "Today is the 88th anniversary of the Declaration of Independence, and an eventful day it has been to us. We laid quiet until noon, when all the vessels in the fleet fired a grand salute in honor of the day and decorated every masthead with a large American flag and the Union Jack at the bow. I counted upwards of 50 floating at one time. Fort Morgan fired one gun, in token of defiance. As soon as the saluting was over we received orders to go in and shell the blockade steamer ... The day was intensely hot and the men at the guns and the firemen suffered severely. The thermometer in the Engine room stood at 150 degrees while on deck the Sun boiled the Turpentine out of the Decks. And before we could wet the whole of the deck with water, one portion would be dry. My position is below at quarters, most of the time I was occupied in finishing the quarterly muster roll, the rest of the time I was on deck, intently observing affairs." (11)

Paymaster William F. Keeler Aboard the USS Monitor

Perhaps the most famous of the Civil War navy paymasters is William F. Keeler. Keeler, a native of Utica, New York, was appointed to his position later in life (at the age of 40) after achieving considerable success in the business world. He was selected for service aboard the newly constructed USS Monitor because of his engineering as well as his financial background. He joined the Volunteer Navy, which was formed as a reserve force for the War, as a Lieutenant. (12)

Exhibit 7-5: William F. Keeler (c. 1862-1865); Aboard the USS Monitor; United States Naval Institute; Annapolis, MD; 1964; Courtesy of United States Naval Institute

Paymaster Keeler (Exhibit 7-5) was an avid writer and wrote to his wife and family constantly throughout his years of naval service, first aboard the USS Monitor and then on the USS Florida. His letters have been compiled into two books. William F. Keeler was released from service on April 25, 1866 and in later life preceding his death in 1886 was referred to as "Major" Keeler. (12)

William F. Keeler is also being profiled in this book because he played an important and hero-

ic role in the battle of the USS Monitor and the Merrimack. Paymasters assigned to naval vessels during this period often had other duties outside of those related to pay. In this case, Paymaster Keeler did not only observe but was an active participant in this historic battle. In addition, he served as the ship's public relations officer and he had several opportunities to meet key public figures of the day, including President Lincoln who on several occasions boarded the USS Monitor. Paymaster Keeler's comments and observations regarding the battle between the USS Monitor and the Confederate Virginia are of historic interest. Note: The Merrimack had been previously captured by the Confederates and was renamed "The Virginia" when it reentered service as part of the Confederate fleet. (12)

The USS Monitor was launched on January 30, 1862 without a full shakedown cruise due to fear that the Virginia would steam up the Potomac and shell Washington itself. It had already crippled three Union vessels, killing 120 crewmembers when the Monitor arrived at Hampton Road, a key Federal strategic point at the mouth of the Potomac. In a battle that only lasted four hours and without a clear victor, the Monitor (Exhibit 7-6) prevented the Virginia from proceeding up the Potomac while the Union suffered significant damage to its fleet. During this battle, Keeler and Toffey (Keeler's clerk) personally passed orders back and forth between the captain and the turret. They performed these duties without regard to their personal safety and later received a commendation from the Secretary of the Navy. (12)

Typical of a paymaster's devotion to his duties, Paymaster Keeler almost drowned while attempting to save pay records during the sinking of the Monitor. "During the abandonment of the floundering Monitor on New Year's Eve 1862, Keeler had tried to save and carry off his Paymaster records, but was ordered to save himself while he could. Subsequently, he was employed for many weeks in trying to reconstruct the pay accounts of the crew." (14)

Finally, the letters of William F. Keeler provide a clearer understanding of a paymaster's role than is evident in the journals of other paymasters of the time.

"I have charge of all the provisions, clothing, stationery, what are called Small Stores, such as tobacco, soap, candles, thread, buttons, needles, jack knives, and all the thousand and one little things a Sailor will stand in need of – besides

THE ERICSSON STEAM BATTERY "MONITOR."

Exhibit 7-6: USS Monitor; Scientific American; Volume VI – No. 12; March 22, 1862, New York, NY

the money. My Steward's business is to give out the men's rations daily and render me an account; Clothing, Small Stores and everything but the daily rations I issue myself. I give my requisition upon the government stores in the yard here for such stores as I deem necessary; making my calculation from tables furnished me by the department. Anyone not drawing these rations is allowed 20 cents per day in lieu." (13)

"For the gratification of my inquisitive friends I will say here that I rank as Paymaster nothing more, nothing less. In the navy a Paymaster is a Paymaster; a Captain is a Captain and a cook, a cook…As other officers I rank with, my copy of "General Orders" says, Paymasters of more than 12 years will rank with Commanders. Paymasters of less than 12 years will rank with Lieutenants." (13)

"I am neglecting my returns to the Department to write you this – I find it no small task to make out my returns correctly this first time, as I have it all to learn with few facilities." (13)

"With the Paymaster 'everything is serene.' I make it a point to see that every duty revolving upon me is done thoroughly and at the proper time and I have now been in the service a sufficient length of time to know what my duties are and how to perform them, besides I am responsible to no one on board for the correctness of my accounts. So long as the ship is properly provisioned and a supply of money kept on hand and the men are fed and clothed my duty with those on board is performed." (14)

"The last quarter is at hand and I am up to my eyes in red tape, returns, reports and papers of various kinds…New orders issued from the Department from time to time keep adding to my work and this with the constant changes being made among the officers and the discharges and enlistment of men keep me pretty busy." (14)

"A sailor is never paid in full till his time of enlistment expires. I usually pay them 3 to 5 dollars a month as spending money. Sometimes they come to me with a doleful tale of sickness, death or destitution at home and a request for 15 or 20 dollars to send to their families. 'You say your wife wrote you that one of the children was dead?' 'Yes sir.' 'Well, where's the letter?' If their tale was a true one and the letter is produced, I give them as I think they need – if on the contrary the letter, as is frequently the case has been torn up or thrown overboard they meet with a pretty abrupt refusal. If they choose, they can appeal through the 1st Lieutenant to the Captain; he, however, very seldom changes the decision of the Paymaster…" (14)

"I suppose for the last few days my signature has been attached to over one hundred papers of various kinds a day, most of them requiring a good deal of care in making out. I have never had as yet but one paper returned to me by the Department for correction…" (14)

"My clerk, a Mr. Gilbert, I took from among the men, on trial and like him very much. He has kept books for seventeen years and entered the Navy thinking that a sea voyage would be good for his health without any idea of the kind of life it was to be. As you may suppose the change from the rough life, hard diet and still harder associates of the berth deck, to the increased pay and rank and privileges of steerage officer is a most agreeable one to him. He writes a fine business hand and is quick and correct at figures." (14)

"Constant changes are being made by the Department in all officers but Paymasters. They are seldom detached from a vessel till the expiration of the cruise. All the stores…accounts…being in their charge renders a great deal of work necessary if a change is made in them – they are seldom detached unless for sickness or some similar reason…." (14)

In April 1865, Paymaster Keeler is assigned escort duty for millions of dollars being transported from the New York Navy Yard to the Gulf. "I take out with me over one million dollars for distribution to the Squadron in the Gulf and I was told to day that I was to receive nine million more to take to New Orleans for the army…Should I take it all out with me it will be more than has been entrusted to any one Paymaster during the war….." April 5, 1865: "I have been busy the greater part of the day with money matters in the Sub Treasury New York. Tomorrow I expect to get my money on board and leave for the sunny South…." April 6, 1865: "This has been a busy day with me. I got on board my 'Greenbacks' between one and two millions. I have been relieved of the other eight million by an army paymaster who goes down with us for the purpose. We sail tomorrow afternoon." April 27, 1865: "Major James Mann who had charge of eight millions for the Army had just got a tug

alongside and had his money on deck, in twenty six iron safes. To this I added mine and persuaded him to see it safe to the Treasury with his own though the Captain wished me to go on shore with it, but my desire to see a rebel ram over came my anxiety for the safety of the money. The safes went over the side into the tug in a hurry I assure you." (14)

Assistant Paymaster Douglas French Forrest Aboard the C.S.S. Rappahannock

Confederate Paymasters such as Assistant Paymaster Douglas French Forrest, also kept journals and wrote letters to families and friends. Douglas's father was a naval officer and his mother was the daughter of the Chief Clerk of the Navy Department. He graduated from Yale in 1857 and earned a law degree from the University of Virginia. On the day that Virginia seceded from the Union he joined the Confederate Militia. In 1862, he was appointed assistant paymaster in the CSS Navy which may have been arranged by his father, then a Navy Commodore. His tour of duty took him to the Caribbean and Europe until Lee surrendered and the War had ended. Douglas French Forrest, somewhat uncomfortable with his appointment, wrote "I am ashamed to be a paymaster at a time like this. I have always been ill at ease in my professions of health and vigor and in the comforts and appliances by which I am surrounded out here. I have felt a something within me, reproaching me for enjoying in my country's agony.. when there really seems to be need for every son of the South to rally to shield her from the detested foes!" After the War, Forrest returned to his legal practice before entering a Theological Seminary and pursuing a career as a priest in the Episcopal Church. (15)

Paymaster George Foster Robinson Saves the Life of Secretary of State Seward

"While John Wilkes Booth was leaping the balustrade of the Presidential box at Ford's Theatre another assassination attempt was underway elsewhere in Washington, D. C." Lewis Payne, pretending to deliver medication to the home of Secretary of State, William H.

Seward, gained access to the Secretary's home. Seward was recuperating from a carriage accident. George F. Robinson, his army nurse, saved his life. Robinson was assigned by Surgeon Norris of Camp Douglas to act as nurse to the recovering Secretary of State while recovering himself from serious wounds suffered during the battle of Bottom's Church in Virginia. Robinson, while attending to the Secretary of State, was able, with Seward's son, to fend off the attack. In 1871, the House and Senate awarded Robinson a formal medal and $5,000 in recognition of his heroic deed. With the help of the Seward family, Robinson was later appointed Major and Paymaster in the U.S. Army, a post he held for 17 years, serving both at Fort Brown in Texas and Fort Union in New Mexico. In 1965, Senator E.L. Bartlett sought to have a 10,000 foot peak in Alaska named in his honor on the basis that without Robinson's act of courage, Alaska may never have been purchased by the United States. (16)

Paymaster's Steward John Swift Aboard the Silver Cloud

John Swift was an Englishman who enlisted in the U.S. Navy in 1863. He served with the Mississippi Squadron aboard the tinclad Silver Cloud. Swift was chosen for the paymaster steward position for the same reason that many others who served as paymasters, paymaster clerks, and paymaster stewards were selected and that is because he was able to clearly express himself and because he had good penmanship. He said "of all the officers on board here there are only three besides myself who can write and spell correctly." His promotion created some friction among some of his peers, especially the younger men. Throughout his tour, John Swift performed other sailor duties including guard and sentry and was wounded in battle, although not seriously. (17)

Money During the Civil War

Greenbacks (named for their color) were issued in mid-1861 by the Federal Government to pay for domestic war materials. These non-interest bearing notes (payable upon demand) were issued in denominations of $5, $10 and $20. Over $60 million of greenbacks were issued

during 1861 and 1862 to offset the hoarding of metallic coins. There was little backing for the greenbacks other than faith in the government. Under the Legal Tender acts of 1862 and 1863, Congress issued insured United States notes and retired the greenbacks and began to offer smaller denominations of $1 and $2 as well as larger denominations. At the peak of the Civil War, there was close to $500 million in United States notes outstanding. These notes, also backed largely by faith in the government, served as legal tender throughout the duration of the war and, by law, had to be accepted. It can be assumed that wages for both soldiers and civilians were paid via this media during this period. (18)

Pay Discrepancies and Disputes

During the Civil War there were many pay discrepancies and disputes, within both the Federal and Confederate Armies.

One of particular note involves Robert E. Lee. A controversy arose as to whether Lee was paid by both the United States and Virginia after he resigned his post as Colonel of the 1st U.S. Cavalry and before his appointment as major general of the Virginia troops. His new appointment was effective April 23, 1861, but his resignation as colonel of the 1st US Cavalry was not finally accepted until April 25. Although original records have been destroyed, a notation made from these records indicates that Lee was last paid for his U.S. Army service on March 5, 1861 and that compensation was for the months of January and February. Evidence suggests that if anything, Robert E. Lee was more likely underpaid for his last 50 days of service in the U.S. Army. (19)

Disputes were not limited to the military, as is evident in the following story about workers building the ironclad CSS Neuse, in what may be one of the earlier disputes regarding overtime pay. (20)

"By the end of the month the ironclad was, understandably, still not completed. If the unavailability of iron wasn't enough to dampen the spirits of the crew and builders, another problem arose in April when the ironclad was on the brink of completion. A dispute erupted over pay for the ship's carpenters, and Benjamin Loyall sought to settle the matter:" (20)

'My dear Minor. There has been a flare up

with the mechanics employed here…Mr. Howard….declares that they understood you to authorize a man employed four hours at night should receive a day's wages for the work…a new paymaster was ordered here, and, when the mechanics' rolls were being made up, he called upon me for authority to pay double for Sunday, and double for four hours of night work.' (20)

"Commander Loyall told the new paymaster that 'arrangements' had been made with Lieutenant Sharp concerning the mechanics' pay before the former assumed his duties on the Neuse. The paymaster then wrote to John Porter (the Neuse's designer), at Loyall's suggestion, to clarify the matter. Porter replied that if a mechanic worked on a Sunday, it would count as two days' work, and one hour of night work would amount to one and one-half hours of regular pay. Loyall wanted the dispute resolved quickly so construction would not be held up any longer than was necessary. Four of the mechanics had already walked off the job." (20)

"Loyall promptly received a reply from Minor about the pay dispute, but contractor Howard stepped into the argument and appealed to Loyall on behalf of the mechanics. The conservative Loyall gave in to the mechanics' request but wasn't pleased with their grumblings. 'Confound them they should all be enrolled and made to work at Government price with rations or go into the Army." (20)

African-American Soldier's Equal Pay Letter to Abraham Lincoln

Paymasters, over the course of history, have been required to issue payments in behalf of their employers (in this case the U.S. Government) that are sometimes unfair and unjust. In this case, an African-American Union soldier, James Henry Gooding, is writing to Abraham Lincoln requesting equal pay for equal work. The eloquence and objectivity of the author's words present a powerful argument in behalf of all African-American soldiers. At the time, soldiers received $13.00 plus $3.50 clothing allowance a month. African-Americans received $10.00 minus a $3.00 clothing deduction for the same period. Due to this difference, two African-American regiments refused their pay. Although not in response to this letter

alone, Congress, much to their credit, granted equal pay on June 15, 1864. (21)

Your Excellency, Abraham Lincoln;

"Your Excellency will pardon the presumption of a humble individual like myself in addressing you, but …… on the 6th of the last month, the paymaster of the department informed us that if we would decide to receive the sum of $10 (ten dollars) per month, he would come and pay us that sum but that, on the sitting of Congress, the regiment would, in his opinion, be allowed the other $3 (three). He did not give us any guarantee that this would be as he hoped; certainly he had no authority for making such guarantee, and we cannot suppose him acting in any way interested." (21)

"Now the main question is, are we soldiers or are we laborers? We are fully armed and equipped; have done all the various duties pertaining to a soldier's life; have conducted ourselves to the complete satisfaction of general officers who were, if any, prejudiced against us, but who now accord us all the encouragement and honor due us; have shared the perils and labor of reducing the first stronghold that flaunted a traitor flag; and more, Mr. President, today the Anglo-Saxon mother, wife, or sister are not alone in tears for departed sons, husbands, and brothers. The patient, trusting, descendants of Africa's clime have dyed the ground with blood in defense of the Union and democracy. Men, too, Your Excellency, who know in a measure the cruelties of the iron heel of oppression, which, in years gone by, the very power their blood is now being spilled to maintain, ever ground them to the dust."…… (21)

"We appeal to you, sir, as the executive of the nation, to have us justly dealt with. The regiment do pray that they be assured their service will be fairly appreciated by paying them as American soldiers, not as menial hirelings." (21)

Letters With References to Paymasters and Pay

Further insights into the pay situation and process during the Civil War can be gained from letters such as the following:
John G. B. Adams writes in his "Reminiscences of the 19th Massachusetts Regiment" in 1899 of his Civil War experiences

regarding the arrival of the paymaster while he was in the hospital recovering from wounds: "I did a foolish thing while in the hospital which came near ending my earthly experience. One day an officer, slightly wounded, came in and said the paymaster was at the Custom House and if we could get there we would receive two months' pay. On the bed next to mine lay Lieut. 'Bob' Stewart of the 72d Pennsylvania, wounded in the leg; neither of us had a dollar, and the thought of two months' pay in our pockets was pleasant. We talked it over that night; Bob was sure he could stand it, but thought I had better not try; still I was anxious to go, so we bribed the nurse, and the next morning, after the surgeon made his rounds, we took a carriage and with the nurse started for the Custom House. I fainted before we had gone a block, but kept on and was able to sign the roll which a clerk brought to the carriage, and received the money. We returned to the hospital and I suffered from fever all day, and when the surgeon made his rounds the next morning he was alarmed at my condition. I dared not tell him what we had done, for the nurse would be discharged if I did. In front of me was a man who suffered from a shell-wound in the back; he was forced to lie on his face and was very restless. I told the surgeon that this man suffered so much that it made me nervous, and he ordered him changed to another ward. It was several days before I regained what I had lost by my foolishness." (22)

Confederate Paymasters and Pay Processes

"Two able, professional paymasters operated the Office of Provisions and Clothing, the bureau responsible for paying, clothing, and feeding the navy – John De Bree (1861 – 1864) and James A. Semple (1864 until the end of the War). Under their control the navy never wanted

for food and , most of the time, had adequate clothing. Their only failure, if indeed it was their fault, was that they could never provide adequate pay." (23)

Pay records played an important role in the pay process. "This pay record, endorsed by the sailor and the paymaster, followed the seaman wherever he went, except on short trips to the naval hospital. His pay record consisted of enlistment papers, advancements in grade, previous payments, commutation of the spirit ration, and any pay advances." (23)

As with Union payrolls, the pay for Confederate sailors was infrequent and usually inadequate. "When a crew did get paid it was usually a very small amount, usually ten percent of the total due." It was not uncommon to go an entire year without receiving any pay. Sailors could have allotments sent home but had to retain a minimum of $6 to pay for government issued clothes, pay advances, or small stores purchases. In 1864, the situation was so bad that sailors often sold (against regulations) their clothing to supplement their incomes. (23)

"When a sailor died in service, his possessions remained the property of the navy until the paymaster received approval from the Treasury Department to release them to his executor or representative. If he were in debt to the government his clothing might be seized by the navy and sold at auction." (23)

Women Hired by U.S. Treasury

Due to a shortage of office workers during the Civil War, the U.S. Treasurer General, Francis Elias Spinner, hired under opposition women clerks for sorting and packaging bonds and currency on a "trial" basis. Spinner would later declare the experiment a complete success. This action opened the door to more women and by the end of the decade there would be women bookkeepers, cashiers, and accountants. (24)

Reference Sources

1. The Army's Paymaster's Manual or Collection of Official Rules for the Information and Guidance of Officers of the Pay Department; Eaton, J.H., Additional Paymaster, U.S. Army; Government Printing Office; Washington, D.C.; June 9, 1864. "Boston Public Library/Rare Books Department. Courtesy of the Trustees."

2. A Sketch of the Organization of the Pay Department, U.S. Army, from 1775 – 1876; Carey, Paymaster A. B.; United States Army Paymaster General's Office, Washington, D.C.; 1876

3. America – Its History and Biography; Newman, Stephen Morrell; B.H. Barnes; Marshalltown, IA; 1882; p. 45

4. The History of the United States; Lossing, Benson J.; Volume V-VI; Lossing History Company; New York; 1901; pp. 1621-1622

5. "U.S. Army Paymasters in the Trenches; American Civil War 1863 – 1865; Wheeler, Dr. Marilyn A.; U.S. Army; http://160.150.33.33/values03.htm

6. Laws of the United States Relating to Navy and Marine Corps, from the Formation of the Government to 1859; Callan, J.F.; Clerk to U.S. Senate Military Committee; John Murphy & Co. Publishers; Baltimore; 1866 ; pp. 133 & 173

7. Memoranda During the War; Whitman, Walt; Author's Publication; Camden, New Jersey; 1875-76

8. Winslow Homer; Goodrich, Lloyd; Whitney Museum of American Art; The Macmillan Company; New York; 1944; pp. 9, 14-15

9. "Paying the Teamsters"; Harper's Weekly; Volume VI; No. 323; March 7, 1863; p.150

10. "Yankee Paymaster"; Plumb, Robert J.; U.S. Naval Institute Proceedings; Volume 103 (10); 1977; pp. 50-57

11. "Aboard the Galena at Mobile"; Hults, E.H.; Civil War Times Illustrated; Volume 10 (1) 1971; pp.12-21

12. "The Clangor of that Blacksmith's Fray – Technology, War, and Experience Aboard the USS Monitor; Mindell, David A.; Technology and Culture; 1995; Volume 36 (2); pp. 242-270

13. Aboard the USS Monitor; Naval Letters Series; Volume One; United States Naval Institute; Keeler, William F.; Edited by Robert W. Daly; Annapolis, MD; 1964; pp. 6, 54, 72, 92-93, 159; Reprinted by permission of U.S. Naval Institute

14. Aboard the USS Florida: 1863 – 1865; Naval Letters Series; Volume One; United States Naval Institute; Edited by Robert W. Daly; Annapolis, Maryland; 1964; pp. 3, 97-99, 108, 179, 207, 211, 217; Reprinted by permission of U.S. Naval Institute

15. "An Odyssey in Gray – Selections from a Diary of Confederat Naval Life with the C.S.S. Rappahannock"; Forrest, Douglas French; Virginia Cavalcade; 1980; Volume 29 (3); pp. 124-129

16. "Seward's Savior: George F. Robinson"; Cooney, Charles F.; Lincoln Herald; 1973; Volume 75 (3); pp. 93-96

17. "Letters from a Sailor on a Tinclad"; Editor: Swift, Lester L.; Civil War History; 1961; Volume 7 (1); pp. 48-62

18. Money – Its Origin, Development and Modern Use; Moore, Carl H.; Russell, Alvin E.; McFarland & Company, Inc., Publishers; Jefferson, NC, and London; 1987; pp. 38-39

19. "Did Lee Receive Double Pay?"; Parker, Elmer, Oris; Prologue: Journal of the National Archives; 1970; Volume 2 (1); pp. 15-18

20. "The Ram is No Myth:The Life of CSS Neuse"; Courtesy of Historical Publications Section, Division of Archives & History, North Carolina Department of Cultural Resources

21. The Black Soldier; David, Jay & Crane, Elaine; Editors; William Morrow and Company, Inc.; New York; 1971; pp. 88-91

22. "Reminiscences of the 19th Mass. Regiment;" Adams, John Gregory Bishop; Boston; 1899

23. "Clothing, Pay and Provisions for the Savannah River Squadron" Kennington, John; http://members.aol.com/isnmr/csn1.htm; Gray Jackets in Savannah; White Mane Publishing; Kennington, John (to be published)

24. Woman's Place Is at the Typewriter; Davies, Margery W.; Temple University Press; Philadelphia; 1982; p. 51

CHAPTER 8:
The Post-Civil War Period

U.S. ARMY AND CAVALRY PAYMASTERS AND PAY PROCESSES

During and following the Civil War, more and more citizens moved westward. By 1890 the Department of the Interior declared the frontier "officially closed." The U.S. Army and Cavalry played important roles in this process. At its peak, the troops in the U.S. Cavalry totaled 10,970 men. (1) For most of the period, the Army and Cavalry were under the management of Paymaster Generals Benjamin W. Brice (1862 – 1872) of Virginia and Benjamin Alvord (1872 – 1880) of Vermont. Following is a composite profile of the military paymaster of the day as presented by several first-hand observers.

Elizabeth B. Custer, Wife of General Custer

In her book, *Following the Guidon*, of her days of military life with her husband during the period 1869 – 1876, Mrs. Custer reports:

"Another excitement besides the promotion of an officer was the advent of the paymaster. If the country over which he had to travel would admit of it, he came every two months; and money, even out there in that desert, where there was little chance to use it except for the prosaic necessities of life, had much the same effect on everyone as it has in the States. The officers often found roll-call a farce for a day or two as the soldiers drew their pay and slid off around the quarters to the sutler's store, or waited till nightfall and went in groups to the little collection of gin-shops usually just outside the confines of the reservation, and invariably called a city, even if there were but six huts. ....If there could be a country where no whiskey was ever imported, and to which the paymaster never came, there would not be the difficulty that exists; but fortunately all the money in the possession of the easily tempted men changed hands soon, and peace reigned until the two months were up." (2)

"The paymasters of our army get little honor-able mention of their service, which, in the Territories, is often very perilous. They have for many years traveled with comparatively small escorts through the most hotly contested of the Indian country, and as the railroads were being built and the towns laid out, a class of outlaws were the first to populate them. These despera-does followed and robbed the paymaster unless the utmost vigilance was observed. On the open plain the escort could guard against an attack, but where a mountain defile was entered, or a canyon was being crossed, or the way lay through the Bad Lands, behind whose columnar buttes many Indians might hide or desperadoes lie in wait, the danger was often very great. Part of the escort dismounted and were deployed in advance of the ambulances containing the pay-master and his travelling outfit, and the drivers and officer himself rode over these dangerous routes with rifles in hand." (2)

"We often entertained the paymaster, and on one occasion I remember that he was going to luncheon with General Custer and me. Suddenly the innocent little valise that he carried attracted our attention, and General Custer asked me if I would mind staying in our room with it until the paymaster was through with his luncheon. Certainly I did not mind, but I was curious, of course. What daughter of Eve would not be? However, I shut myself in, and after a little I divined what this mysterious seclusion meant. One woman out of all those hundreds of men was sitting up there on guard over the fifty to seventy thousand dollars in bills, for it took fully that to pay officers, soldiers, and quartermasters' employees." (2)

In the summer of 1876, Custer and his 7th Cavalry left Fort Lincoln and moved up the Missouri toward their destination (Yellowstone) to resolve the Indian issue. One entry in Elizabeth B. Custer's book, *Boots and Saddles*, is of particular interest as it references a visit by the paymaster to the troops the evening before that fateful and historic battle. "We made camp the first night on a small river a few miles beyond the post. There the paymaster made his disbursements, in order that the debts of soldiers might be liquidated with the sutler. In the morning the farewell was said, and the paymaster took sister and I back to the post." (3) NOTE: A sutler was an individual under contract to the government who provided commissary and other services to soldiers at military posts.

A Cavalryman Remembers Life With the Sixth and Paymasters And Paydays

H.H. McConnell provides the following pictures of paydays at Fort Richardson, Texas in the second half of the nineteenth century: "One of the events in the life of the soldier is the advent of the paymaster; it is looked forward to with varied kinds of interest by men of different temperaments and habits; his arrival marks an era in the otherwise monotonous life of the camp...."

Quotation:

"They Say Some Disaster Befell the Paymaster"

- from an army "proverb"

"The intervals between pay-days were sometimes considerable, during which all kind of speculations as to the causes were indulged in. Now and then a witty soldier would quote Micky Free: '*They say some disaster befell the paymaster,*' but on me conscience I think the money's not there." (4)

H.H. McConnell also provides further understanding into two key personages at all military forts of the time, the sutler and the laundress.

"Before and during the war, and up to about the period of its close, the "sutler" – so called – was appointed by the President and Secretary of War, one for each regiment....The sutler, under the regula-

tions of the old army, had many privileges; his bills against the men were collected at the pay-table, he was provided with transportation under some circumstances, his charges were regulated by law, and, upon the whole, he was not a necessary evil, but a real convenience to both officers and men.... The sutler was compelled to make both ends meet by charging exorbitant prices to the enlisted men, he having a 'dead thing' on them, collecting his pay, as he did, at the pay-table. Again, he got even with the officers by 'shaving' their pay-rolls in advance at fabulous and ruinous rates of discount, for be it remembered that at this time on the frontier money commanded five percent per month interest, and often ten percent was demanded and paid." (4)

"Situated on the outskirts of huts, old tents, picket houses and "dugouts," are the quarters of married soldiers and of the laundresses, known in army parlance as "*Sudsville.*" Each troop of cavalry was allowed four laundresses, who were rationed, and did the washing of the men at fixed prices, the same being guaranteed them, they receiving their pay at the pay-table." (4)

Paymaster as Historic Figure of The Old West

The "Paymaster" is a historic figure of the Old West – an individual trusted to carry money, make loans and offer advice on financial matters. This image would not fade with time. (Exhibit 8-1).

Paymaster as "Angel"

"Theoretically, pay came every two months, assuming that hostiles had not cut off the posts for protracted periods and that nothing had happened to the paymaster en route. One soldier likened the arrival of the paymaster to the appearance of an angel; it seemed just as miraculous." Six or eight months frequently passed between paydays and when the paymaster did arrive and disburse his funds, money was spent quickly and the next day the hospital would be full of "pay-day casualties." (5)

Paymaster as "Collection Agent"

"An officer's pay was not always free and clear – he pretty constantly faced that bugaboo known as 'accountability,' or responsibility for all government property for which he had signed, personal as well as troop. The bloodhounds in Washington were always vastly interested in the whereabouts of wandering inkstands, misplaced supplies, dead horses and an apparently infinite number of other things. ….anything not definitely proved as lost in combat or used up in service according to regulations, the errant officer had to pay for." (1) The commanding officer and paymaster had to maintain records of such debts and subtract such from the officer's pay as a regular part of the pay process.

Description of Paymaster's Office, Paymaster's Arrival and Pay Clerks

"Opposite Officers' Row were the barracks of the men, and on either side, the guardhouse, quartermaster storehouse, offices, and the hospital. Offices housed the commanding officer, the long-suffering adjutant, that harassed factotum, the quartermaster, and the paymaster whenever he reached the post which was often six or eight months late. Clerks handling the rolls and requisitions were usually men of some education whose careers in civil life had been ruined by drink. When one of them was reprimanded for his habits by his captain who asked: 'How is it that whenever I get a clerk worth anything, he is a drunkard?' The backslider replied 'Sir, if it weren't for whisky there wouldn't be any clerks in the Army." (6)

Stories and Folklore of Army and Cavalry Paymaster Escorts and Robberies

Over the course of this period, there were many reports and stories about paymaster and paymaster escort robberies or attempted robberies. In truth, many paymasters (Exhibit 8-2) and escorts were held up and/or killed while delivering payrolls to troops in their districts as illustrated in the following assortment of such accounts.

Exhibit 8-2: "The Paymaster's Escort;" Lockwood, John A; Painting "His Saddle-Bags Seemed Full;" by A. Fairmuth (?); Harper's Weekly; February 1899; Volume 33; No. 194

In *Horse, Foot, and Dragoons*, Rufus F. Zogbaum (author and artist) reported that in a journey down the Missouri by steamboat, "a band of desperadoes had carried their audacity to such an extent as to attack the escort of an army paymaster en route to a military post to pay the troops stationed there, and although they failed in their object, at least one of the soldiers guarding the treasure had met with his death in the discharge of his duty while protecting the property of the Government." (7)

Infantrymen also faced similar dangers along with cavalrymen, especially when assigned payroll escort duty. On May 11, 1889, African-American infantrymen of the 24th and cavalrymen of the 10th were escorting Major Joseph W.

Exhibit 8-3: Painting "Paymaster's Escort" by Rufus F. Zogbaum; "Following the Guidon;" Custer, E.B.; Harper & Brothers; 1890; New York, NY

such folklore, the James Boys rank high. They too have been linked to at least one army payroll robbery at Muscle Shoals, Alabama in 1881. (11) Even today, there are accounts of lost treasures resulting from such paymaster robberies. (12)

Paymasters in the Arts, Science And Literature

Rufus F. Zogbaum, Painter of Military Life

Rufus Fairchild Zogbaum, born in 1849 and a predecessor of Frederick Remington, was best known for his military paintings and for his coverage of the Spanish American War. (13) Zogbaum's painting of *"The Paymaster's Escort"* (Exhibit 8-3) appeared in Elizabeth B. Custer's *Following the Guidon.*

Wham, paymaster, U.S. Army in Arizona. Between Forts Grant and Thomas, the unit, transporting over $28,000 in gold and silver was ambushed. A heavy exchange of cross fire ensued. Nine soldiers in the contingent were wounded. The entire escort was cited for bravery. Unfortunately, the bandits were successful in escaping with the money and never were apprehended. (8)

Paymasters often had to take special measures to disguise themselves and their cargoes to ensure safe passage. One such case involved a paymaster who was moving the Army payroll to Fort Yellowstone in 1887. As there was common knowledge regarding this practice….the paymaster sensing the need to alter the procedure passed by the unsuspecting robbers in a buggy and delivered his precious satchel to Fort Yellowstone safely. (9)

"Paymaster robberies have become an endemic part of the legendary stock in trade of almost every part of the American west." (10) Among

Frederic S. Remington, Painter of The American West

Frederic Sackrider Remington, artist of over 3,000 paintings, largely of western America, was born in 1861. (13) One such painting is titled "Captain Dodge's Troopers to the Rescue." (Exhibit 8-4) Captain Dodge was a U.S. Army Paymaster who served in the Civil War, in the U.S. Cavalry following the War, in the Spanish American War, and then subsequently was appointed Paymaster General of the U.S. Army. During the first half of his career, Captain

Exhibit 8-4: Painting "Captain Dodge's Troopers to the Rescue" by Frederic Remington; 1880; Courtesy of Frederic Remington Art Museum, Ogdensburg, NY

Dodge promoted and led all black regiments and was awarded a Congressional Medal of Honor for his valor on October 18, 1879.

Additional Paymaster Samuel C. Staples and His "*Random Sketches*"

At the outbreak of the Civil War, Samuel C. Staples, age 25, was appointed Additional Paymaster of the Army and in 1864 journeyed to Santa Fe, New Mexico to pay off volunteer and regular army troops. (14)

In her book, "*Across the Plains in 1864 With Additional Paymaster Samuel C. Staples*", Darlis A. Miller credits Staples for capturing this period of time in the United States which was not otherwise well recorded. "…. First, there are relatively few overland journals for the year 1864, and Staples observed first-hand the settler-Indian hostilities and tension of the Plains preceding the Sand Creek Massacre. Second, Staples offers insights into overland travel during the war years and gives unique and sometimes charming descriptions of well-know landmarks on both the Smoky Hill and Santa Fe trails. Third, Staples provides interesting commentary on people and localities within his pay district, which included parts of New Mexico, Arizona, and Texas." (14)

Congress Authorizes U.S. Mail And Express Services to Deliver The Payroll

The process of delivering mail became a little safer and more reliable when the government began to utilize other mechanisms for delivering pay to military facilities toward the end of the century.

"In 1892, Congress authorized paymasters to use the mails or express delivery to send either checks or currency to soldiers serving at posts where there were no paymasters. Only after the passage of this act could Paymaster General T.H. Stanton report to Congress that all military posts and arsenals were now being paid each month." (15) Paymasters in the latter part of the 19th century often issued Pay Authorization Forms to soldiers (Exhibit 8-5) instead of cash directly and soldiers, in turn, would cash these with local merchants, thereby making the pay process more timely and somewhat safer.

Exhibit 8-5: U.S. Cavalry Paymaster's Pay Authorization Form (c. 1870s); Courtesy of U.S. Cavalry Museum, Fort Riley, Kansas

EARLY RAILROAD PAYMASTERS AND PAY PROCESSES

The first "rail-road" in the United States was built in Quincy, Massachusetts in 1827 to transport granite from a quarry to a river some three miles away. By 1831, hundreds of East Coast residents were traveling railroads like the Boston and Lowell, Ithaca and Susquehanna, Boston and Worcester, Boston and Providence, and Hudson and Mohawk daily. Within 10 years, there were over 2,800 miles of railroad in the United States. Railroad miles had tripled by 1850 and the standard American-type steam locomotive was in use and would remain the backbone of the American fleet until nearly the end of the century. (16) By that time, the national railroad network had expanded to over 164,000 miles and steel rails, refrigerator cars, oil tank cars, automatic couplers, and air brakes had all been invented, patented, and implemented. (17)

But it is the expansion of railroads westward following the Civil War that epitomizes the role that railroads have played in the development of America. Railroad paymasters played an integral part of this story as illustrated by the following examples:

Paymasters and Pay Processes of The Central Pacific Railroad

As the transcontinental railroad neared completion, many newspapers like the *California Vallejo Evening Chronicle* followed every facet of the project with intense interest, including how the workers were paid. When asked this question, the engineer, J. M. Graham responded "East of the state line of Calif.-Nevada,. W. E. Brown, who was secretary of the Contract & Finance company, would come to the end of the track and would often drive more than 100

53

miles in order to get in touch with the men along the line where they were working, to pay them. He carried the coin in a spring wagon and had guards along with rifles, on horseback. Sisson and Crocker Company paid all the Chinese. We always accompanied them and got paid at the same time. Sisson and Crocker Company had an interpreter named Sam Thayer and also a Chinese interpreter. When they came up to these gangs of Chinese, the money due them would be already counted out and they would dump the money in one of the Chinese' hats for that gang with a statement written in Chinese. There would be no time for explanations. They had to take it whether they liked it or not. This Sam Thayer claimed he could speak half a dozen Chinese dialects. If there was any

Camp 21

C. CROCKER.

C. P. R. R.

PAY ROLL No. *15 6*

Division No. _____ $1958.49

Sections, *Turnay & Tracy*

For the Month of *April* 1866

claims about the pay, they would take it up with Sisson and Crocker Company later." (18)

Contractors hired by the railroads were responsible for not only managing and paying the workers but for maintaining worker pay records as illustrated in this April 1866 pay roll log for men paid out of Camp No. 21 (Exhibit 8-6).

Paymasters and Pay Processes of The Union Pacific Railroad

"The Casement brothers were a team, Jack being the field boss, driving the tracklayers at the front, his brother Dan handling the paperwork, making sure the men were paid and supplies ordered. Here (Exhibit 8-7) Dan stands in the doorway, strategically placing his clerks on the ground a few inches below him. Both Casements were physically small men – but the men who worked for them would swear the Casement boys were seven feet tall and tough as nails." The second and third clerks, based on their army attire, are probably veterans of the Civil War. (19).

The Paymaster's Car at Promontory

When the work started in Omaha there were only 250 workers, but by the time they reached Promontory, Utah there were over 10,000 workers employed by the Central and Union Pacific Railroads. On the average they made three dollars a day, good wages for the period. The pay car or paymaster's car (Exhibit 8-8) is pictured here at Promontory. (19)

The term "paymaster's car" is uniquely American, and was first seen in print around 1867. (20) Eastern railroad companies, like the

Baltimore and Ohio (B&O) reported the existence of customized paymaster cars in their annual reports as early as 1865. In 1882, the Louisville and Nashville Railroad had a combination pay and track inspection car. "The paymaster's compartment at the forward end contained tables, seats, a cage, a safe, and a signal bell. The end of the bulkhead had extra-large windows for a clear view of the tracks. Double-glass windows were an interesting feature." (21).

Pay Tickets

On some railroads, workers received pay tickets (or vouchers) and then cashed them with company agents as illustrated in this Alabama & Chattanooga Railroad pay ticket (Exhibit 8-9). Both the timekeeper and the auditor had to sign the ticket. Also of interest is the 50 cents that was withheld from this pay ticket to cover doctor costs.

"The Day the Eagle Screams" — Better Known as Payday

Payday has been a festive occasion for many workers throughout history and this photo (Exhibit 8-10) of railroad workers on the Mobile division of the Southern Railway System in 1890 certainly conveys this feeling. (22)

The term "the day the eagle screams" may have originated back in 1792 when Congress passed comprehensive laws creating the first U.S. Mint and establishing the initial denominations of paper currency and coinage. The reverse side of gold and silver coins were to carry the inscription "United States of America" along with the representation of the eagle. While it is uncertain when the phrase was first used, references to the term or variations of the term have appeared throughout the nineteenth and twentieth centuries.

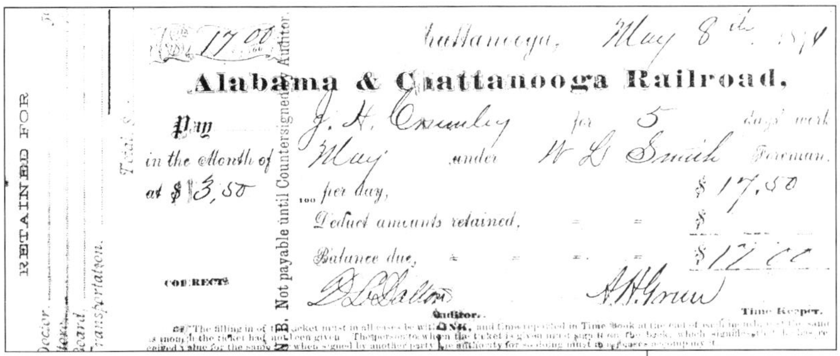

Railroad Paymasters With Towns Named After Them

David L. Gallup

While some railroad paymasters have been captured in photos, other railroad paymasters have obtained "immortality" by having towns named after them. "In 1880, a paymaster for the Atlantic and Pacific Railroad, David L. Gallup, established headquarters along the construction right-of-way of the southern transcontinental route. The railroad workers began 'going to Gallup' to get their pay; thus a town (Gallup, New Mexico) was born and named in 1881." (23)

James Madison Hanford

A similar story is associated with the California town of Hanford. "This city had its roots in the expansion of the Central and Southern Pacific Railroad system in the 1870s. The railroad was built along the spine of the interior valley. James Madison Hanford, the highly respected railroad paymaster, land agent, and assistant to the railroad president was given the honor of selecting the new town site and giving it his name. The site was established in 1877 near a Chinese shepherd's simple camp. The city was incorporated in 1891." (24)

PAYMASTERS AND PAY PROCESSES OF THE EARLY INDUSTRIAL ERA

Overview of the Period

Following the Civil War, company dynamics began to change dramatically. Small workshops became large manufacturing plants controlled by industry giants. Competition for workers

Exhibit 8-9: Old Alabama and Chattanooga Railroad Pay Ticket; (c. 1879); TIES – The Southern Railway Magazine; December 1957; Courtesy of TIES

Exhibit 8-10: "The Day the Eagle Screams;" Payday in 1890 on the Mobile Division of the Southern Railroad; TIES – The Southern Railway Magazine; August 1958; Courtesy of TIES

increased. So called "welfare companies" offering worker housing, new company benefits and other community services were created to attract and retain a stable and productive workforce. New systematic approaches to the organization and the performance of work were introduced. Unions and reform groups began to influence worker conditions and treatment and progressive governments, especially at the state level, began to enact laws to respond to these needs.

The nature of work was also changing dramatically. Administrative workers were being added to company payrolls at a record pace. Women, taking advantage of the openings provided during the Civil War and the new job opportunities created after the War, were entering the job market in ever-increasing numbers. The typewriter and carbon paper were proven to be commercially viable; the punched card tabulating machine was invented; and a flood of office technology was about to come forth. Finally, groundwork for the banking industry was being laid in the form of a check payment system.

Much of the impact of these seemingly unrelated changes would not be fully realized until the first or second decade of the twentieth century, so it was both a time of excitement and confusion, of letting go and holding on – a period of wonderful possibilities and conflicting forces.

In regards to payroll, this was probably the era in which the administrative needs of larger companies and the movement toward division of work into specialized functions gave birth to the contemporary payroll organization. Time keeping may very well have been the first payroll-related process to be impacted by technology.

Establishment of the Factory System

By "1880 the manufacturer was likely to be a factory owner or manager, the employee a machine operator, and the plant a massive multistoried brick or stone structure driven by water or steam. Economic growth and technological innovation had created the factory system." (25)

Small Firms Give Way to Giant Corporations

By the end of the nineteenth century, the number of wage earners in manufacturing would exceed 4.5 million. (25)

"The small and highly competitive firms that had dominated production in the antebellum United States gave way to giant corporations integrated vertically and horizontally in the merger movement that swept through industry during the 1890's. In the steel (United States Steel Corporation), oil (Standard Oil Company), tobacco (American Tobacco Company), food, and meat-packing sectors (Armour and Swift Companies), to name just a few, such corporations enjoyed virtual monopolies." (26).

With the introduction of the Bessemer process and the business recovery of the late 1870s and early 1880s, the steel industry became the giant of the manufacturing world (displacing textiles) - a status it would retain for the next 30 years. (25)

A few of the many other companies established during this period include the Westinghouse Electric and Manufacturing Company (1886), the General Electric Company (1892), the Goodyear Rubber Company (1898) and the United Shoe Machinery Company (1899).

Seeds for New Organizational Structures and Processes Are Planted

The late nineteenth century was an exciting period. Many new ideas and concepts on how to better organize and perform work were introduced. The status quo approach to manufacturing management, with its heavy emphasis on foreman control of work and workers was being challenged by the concept of plant management. Companies were beginning to recognize supervision and personnel management as distinct administrative functions. Finally, companies had begun to experiment with the concept of "scientific" or systematic management techniques, all in response to larger and more complex operations. (25)

"Among the outstanding features of the reorganization of the office was the division of businesses into departments. This became necessary as firms grew so large and complex that it was no longer possible for one capitalist, or even a small group, to make all the decisions." Railroad industry management was the first to recognize this need and soon began to introduce separate offices for different classifications of work, including accounting. "Thus the post-Civil War expansion and consolidation of capitalism drastically rearranged the office by partitioning firms into departments and dividing up clerical work into specialized tasks." (26)

At the same time, it was a period of intense resistance to change from those interested in preserving the status quo, like the traditionally all-powerful foreman, who actively opposed any kind of change that would lessen his span of control. To some extent, this resistance delayed any dramatic change in process until the first two decades of the twentieth century. (25)

Rise of the "Welfare Company"

"Early paternalistic or philanthropic activities were as old as the factory system and later facilitated the move to welfare work – company towns, relief funds for injured employees, reduction in work hours (although debatable) were all early forerunners of the twentieth century welfare state." (25)

In order to attract and maintain a qualified and stable workforce, companies began offering other benefits to their employees on the basis that it would inspire employees to become better workers. H. J. Heinz was a leader in this area offering his employees uniforms, dressing rooms (for women), washrooms, lockers, "roof-gardens" for lunchtime strolls and in 1890, recreation centers along with a relief association, annual outings, and the first "welfare" secretary responsible for hiring, firing, attendance, and counseling. Some companies, like Pacific Mills, deducted a small amount from each employee's weekly pay to offset the cost of some of these services, like their employees' library. (25)

Beginning of Progressive Government

Labor unions and reform groups working with more progressive states helped enact a number of laws during this period to improve worker conditions and treatment in the following areas:

Payment of Wages

"In the 1870s northern lawmakers began to legislate against long intervals between wage payments and the use of scrip or store orders." These early laws on pay frequency were usually designed to aid miners, but they also benefited factory workers. (25)

However, in many industries, changes came slowly. For example, up until the 1890s "Workers in the lumber industry were not paid in cash, or at least not entirely in cash. As a rule, cash was scarce and the workers received due bills payable in the fall or spring at the close of the logging or sawmilling season. In many places, also, the sawmill workers were given 'store orders' or took part of their pay in kind from the company store. In many cases sawmill workers were forced to trade at the company stores and were often exploited. There were cases in which, as a condition of employment, employees were required to sign written agreements that they would buy everything they needed at the company store. Frequently, liberal credit was extended in order to capture future earnings. If due bills were not used, workers had to wait until the 'end of the season' to collect their wages. When workers had to have some cash employers stood ready to discount the due bills for 10 per cent or more." (27)

Work by Women and Children

While laws establishing minimum ages and maximum hours for women and children had been enacted prior to the Civil War by many Northeastern States, they were dependent on local enforcement. In the late 1870s and 1880s, a number of northern states passed stronger laws and created state factory inspectors to ensure compliance. (25)

Maximum Work Days and Work Weeks

By 1900, the uniform standard was 10-hour days and 60-hour weeks for northern states. This standard was a long time in coming. Workers even in the first half of the nineteenth century had been pushing (Exhibit 8-11) for

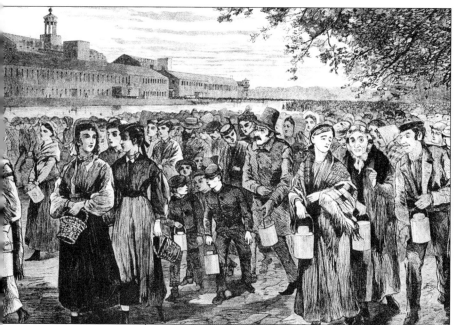

Exhibit 8-12:"Bell-Time;" Sketch by Winslow Homer; Harper's Weekly; July 25, 1868

shorter work weeks. Petitions would turn into confrontations and strikes long before companies would introduce lower standard workweeks. (25)

Health and Safety

Beginning in the late nineteenth century, state governments began to take a more active role in such matters as worker comfort and safety on the basis that "if an employer becomes satisfied by experience that his profits increase in proportion as his employees are protected against accidents and the destruction of their health, he will, in accordance with an immutable law that governs the conduct of mankind, be more careful as to their welfare, and begrudge the expenditure of a few dollars for the purpose of securing their comfort and safety." (25)

In 1877, Massachusetts began to address employee working conditions when it passed a general factory act modeled after British statutes covering fire escapes, ventilation, dangerous machinery, and elevators and provided inspection and enforcement procedures. (25)

To Chs. S. Storrow Esq., Agent of the Essex Company, Lawrence, Mass.

Those whose names are hereto appended are Workmen and Operatives in the employment of the Company for whom you are Agent; who, feeling that it will be alike for the interests of themselves and the Company that employs them, if the hours of labor are changed from the present rate to ten hours per day, very respectfully beg your earnest consideration of the subject, that you may lay our petition before the board of Directors, and that they may deem it expedient to adopt the Ten Hour System instead of the one at present in operation. They regard the justice of their petition too self-evident to need any argument with you or other rational men. You are well aware of all the circumstances of complaint, and we can but hope that it will be your pleasure as we are happy to have it your privilege, to aid us in our efforts to bring about so beneficial a reform.

Names Names

G. Smith
S. D. Yates
S. P. Nelson
J. Hoarriman
Dollar
W. Durker
M. O. Ready
R. C. Annan

Wm. W. Snell
S. C. Kingman
Benj. B. Berry
Rufus S. King
S. W. Robinson
Freeman Higgins
R. C. Hayes

Exhibit 8-11: Essex Company Workers Petition for Ten Hour Day; 1852; Essex Company Documents, Lawrence, MA; Document MS 69 & 306; 149.10; Accession: 0022.69; Courtesy of American Textile History Museum, Lowell, MA

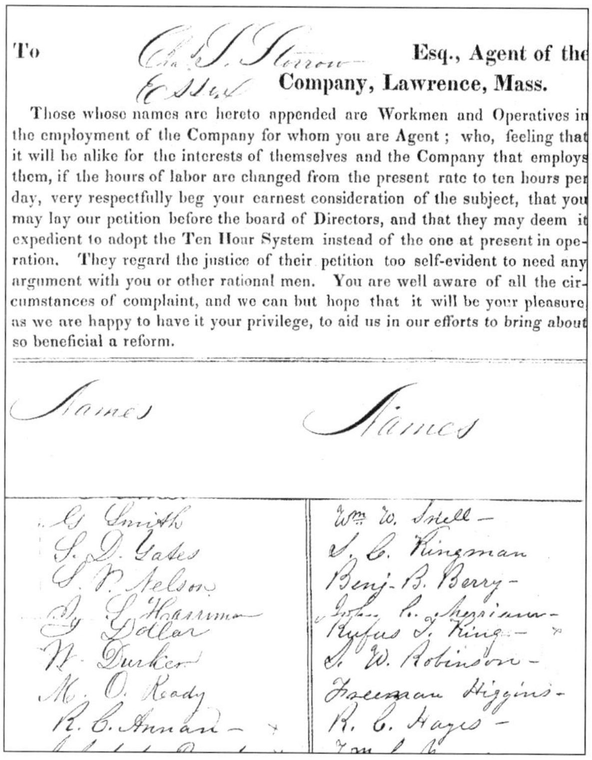

Time Keeping Methods of the Mid and Late Nineteenth Century

As illustrated in Winslow Homer's drawing "*Bell-Time*" of the workers pouring out of the mills at Lawrence, Massachusetts in 1868 (Exhibit 8-12), the work day at large factories, prior to and immediately following the Civil War, was often signified by the sounding of the factory bell.

With larger corporations and specialization of tasks, the need for automated tools arose and inventors and engineers responding to market demand soon would deliver a myriad of technological solutions to solve these growing needs. However, the overseer (supervisor) of workers along with designated "timekeepers" through most of the nineteenth and well into the twentieth century would continue to utilize pre-formatted time books to record the comings and goings of their workers.

MONTHLY TIME BOOK.

Month of April 1874

C. W. Davis
J. W. Copeland
George Smith
J. H. Thompson
Susie Shackley
Carrie Stolworthy
Annie Raynor
M. J. Sutcliffe
Annie Hefron

Price per Spool 14 Ct.
Susie Shackley 120 Spools 16 80
M. J. Sutcliffe 100 " " 14 7
Annie Hefron 8 " " 1 12
Carrie Stolworthy 111 " " 15 61
Annie Raynor 124 " " 17 36

Exhibit 8-13: Overseer Time Book for Dressing Room; National Stevens & Company; Franklin Mills; December 1870 – October 1874; Item I.D. MS 60 1535.1; p. 1874; Courtesy of American Textile History Museum, Lowell, MA

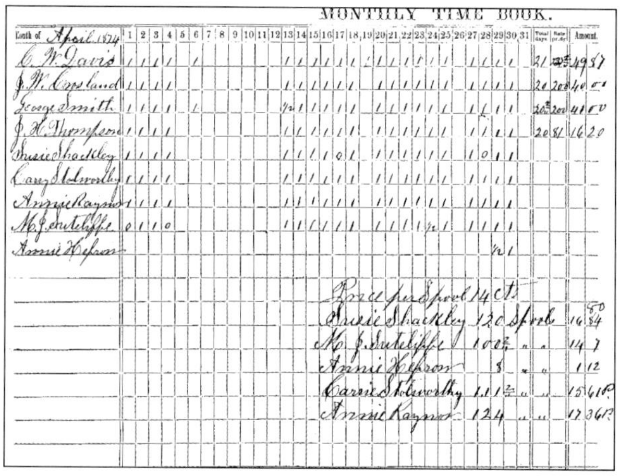

For much of the nineteenth century factories normally recorded worker times in increments of whole days as illustrated (Exhibit 8-13) in the overseer's "Monthly Time Book" of the Dressing Room of the Franklin Mills in 1874. Workers were either present or absent. Workers who

were absent for portions of a day were often docked for half or all of the day. (28)

Factories Change Time Record Keeping From Units of Days to Hours

In the latter part of the century, however, companies, perhaps in response to growing worker time reporting requirements, began to transition to increments measured in hours as reflected below in the time keeping records of the Number 8 Spinning Room of the Hamilton Woolen Company of Salisbury, Massachusetts, dated July 1, 1881:

Note to Overseers from Agent: "On and after July 1st, overseers will keep the time in hours instead of days, giving convenience 5 hours on Saturday and 11 hours on other days. They are also expected to write the names every month, add the time, record the price per hour (which will be 1/10 of former price per day) and carry out the amount in full. – Agent." (29)

Wage Calculation Tables and Aids

Wage calculation tables with pre-calculated wages based on various combinations of pay rates and hours were the primary pay tool of the day, although much improved over earlier versions.

These aids were now available from very general formats as illustrated in the *Safe Methods of Business* version (Exhibit 8-14) to highly customized industry-specific formats such as illustrated in the *Hayes' Railroad Fast Express Daily and Hourly Wages Computing Tables* (Exhibit 8-15). The visibly worn tabs of the Hayes edition give evidence of extended and heavy use of certain sections of the tool.

Birth of the Time Recording Industry and the "Time Clerk"

But automated time recording devices were soon available to help facilitate the process. One of the pioneers in their development was Edward G. Watkins, son of Gardner A. Watkins, inventor of cane splic-

ing and weaving equipment used in the production of cane chairs. His father hired Edward in 1886 to work at the Heywood Brothers Company in Gardner, Massachusetts, and his first assignment was to design a time recording machine. (30)

Exhibit 8-14: The Business Guide or Safe Methods of Business; Nichols, J.L.; J. L. Nichols & Company; Naperville, Illinois; first edition; 1886; p. 364-5

IMPROVED EDITION

HAYES'

RAILROAD FAST EXPRESS

"DAILY AND HOURLY" WAGES

COMPUTING TABLES

ARRANGED ON AN ORIGINAL PLAN

By Whole Days, Tenth and Quarters, so that the amount at a given rate Per Day, or Per Hour, for any portion or fraction of time under Forty Days, or 400 hours, is found expressed in ONE AMOUNT DIRECTLY UNDER figures representing the time for which it is computed.

INCLUDING RATES OF ALL FORMER EDITIONS

—AND—

ONE HUNDRED AND EIGHTEEN NEW RATES

—WITH—

STAHLE'S IMPROVED INDEX

EIGHTEENTH EDITION

The "Daily" and "Hourly" Tables are both included in this volume

PRICE - - $5.00

THE W. C. STAHLE COMPANY, Publishers
PITTSBURGH, PENNA.

Exhibit 8-15: Hayes' Railroad Fast Express "Daily and Hourly" Wages Computing Tables; W.C. Stahle Company; Pittsburgh, PA; 1904; cover page; Courtesy of American Textile History Museum, Lowell, MA

"With more people working in factories it was becoming difficult to keep track of the numbers of employees and paying them by the piece was difficult and time consuming. It was much simpler to pay by the hour. To maintain a system of paying by the hour it was necessary to keep a record of the number of hours each employee worked. "Time Clerks" were introduced to keep records. They were positioned by the factory door where they checked workers in and out and recorded the details. It quickly became apparent that this was not an efficient or accurate way of keeping a check on workers' hours. A better way had to be found." (30)

Earlier versions of time clocks like the "Telltale Clock" built in England by John Whitehurst were designed for use by night watchmen and were not adaptable for recording the comings and goings of hundreds of factory workers. "Subsequently other industrial time recorders were invented and produced, but none could make a written record of the workers' times. Until the 1870s, the Check Clock was in wide use. Each worker was given a token or "chink" with a number on it which was then deposited in a slot upon arriving at work. Behind the slot were separate bins which turned with the clock

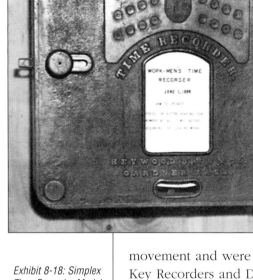

movement and were marked with the time. The Key Recorders and Dial Recorders of the late 1870s and early 1880s offered the employer an automatic written record from which to produce the payroll." (30)

Watkins' first time recording machine (Exhibit 8-16) was introduced in 1888, but it was never patented as it did not offer any new technology and couldn't, as was the case with other time recording clocks of the day, service large numbers of workers. By 1894, however, Watkins had solved some of these problems and the Heywood Brothers Company began manufacturing time clocks. (Exhibit 8-17) Due to stiff competition from other manufacturers (including the Bundy Time Recorder Company and the International Time Recorder Company), the Heywood Brothers Company decided to discontinue the product line and sold their patents, machinery, and stock to Watkins. In 1902, the Simplex Time Recorder Company was incorporated and soon was manufacturing time clocks under its own name. (30) (Exhibit 8-18)

Typewriters and Carbon Paper Come of Age

While the concepts of the typewriter and carbon paper had been envisioned for many years, it was not until the late nineteenth century that the need was strongest and the technology available so that practical models were developed. The introductions of these two separate inventions went hand in hand. These along with the commercial application of electric lighting and power, the telephone, and linotype all supported the centralization of work and the advancement of office workers.

Women Become a Major Part of The Workforce

"During the Civil War the government, now a major employer, gave hiring preference to war widows and children of soldiers killed in action. Increasingly, women also held jobs as clerks and copyists..." "The story of women entering the field of office work is again that of employers discovering that women could do the job as well as men and would work for less. Bookkeepers in the 1860s received $500 a year if female, closer to $1800 a year if male. The growth of business and industry, however, opened the door for the employment of women in secretarial as well as typing work. With the introduction of the commercial typewriter in 1873 and the shift-key model in 1878, business schools began to train women as 'typewriters' (as those who operated typing machines were called at first), stenographers, and bookkeepers. So rapidly did opportunities for women open in these jobs that by 1900 one-half of all women in high schools were enrolled in business courses and over half of all business school students were women." (31)

Banking and Its Contributions to The Transition

During the second half of the nineteenth century, the banking and financial infrastructure needed to support the emerging industrialization of America was coming into place. Payment by check currency was becoming more and more prevalent, although the payment of wages by cash would continue until the 1930s. The New York Clearing House, established by banks in New York City in 1853, would play a major role in bringing about standardization of processes.

Origins of American Accounting Association

The American Association of Pubic Accountants was incorporated under New York law in 1887. Within 10 years of this date, the state had established licensing requirements for those wishing to practice in the state. By 1902 the Federation of Societies of Public Accountants was founded in America. (32)

By 1920 most large universities were offering degrees in business administration with a major in accounting. While Italy is credited with the birth of the profession, the United States was the first nation to recognize accounting as a discipline worthy of inclusion in college curriculums. The University of Pennsylvania was the first institution to offer courses on the subject. In 1916 the American Association of University Instructors was organized. It would later go on to form the American Accounting Association. Payroll is often considered to be a specialized branch of accounting and over the coming decades, the accounting profession would establish the basic accounting framework under which payroll professionals would operate.

SPANISH-AMERICAN WAR ARMY PAYMASTERS

Without focusing on the Spanish-American War itself, inclusion of this period in American history in this book permits the author to profile three army paymasters who deserve special recognition - Francis S. Dodge, John R. Lynch, and Richard R. Wright.

All three of these individuals were not only successful paymasters, but were important contributors to social change. Each was different and yet each shared some common beliefs and values. They should be remembered for what they have taught us. Their lessons go far beyond their contributions as paymasters.

Brigadier-General Francis S. Dodge, Paymaster General in the United States Army

In 1899, Dodge was made chief paymaster, Division of Cuba, and was responsible for paying 39,000 Cuban soldiers who had fought against the Spaniards. (33)

After the War he was first appointed Deputy Paymaster General of the Army in 1901 and then Paymaster General with the rank of brigadier-general in 1904. Shortly thereafter he retired in 1906, never having fully recovered from yellow fever contracted during his days in Cuba. He passed away on February 19, 1908 and was buried at Arlington National Cemetery. (34)

Exhibit 8-19: Brigadier-General Francis S. Dodge (c. 1900); Photographer Jack Andersson (1999); Courtesy of Danvers Historical Society, Danvers, Massachusetts

Throughout his career, Francis S. Dodge (Exhibit 8-19) had developed a reputation for honesty and integrity. As Paymaster General, he had subordinate paymasters arrested and tried for keeping double sets of books and never tolerated any cover-ups during his administration. (33)

Above all he is being remembered here for his courage and his leadership in demonstrating the equality of all soldiers within the constraints of the times. Dodge, an idealist, commanded one of the earliest African-American units in the Civil War and subsequently in the West and risked the consequences. "Most white officers did not want an assignment with any of the four black regiments, afraid it would be considered 'a blot on their record.' Dodge had lived and fought too long beside his men to be influenced by such considerations; living his isolated life on lonely outposts, he developed a sense of fearless rectitude and was not tempted to hide his connections with the colored cavalry. He was an incorruptible army officer who had served his country well and in so doing had demonstrated, without chauvinistic exploitation, that an oppressed segment of our society was worthy of the rights of free citizens under the American Constitution." (33)

Major John R. Lynch, Politician, Author and Paymaster in the Regular Army

Obtaining the rank of major in the U.S. Army during or immediately following the Spanish-American War was an accomplishment by itself. But as an African-American citizen, it was a major milestone for the times. In fact, John R. Lynch may have been the first African-American to rise to this level. (35)

In 1898 he was appointed by President McKinley to the rank of captain and to the position of additional paymaster of volunteers. In 1901, he received a presidential appointment to a position of paymaster in the regular army. He served in this capacity until the date of his retirement in 1911. (35)

John Roy Lynch was born a slave on a plantation in Concordia Parish in Louisiana in 1847. After his emancipation in 1863, Lynch soon was participating in Republican politics and by 1869 (at the age of 22) he had been appointed a justice of the peace by the Governor. In the same

year, he was elected to the state house of representatives. (35)

In 1872, Lynch was chosen speaker and used this powerful position to launch a bid for a seat in Congress. On March 4, 1873, the twenty-five year old Lynch became a member of the Forty-third Congress. (35)

From 1881 to 1892 he was chairman of the Republican State Executive Committee and a member of the Republican National Committee from Mississippi for many of these years. Lynch also was the first African-American to deliver the keynote speech at the Republican National Convention. (35)

In 1896, Lynch was admitted to the Mississippi bar, and he opened up law offices in Washington the following year. It was during this period in his life, after so many other accomplishments, that John R. Lynch accepted the appointment of paymaster in the volunteer army under the McKinley administration. (3)

Major Lynch had the following to say about his appointment as paymaster in the regular army:

"Shortly before peace was declared, I had occasion to pass through Washington while on leave of absence and called at the White House to pay my respects to the president. In the course of the conversation the president asked me how I liked the position. I replied that I was better pleased with it than I supposed I would be. Then replied the President, 'you shall be retained in the regular establishment,' for which I cordially thanked him. The President informed me that my record at the War Department was one of the best of the volunteer paymasters." (35)

Lynch (Exhibit 8-20) was the author of *The Facts of Reconstruction* and an autobiography *Reminiscences of an Active Life*, the latter of which was not published until some 31 years after John R. Lynch passed away in Chicago on November 2, 1939. John R. Lynch is buried at Arlington National Cemetery. (35)

Major Richard R. Wright, Educator, Banker and Paymaster In the Spanish-American War

Born a slave on a plantation, Wright's family moved to Atlanta after emancipation where he attended missionary schools. After graduating from Atlanta University's first graduating class of 1876, Wright went on to organize a farmers' cooperative, a teachers' association, and publish a weekly newspaper. (36)

Wright (one of eight children) soon earned his doctorate in economics from the Wharton School of Finance. In 1921, Wright (Exhibit 8-21) opened the Citizens and Southern Bank and Trust Company in Philadelphia. It was one of the few African-American banks that would later survive the Great Depression. Wright was a "progressive" banker who recognized the central role of money and the need for wealth accumulation to advance African-Americans and bring greater freedom. (36)

By the time Wright was appointed paymaster in the voluntary army by President McKinley, he was a successful banker. (36)

Exhibit 8-20: John Roy Lynch (c. 1881); Photograph, albumen silver print; NPG. 89.190; Courtesy of National Portrait Gallery, Smithsonian Institution, Washington, D.C.

Exhibit 8-21: Richard R. Wright (estimated date c. 1920); Courtesy of Archives and Special Collections, Atlanta University Center, Robert W. Woodruff Library, Atlanta, Georgia

Reference Sources

1. The Troopers; Whitman, S.E.; Hastings House Publishers; New York; 1962; pp. 25 & 102

2. Following the Guidon; Custer, Elizabeth B.; Harper & Brothers; New York; 1890; pp. 286-288

3. Boots and Saddles or Life in Dakota with General Custer; Custer, Elizabeth B.; Harper & Brothers; New York; 1885; p. 265

4. Five Years a Cavalryman: Sketches of Regular Army Life on the Texas Frontier; McConnell, H.H; University of Oklahoma Press; Norman, Oklahoma; 1996 (originally published: Jacksboro, Texas; J.M. Rogers; 1889); pp. 156-161, 208-209, 211

5. The Soldiers; The Old West; Time Life Books; Nevin, David (Text); New York; p. 72

6. Indian-Fighting Army; Downey, Fairfax; Charles Schribner's Sons; New York; 1941; p 32

7. Horse, Foot, and Dragoons, Sketches of Army Life at Home and Abroad; Zogbaum, Rufus Fairchild; Harper & Brothers; New York; 1888; p. 150

8. "Walk-A – Heaps: Black Infantrymen in the West;" Langellier, John P.; WildWest; February 1997; Volume 9, No. 5

9. Lacey's Legacy; http://www.nps.gov/yell/may-12pr.htm; 5-20-97

10. The Paymaster's Escort; Lockwood, John A.; Harper's Weekly; Volume 33, No. 194; February, 1899; pp. 109-111

11. The James Boys Rode South; Hoole, W. Stanley; SWS Printers; March 1955; pp. 17 & 25

12. Buried Treasures of the American Southwest – Legends of Lost Mines, Hidden Payrolls and Spanish Coins; Jameson, W.C.; August House; Little Rock, Arkansas; 1989

13. Who Was Who in American Art; Falk, Peter Hastings; Editor; Sound View Press; 1985

14. Across the Plains in 1864 with Additional Paymaster Samuel C. Staples; Miller, Darlis A.; Sunflower University Press; Manhattan, KS; 1970

15. Finance Branch at USMA; http://dmi.usma.edu/Branch/FI/Fi.htm; 1/27/1999

16. Book of the United States; Mellen, Greenville; Editor; H.F. Sumner & Company; New York; 1836; pp. 369-378

17. American Railroads; Stover, John F.; The University of Chicago Press; Chicago, IL; 1961; pp. 266-267

18. High Road to Promontory; Kraus, George; Castle Books; New York; 1969; p. 221

19. Westward to Promontory; Combs, Barry B.; Promontory Press, New York; 1969; pp. 50, 62-63

20. Random House Historical Dictionary of American Slang; Lighter, J.E., Editor; Random House, New York; p. 1211

21. The American Railroad Passenger Car; White, John H.; John Hopkins University Press; Baltimore, MD; 1975

22. "TIES" – Southern Railway Magazine; December 1957

23. "City of Gallup – Brief History"; http://www.ci.galup.nm.us/shst.htm

24. "Short History of Hanford"; http://www.sirius.com/~pterrell/ROK/Hanford_Hisotry.html

25. Managers and Workers; Nelson, Daniel; The University Press of Wisconsin; Madison, WI; 1975; pp. 3-6, 102, 122-125

26. Woman's Place Is at the Typewriter; Davies, Margery W.; Temple University Press; Philadelphia; 1982; pp. 29, 31, 51

27. Lumber and Labor; Jensen, Vernon H.; Arno and the New York Times; New York; 1971; p. 58

28. Documents: Overseer's Monthly Time Book for Dressing Room Workers; December 1870 to October 1874; Nathanial Stevens & Company, Franklin Mills; Item I.D. MS 60 1535.1; 1874; American Textile Museum Library, Lowell, MA

29. Documents: Time Keeping Records of No. 8 Spinning Room of Hamilton Woolen Company; Salisbury, MA; 1881-1882; Call Number F.Ms H222; Peabody Essex Museum and Library, Salem, MA

30. "The Watkins Family and Simplex…the first 100 years"; Simplex Corporation; Gardner, MA

31. We Were There; Wertheimer, Barbara Mayer; Pantheon Books; New York; 1977; p. 158

32. A History of Accounting and Accountants; Brown, Richard; Verlag Sauer & Auvermann; Frankfurt, Germany 1968; pp. 271-278

33. "General Francis S. Dodge and His Brave Black Soldiers"; Zollo, Richard P.; Essex Institute Historical Collections; 1986; Volume 122 (3); pp. 181-206

34. Chronicles of Danvers; Old Salem Village 1632 - 1923; Newcomb & Gauss; Salem, MA; 1923; p. 187

35. Reminiscences of an Active Life – The Autobiography of John Roy Lynch; Lynch, John Roy; Franklin, John Hope, editor; The University of Chicago Press; Chicago and London; 1970 and secondary references to:

- "John Roy Lynch - A Measure of Hope, Black Officers in the Post Civil War Army"; http://www.usbol.com/ctjournal/JRLynchbio.html

- "John Roy Lynch, Major, U.S. Army & Member of Congress;" The Arlington National Cemetery; http://www.arlingtoncemetary.com/jrlynch.htm

36. "Banking Pioneers – The Steadfast Richard R. Wright;" http://afgen.com/blkbus7.html; pp. 8-9

CHAPTER 9:
The Twentieth Century: The Pre-World War I Years

Key Events: Year 1913
The Federal Reserve System is established under the authority of the Federal Reserve Act of December 23, 1913.

Congress reinstates the income tax and enacts a progressive tax rate of 1%-7% beginning at $3,000 of taxable income. Form 1040 is born!

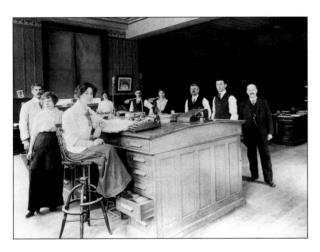

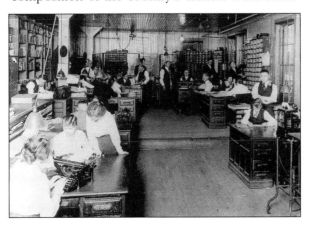

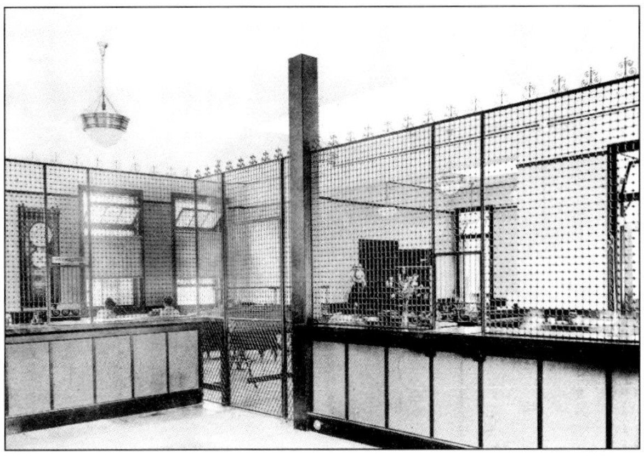

Exhibit 9-1: Royal Weaving Mill Offices, Pawtucket, RI (c. 1910-1918); Silver print. Anonymous; Neg.No. RH: (x3) Photograph, Lot 34; Courtesy of Rhode Island Historical Society, Providence, Rhode Island

During this period, immigrants represented a significant portion of the unskilled labor force. In addition, by 1910 over eight million women (almost one out of every four women in the U.S.) were employed outside the home and filled 31% of all bookkeeping positions. (Exhibits 9-1 and 9-2) "The change in gender composition of the country's clerical work force was reinforced by a rigid sex-role differentiation in offices around the turn of the century. In most American offices men predominantly served as general clerks, accountants, shipping clerks, weighers, and messengers, while women accounted for a majority of bookkeepers, cashiers, stenographers, machine operators, and filing clerks." (1, 2, & 3)

Exhibit 9-2: Clerical Workers at Signal Corps (1910); No. 111-SC-2482; Courtesy of National Archives, Washington, D.C.

United States Manufacturers in 1900

While the average manufacturing plant employed 125 workers in 1900, there were more than 70 U.S. manufacturers with plants with 2,000 or more workers. In total, these companies employed over a quarter of a million workers. Of these, there were four companies with plants employing 8,000 to 10,000 workers, including Cambria Steel, Carnegie Steel, Jones & Laughlin (steel) and Baldwin Locomotive. (4)

Images of the Office Environment and Office Worker Of the Day

The following images present a fairly accurate collective picture of the payroll environment of the period.

The paymaster's office (Exhibit 9-3) was now located in a separate office space and was well

Exhibit 9-3: Paymaster's Office, Palmer Mills (c. 1910-1920); Photographer Deer; Gelatin Silver Print; P1277.109; Courtesy of American Textile History Museum, Lowell, Massachusetts

"EVERY *time an accountant carried a fifteen-pound ledger across the room, he recalled the picture painted by the loose-leaf salesman*"

Exhibit 9-4: Fifteen-Pound Ledger Books (1913); System; Volume 23, No. 1; January 1913; p. 121

Felt & Tarrant Comptometer

An early Comptometer, with the listed patent dates ending with July 14, 1908 and the serial #26890. This model has 8 columns of keys and a 9 digit register. Alternate rows (odd numbers)of the octaganal keys are more deeply concave than the adjacent even rows, to aid the typist in finding the correct keys. These were business machines and the Comptometer users became very fast at data entry, even taking Comptometer courses, much as typists did. The beauty of the early Comptometers was that they could handle such high speed data entry without jamming. The copper finish is very good and the machine is in working order. The metal cover has a large decal on each end, reminding us that "Comptometer is pronounced like thermometer"

organized and lighted. The office cage screening provided an open working environment along with the additional protection that was necessary for confidential pay information and for large payroll cash distributions.

Male payroll clerks (Exhibit 9-4) of the period projected the classic image of the old time accountant with head visors, arm bands, and heavy ledger books.

No.	NAMES.	S	M	T	W	T	F	S	No. of Days.	Rate Per Day.	Amount.	Rent.
1	Arthur Goguen		1	1	1	1	1	1	6	2 00	12 00	
2	John S McCormick		1	1	1	1	1	1	6	3 00	18 00	
3	Alfonsine Lemay		1	1	1	1	1	1	6	90	5 40	
4	Mary L McCormick		1	1	1		1	1	1/2 5½	90	4 95	
5	Ira Leur Hired Sep 3 - 1907 = age 19 = years											
6	Mina Boulton Hired Sep 3 " age 13 "											
7	Henry L Jarvis	1	1⅝	1	1	1	1	6⅝	1 75	11 60	

Property of HISTORICAL SOCIETY FITCHBURG, MA 01420

Crocker, Burbank & Co.

Time, Week ending, Aug 3 1 1907

Exhibit 9-5: Pay Registers (August 31, 1907); Crocker, Burbank & Co.; Courtesy of Fitchburg Historical Society, Fitchburg, Massachusetts

Exhibit 9-6: Felt & Tarrant Comptometer (c.1908) www.americanartifacts.com; Courtesy of Richard Van Vleck

While the typewriter was now well established, other office machines that were also invented in the late nineteenth century were catching up and these new labor saving tools were bringing new ways of working. Payroll record keeping (Exhibit 9-5), however, for many companies, especially the smaller ones, continued to be a manual process.

Arrival of Office Technology

One of the key technological advances of the early twentieth century was the comptometer, a crank or key driven calculator. Once the product

permitted an accountant to add faster than he or she could with pencil and paper the industry took off. The comptometer became an "instant success" as one of the first automated tools for the bookkeeper, accountant, and payroll clerk. This early Felt & Tarrant model (Exhibit 9-6) had eight columns of keys with alternate rows of different colors to aid the typist in finding the correct keys. The model provided high-speed capability without the risk of jamming. Comptometers required a high level of concentration and a great deal of physical dexterity and for these reasons, comptometer departments were often filled with skilled comptometer clerks to perform calculation work for various company needs.

Along with the comptometer there was a broad array of overlapping and competing tools including the Morse and Walsh "Calcumeter" (Exhibit 9-7), the Fay-Sholes Company "Arithmograph" (Exhibit 9-8), and of course, machines like the Burroughs Adding Machine manufactured by the American Arithmometer Company (Exhibit 9-9).

In addition to accounting type tools, labeling and addressing machines like those manufactured by the Addressograph Company (Exhibit 9-10) were becoming popular.

New and more sophisticated time recording tools, like the International Time Recorder

We don't ask you to buy it until you have tried it at our expense. Isn't that fair?

Here's Your Ticket

Give Your Brain a 20 Days' Vacation
At Our Expense

Give your brain a twenty days' rest. Stop tiring it with long intricate columns of figures. We will send you

AN 8-DIAL CALCUMETER
FREE FOR 20 DAYS' TRIAL

You can try it right in your own office at your daily work for twenty days without one penny's cost. THEN, if you are not fully satisfied, return it at our expense. We sell it purely on its merits. :: Figures are the drudgery of office work. Continued toiling over long columns of figures brings on brain fag. A tired brain continually makes errors. Save the time spent in locating these mistakes. Save the worry, Save your brain with

The Calcumeter

Adds, Subtracts, Multiplies, Divides
RAPID. ACCURATE. SERVICEABLE. SMALL. PERFECT CONSTRUCTION. AUTOMATIC CARRIER

It combines speed and accuracy to the highest degree and at a cost so small as to place it within the reach of every business man. No office, no business man, should be without a Calcumeter. The saving of time and worry will pay for one in a day. :: Just fill out the attached coupon and mail to us. We will send you the Calcumeter for 20 days' trial free. Give it a thorough test. If at the end of twenty days' time you find it all we claim for it, send us $25.00. If not satisfactory, return at our expense.

ENGLISH MODEL—Pence, Shillings and Pounds, $25.00.

ASK FOR OUR CATALOGUE NO. 1

The Morse & Walsh Co.
TRENTON, N. J.

MORSE & WALSH, Trenton, N. J.

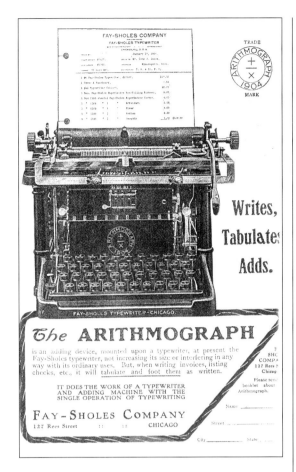

FAY-SHOLES COMPANY
FAY-SHOLES TYPEWRITER

Writes, Tabulates Adds.

The ARITHMOGRAPH

is an adding device, mounted upon a typewriter, at present the Fay-Sholes typewriter, not increasing its size or interfering in any way with its ordinary uses. But, when writing invoices, listing checks, etc., it will tabulate and foot them as written.

IT DOES THE WORK OF A TYPEWRITER AND ADDING MACHINE WITH THE SINGLE OPERATION OF TYPEWRITING

FAY-SHOLES COMPANY
127 Rees Street :: :: CHICAGO

Please send booklet about Arithmograph.

Name

Street

City   State

Exhibit 9-7: The Calcumeter (1904); Morse & Walsh Co; System; December 1904; Volume 6; p. 586

Exhibit 9-8: The Arithmograph (1904); Fay-Sholes Company; System; Volume 6; December 1904; p. 586

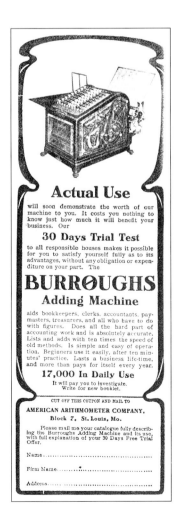

Actual Use

will soon demonstrate the worth of our machine to you. It costs you nothing to know just how much it will benefit your business. Our

30 Days Trial Test

to all responsible houses makes it possible for you to satisfy yourself fully as to its advantages, without any obligation or expenditure on your part. The

BURROUGHS
Adding Machine

aids bookkeepers, clerks, accountants, paymasters, treasurers, and all who have to do with figures. Does all the hard part of accounting work and is absolutely accurate. Lists and adds with ten times the speed of old methods. Is simple and easy of operation. Beginners use it easily, after ten minutes' practice. Lasts a business life-time, and more than pays for itself every year.

17,000 In Daily Use

It will pay you to investigate. Write for new booklet.

CUT OFF THIS COUPON AND MAIL TO
AMERICAN ARITHMOMETER COMPANY,
Block 7, St. Louis, Mo.

Please mail me your catalogue fully describing the Burroughs Adding Machine and its use, with full explanation of your 30 Days Free Trial Offer.

Name

Firm Name

Address

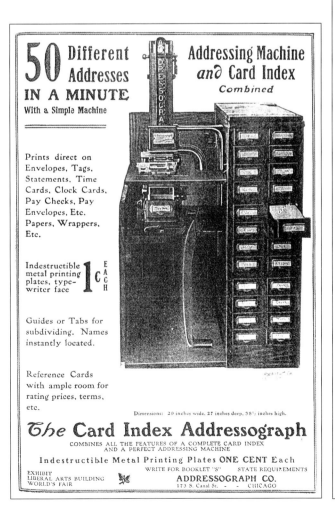

50 Different Addresses IN A MINUTE
With a Simple Machine

Addressing Machine *and* Card Index
Combined

Prints direct on Envelopes, Tags, Statements, Time Cards, Clock Cards, Pay Checks, Pay Envelopes, Etc. Papers, Wrappers, Etc.

Indestructible metal printing plates, typewriter face 1c EACH

Guides or Tabs for subdividing. Names instantly located.

Reference Cards with ample room for rating prices, terms, etc.

Dimensions: 29 inches wide, 27 inches deep, 38½ inches high.

The Card Index Addressograph

COMBINES ALL THE FEATURES OF A COMPLETE CARD INDEX AND A PERFECT ADDRESSING MACHINE

Indestructible Metal Printing Plates ONE CENT Each

WRITE FOR BOOKLET "S"   STATE REQUIREMENTS

EXHIBIT
LIBERAL ARTS BUILDING
WORLD'S FAIR

ADDRESSOGRAPH CO.
173 S. Canal St. - - CHICAGO

Exhibit 9-9: Burroughs Adding Machine (1904); American Arithmometer Company; System; Volume 6; December 1904; p. 586

Exhibit 9-10: The Card Index Addressograph (1904); Addressograph Company; System; Volume 6; September 1904; p. 270

This
International
Time
Recorder
Went
Through
Fire. It is Still
Running
and Keeping
Accurate
Time

NO better evidence of the accuracy, durability and all-round efficiency of

Photo, courtesy of Cotton States Belting & Supply Co., Atlanta, Ga.

International Time Recorders

could be offered than this photographic exhibit.

Our customers, the Cotton States Belting & Supply Co., Atlanta, Ga., write as follows:—

"On January 13th, 1914, our plant was destroyed by fire and we had in use one of your time clocks. This clock was badly burned and defaced, but continued to run during the entire time and is still running and keeping time.

"We should be very glad to box this clock up and send it to you for exhibition purposes, if you so desire."

The reason why this International Time Recorder was able to go through the fire and still keep time is this:

The International clock movement is exceptionally strong and stiff and is mounted on a heavy iron back frame having a three-point bearing. This iron frame is fastened to the back of the recorder case. No amount of warping of wood, even if located in damp and exposed places, can affect the running of an International Time Recorder—nor, we might add, can some fires.

No ordinary time clock movement could have withstood this fire test, because such movements have skeletoned-out clock plates, leaving the plates weak and allowing them to spring out of shape.

The movement of the International Time Recorder has two main springs which give an even, steady power and the absolute accuracy for which our recorders are noted. The winding arbor is exceptionally large and cannot be broken.

The automatic two-color ink ribbon shift prints the regular time in blue and the irregular time—the "in-lates" and "out-earlys"—in red. This two-color ink ribbon shift does not draw upon the power of the clock movement for its operation.

OUR NEW CATALOG shows how an International Time Recorder can be profitably used in YOUR BUSINESS—for recording day, piece, productive, non-productive, clerical and executive time. When writing kindly state your position.

International Time Recording Co.
of New York

LONDON OFFICE:
International Time Recording Co., Ltd., 151, City Road, London, E. C., England

Lock Box 971

Endicott, N. Y.

BERLIN OFFICE:
International Time Recording Co., m. b. H., 135-136 Alexandrinenstr., Berlin, S.W., Germany

Please mention SYSTEM when writing to advertisers

*Exhibit 9-11:
International Time
Recorder (1914);
International Time
Recording Co;
System; Volume 26;
December 1914; p.
advertising section*

model being promoted in this advertisement (Exhibit 9-11), regularly appeared in business magazines reflecting a growing assortment of "smart" time recording machines. International Time Recorder (owned by IBM) would later be acquired by Simplex.

Finally, punched card tabulator technology had also advanced from its first practical application in processing the 1890 U.S. Census to wider acceptance and use. IBM was now producing a mechanical keypunch. (5)

Thomas A. Edison on Office Automation

"In a few years machines will do everything in an office just as they do in the shops. All office workers will have better jobs and comparatively better pay the more they use the automatic devices."

Industrial Management; October 1920; p. 5

Scientific Management Picks Up Momentum

By the end of the first decade of the twentieth century, most companies had accepted

Frederick W. Taylor's theories regarding scientific management and were fully engaged in better organizing and managing their businesses through the scientific management approach. Worker time studies were rampant. Studies on work flow and office layout to achieve maximum productivity were being performed in every aspect of American business. New approaches to worker compensation to spur greater worker motivation were being proposed at a rate and frequency never before seen. New consulting firms, to help companies become more competitive and cost-efficient, were being created to meet these new needs. (4)

Scovill Manufacturing - An Early Leader in Scientific Management And Timekeeping

Scovill Manufacturing was one of the very first companies to apply these techniques to timekeeping. In order to standardize time reporting and achieve reliable cost information, Scovill began in 1905 to implement (in phases) some radical changes including the removal of timekeeping responsibility from the foreman, the creation of a centralized timekeeping department, and the introduction of women timekeepers on the plant floor. Scovill would build on this concept and ultimately create a new central accounting organization under the management of a comptroller's office which would include responsibility for timekeeping, payroll, and cost along with the departments of supply (purchasing, storekeeping, and inventory control) and general ledger accounting. This new model would become the standard for manufacturing organizations for many years to come. (2) Pictured in this illustration (Exhibit 9-12) are two timekeeping clerks working behind an enclosed caged office at the South Bend Watch Company in 1910.

Scientific Management Applied to Payroll

Scovill was not the only company to experiment with new approaches to work and payroll was not excluded from such reviews. *"System,"* a publication of the late nineteenth and early twentieth centuries, published many of these innovative approaches and became an important

Where a close watch is kept on time spent on all work in the factory to minimize errors—the timekeeping office of the South Bend Watch Company

Exhibit 9-12: The Timekeeping Office of the South Bend Watch Company (1910); "How I Check Clerical Errors;" Rider, S.D.; System Vol.10; March 1910; p. 305

educational tool for subscribing companies, especially those in manufacturing:

"Saving Time in Paying Men"

In *"Saving Time in Paying Men"*, author Jedediah Treat provides a more efficient method for paying large numbers of workers at a large, but unspecified, company. The article claims that the process permitted it to pay four thousand employees in less than a quarter of an hour each payday! An outline of one process follows and provides a great overview of the possible pay process of the day, whether efficient or not: (6)

1 "Instead of taking his original data of time and earnings from elaborate statements sent him by the timekeeping departments, as is often done, the paymaster takes the daily time tickets of all departments and transfers the earnings direct to the payroll sheets. The methods of timekeeping, computing wages, and making up the payrolls is all done in the timekeeping department, under the general direction of a single responsible head.

2 Payroll clerks enter earnings on the sheets by departments from the previous day. This

keeps records up to date and 'enables the paymaster to pay off discharged workmen without delay.'

3 Payroll sheets are maintained by department with two lines for every worker; the first for time spent in day labor by day and the second for piecework. The total number of hours is carried out at the right. Deductions are noted and sub-totals recorded.

4 Labor saving devices are utilized. Addressing machines are used to print names on payroll sheets and envelopes while the extension of time and computation of wages including piecework is facilitated by duplex adding machines.

5 Corrections and adjustments are then made to reflect rate changes, transfers, and advances. Following this step the rolls are closed for the pay period.

6 A clerk then draws off on an adding machine the actual amount of each kind of currency and coin required to make up the rolls. With this, money is then withdrawn from the bank and pay envelopes are filled. To ensure accuracy there are three counts, the first two by payroll clerks and the last by the paymaster.

Form 159

Abbot Stevens

To ....

For convenience in keeping the time record and paying off, a number is given, to each man employed in the Works.

Your number will be .... *3093* ....

A Check bearing this number is provided for your use.

1. On entering the Works before regular hours, you will turn your number on Check Board.

2. If you come in after starting hours, you will report to the Time-keeper.

3. If you wish to go out at any time during regular hours, you will obtain of the Foreman a slip on which is marked your number and the time at which you left off working; as you pass out LEAVE THE SLIP at the Time-Office.

4. For all over time a slip must be obtained of the Foreman, and handed to the Time-keeper on the morning of the next day.

5. All work out of the regular line, done EITHER AT THE WORKS OR OUTSIDE, must be reported EACH DAY to the foreman, that a correct record of time and expense of same may be kept.

6. Assignment of Wages Absolutely Forbidden.

By a careful compliance with the above directions, a correct time record will be secured, and liability to mistakes and misunderstanding greatly lessened.

CROMPTION & KNOWLES LOOM WORKS

Exhibit 9-13: Employee Number Card (c. 1900); Crompton & Knowles Loom Works; Stevens Collection; Item 55.1; Courtesy of Merrimack Valley Textile Museum/ American Textile History Museum, Lowell, Massachusetts Note: This exhibit has been recreated for legibility purposes

7 The timekeeper's pay list is another time-saving form. It is made out by departments and sent to the foremen on regular paydays to guide them in giving to their workmen the paymaster's checks, or cash vouchers, on which they draw their pay. Every other Saturday as the men come to work, they are handed their pay checks which they sign in the presence of the foreman or his clerk. The checks act as receipts for the payment of wages specified and at the appointed time they are handed in at the pay wicket (window).

8 Envelopes are handed out to employees at stations located in convenient places in each building. These stations are strong steel cages that accommodate three men and have two wickets. Workers form lines in front of the first wicket. A clerk calls the man's number, another clerk pulls the envelope, and a third, the payer, receives both the pay check and the envelope and compares them. If the name and amount in both

cases agree, he passes out the envelope to the workman."

Advice on How to Avoid Mistakes in Paying Workers

As the number of workers on the payroll began to increase, so did the opportunity for errors. In 1912, *System* offered its readers the following suggestion:

"A contractor had trouble with his employees because of the fact that men of similar names had now and then been confused on the payroll. This not only caused friction between the men but complicated the work of the paymaster unnecessarily. This confusion has been eliminated by a simple change in method. Voucher slips for each department are given to the different foremen. The foreman then distributes the slips to the workmen. He satisfies himself that each man receives his own slip and also makes sure that the amount is correct. The employee signs the slip and presents it in order to receive his pay. This does away with many of the ordinary difficulties in paying off – difficulties that come from mis-identification or discussion over wrong amounts. The slips are also numbered consecutively to save the paymaster's time, although the workman receives his voucher slip in the morning and may draw his pay at any convenient time before night. The employee's signature on the voucher is a good form of receipt." (7)

Employee Badge Numbers Assigned

Partly due to the above problem of proper worker identification and partly due to the need for greater control, some employers began to assign their workers permanent employee identification numbers or badges as illustrated in this 1900 employee card (Exhibit 9-13) for Abbot Stevens of the Crompton & Knowles Loom Works.

Providing Change for the Payroll

A significant problem for the paymaster of the day was the process for determining what denominations of currency and coins would be necessary to cover the payroll. Procedures like the following suggested again in *System* were developed to simplify the process:

"In paying a large payroll in currency, a systematic method of figuring how many bills of each denomination and how much silver is required is essential to avoid delay and confusion. A simple and convenient plan of calculating the necessary change is to analyze the 'amount' column of the payroll into units corresponding with the usual denominations of currency and silver, keeping it in mind always to use the largest denominations possible in each instance. Thus, by adding the fourth column to the left, the amount required in ten- and twenty-dollar bills is quickly ascertained. The number of five-dollar bills is found by noting the number of figures in the third column to the left of five dollars or over, and the one- and two-dollar bills necessary are easily computed by deducting from the total footing of this column the amount of five-dollar bills just determined. The second column analyzed in the same way will show the silver required in half-dollars, quarters and dimes, and the same process applied to the first column will result in the requisite number of nickels and cents. The total of the different denominations will balance the total of the payroll." (8)

To Get the Payroll Through on Time

"In the general office of a large manufacturing company it is a standing instruction that all mill pay rolls are to be rushed through the various departments without delay. This is to insure payroll checks being prepared and sent to the mill superintendent in time for his regular pay day. Frequent delays, which could not be satisfactorily accounted for, led to the installation of a system for individualizing responsibility for any delay. Upon the arrival of a pay roll a tracer slip (Exhibit 9-14) is attached by the mail clerk. Upon this blank is the name of each individual or department through whose hands it must pass. There also is space provided for each to write in the date and time of the day it is handed by him to the next person. ....In this way a complete proof of delivery is obtained. Further, if there is any cause to complain.....the point where the delay occurred will show upon the tracer slip; the reason can be ascertained and steps taken to prevent its recurrence." (9)

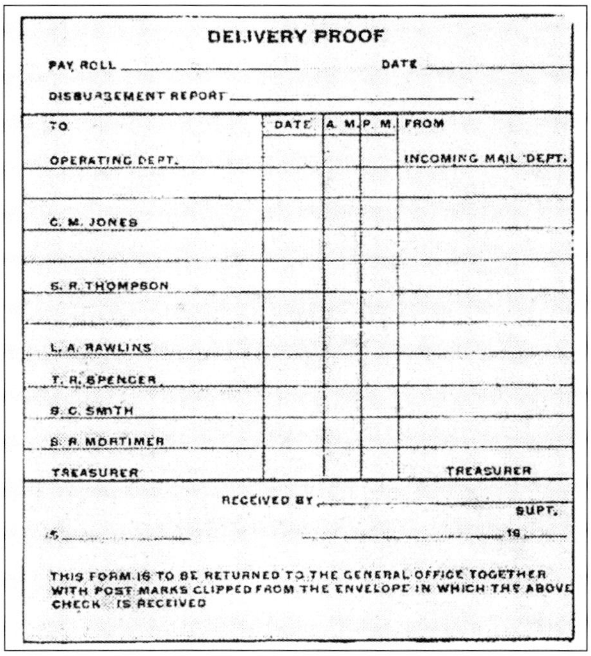

DELIVERY PROOF

PAY ROLL ______ DATE ______

DISBURSEMENT REPORT ______

TO	DATE	A. M.	P. M.	FROM
OPERATING DEPT.				INCOMING MAIL DEPT.
C. M. JONES				
S. R. THOMPSON				
L. A. RAWLINS				
T. R. SPENCER				
S. C. SMITH				
S. R. MORTIMER				
TREASURER				TREASURER

RECEIVED BY ______ SUPT.

$ ______ ______ 19 ___

THIS FORM IS TO BE RETURNED TO THE GENERAL OFFICE TOGETHER WITH POST MARKS CLIPPED FROM THE ENVELOPE IN WHICH THE ABOVE CHECK IS RECEIVED

Exhibit 9-14: Payroll Delivery Proof Form; "To Get the Pay Roll Through on Time;" Stevens, G. F.; System; Volume 19; February 1911; p. 205

More and More Companies Develop "Welfare Consciousness"

The evolution of "welfare companies" overlapped with the application of scientific management, and the list of companies with extensive welfare programs continued to grow. High level Welfare Secretaries (predecessors of future Personnel and Human Resource Managers) were hired to oversee these programs including new stock purchase plans, life insurance programs, etc. (4)

The Nation Recognizes the Need For New Approaches to Unemployment

"The generation before the outbreak of World War I experienced what has been called 'the discovery of unemployment.' Joblessness had certainly existed earlier but had been perceived in a different way. In American society throughout most of the nineteenth century the conviction had prevailed that natural laws cannot be tampered with and that consequently government action in the social sphere would ultimately fail. The belief in the merits of competition postulated the individual's self-reliance. By the time of the American entry into the world war, however, a perceptible change had occurred. Advancing industrialization and the concomitant spells of mass unemployment induced reform-

Exhibit 9-15: Mr. F. C. Henderschott; "Establishing the Science of Personnel Management;" Industrial Management; 12/12/1920; Volume 60; pp. 10-11

oriented thinkers and progressive activists to question the justification of administrative reserve. They laid the seed for future governmental involvement by articulating the problem, devising possible solutions, and broadcasting the need for action. Palpable successes were few as yet, but there could be no doubt that by 1916 a broad public had become acquainted with the issue and governments had grown uneasy about their traditional inertia." (10)

However, it would take some time and a major economic depression before this new consciousness would be translated into state and federal laws and unemployment insurance would be fully conceptualized and made workable.

The Personnel Department Emerges as a Distinct Function And Science

"Overnight the employment department and manager became standard features of a progressive factory – largely due to the demand for labor and in response to the astronomical turnover rates. In Ford alone, 52,000 workers were hired in 1912 to fill 13,000 jobs. Ford Motor Company undertook a massive reform effort and became a leader in personnel management. It stripped the foreman of much of his remaining authority; established seven classes of workers, each with a specific wage rate; and gave the employment department increased responsibility." Employers began to realize the financial implications of turnover and began to concentrate on programs to recruit and retain employees. To accomplish this, companies began to design and utilize applicant testing (including psychological) and job analysis techniques to solve these problems. The welfare company began to evolve into the employment department which in turn began to evolve into the personnel department with a broad array of employee-related duties. (4)

The National Association of Corporate Training began as an experiment to train employees within the commercial department of the New York Edison Company. The effort received public attention and by 1912, Mr. F. C. Henderschott, responsible for the Edison training program, was working with Dr. Lee Galloway of New York University on the concept of possibly developing an association on a national level. By the following year a convention was held with over 31 companies in attendance. Provisional officers were elected and Mr. Henderschott was named its Managing Director. (Exhibit 9-15) Committees were established to address foremen training, industrial housing plans, bonus plans, and the like. The Association's initial goals were to build a University where men would be trained in the

Science of Personnel Management to better handle the human equation in industry and commerce. (11)

The Textile Industry and the Strikes of 1912

The pay envelope of the early twentieth century was exactly that – an envelope for holding an employee's pay. The outside of the envelope included only the employee's identification number or sequential envelope number, the date, and the amount of cash included in the envelope. (12)

On January 1, 1912, textile workers at the Lawrence Textile Mill went on strike following a cut in pay precipitated by a reform law restricting women and children to a maximum of 54 hours per week versus the 56 they had been working. While workers anticipated a cut in pay, they refrained from striking until payday as described in the following:

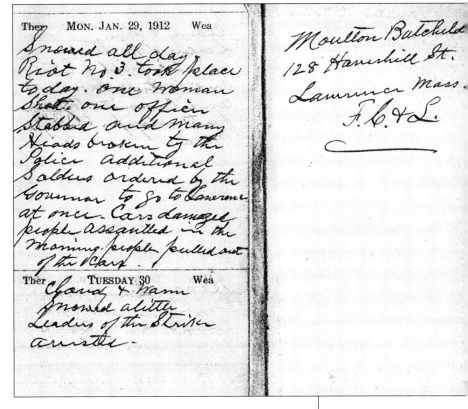

"Just like any other Friday, the paymaster, with the usual armed guards, wheeled a truck containing hundreds of pay envelopes to the head of a long line of anxiously awaiting people…The first ones nervously opened their envelopes and found that the company had deducted two hours' pay. They looked silly, embarrassed and uncertain what to do. Milling around, they waited for someone to start something. They didn't have long to wait, for one lively young Italian had his mind thoroughly made up and swung into action without even looking into his pay envelope. Strike! Strike!" (13)

A sense of the tense times in the City of Lawrence can be seen in this photo of Everett Mills (Exhibit 9-16) where soldiers attempt to maintain order during pay day, in this photo of an overseer at the Pacific Mills (Exhibit 9-17), and in a page from the personal diary of a mill employee (Exhibit 9-18).

Paymasters in the Arts, Science And Literature

The following selection of paintings and writings of the day, which refer to the pay envelope, provide a vivid representation of the paymaster and pay process in a diverse set of industries and geographies.

Exhibit 9-18: Diary of Lawrence Mill Worker (1912); Courtesy of Immigrant City Archives; Lawrence, Massachusetts

Exhibit 9-16: Soliders Keeping Order on Pay Day During Lawrence Mill Strikes (1912); Photo #33; Courtesy of Immigrant City Archives, Lawrence, Massachusetts

Exhibit 9-17: Overseer (Francis G. Brainerd) of Cotton Carding, Pacific Mills (c. 1914); Item P 588.58; Courtesy of American Textile History Museum; Lowell, Massachusetts

Painting ("Pay-Day") by J.C. Leyendecker

Norman Rockwell idolized the work of Joseph Christian Leyendecker and considered him the master practitioner of commercial art illustration. The artist, born in Germany in 1874 and trained in Paris with a career that extended over 50 years, is best remembered for his magazine covers for *Collier's* and the *Saturday Evening Post,* especially for his series "The Arrow Collar Man." Other clients included Hart, Schaffner & Marx and Kelloggs Corn Flakes. Leyendecker had a unique talent to speak to and for Americans through his paintings. (14)

Leyendecker's painting "Pay-Day" (Exhibit 9-19) published in *Collier's Weekly* in 1908 captures the essence of pay-day for the period. The image of the paymaster or pay clerk behind a window or set of bars is an image of the paymaster that would be perpetuated for many years to come.

Extract From "The Jungle" by Upton Sinclair

The state of the meat packing industry and the plight of "Packingtown" workers in Chicago received considerable attention during the first part of the twentieth century from writers such as Upton Sinclair and through the congressional hearings that followed. Excerpts from Sinclair's "The Jungle" from the perspective of the hero, a young man named Jurgis Rudkus from Lithuania, give some insight into the conditions of the day, including those related to the payment of worker wages: (15)

Foremen were constantly looking for ways to take advantage of workers. The lines were constantly being accelerated and workers docked whenever there was the slightest opportunity to do so. "All this was bad, and yet it was not the worst for after all the hard work a man did, he was paid for only part of it. Jurgis had once been among those who scoffed at the idea of these huge concerns cheating; and so now he could appreciate the bitter irony of the fact that it was precisely their size which enabled them to do it with impunity. One of the rules on the killing beds was that a man who was one minute late was docked an hour, and this was economical, for he was made to work the bal-

ance of the hour - he was not allowed to stand round and wait. And on the other hand if he came ahead of time he got no pay for that – though often the bosses would start up the gang ten or fifteen minutes before the whistle. And this same custom they carried over to the end of the day; they did not pay for any fraction of an hour – for "broken time." A man might work full fifty minutes, but if there was no work to fill out the hour, there was no pay for him. Thus the end of every day was a sort of lottery – a struggle, all but breaking into open war between the bosses and the men, the former trying to rush a job through and the latter trying to stretch it out." (15)

Payday in Packingtown was on Saturdays and men, in their best attire, would line up around the Central Time Station (Exhibit 9-20) to receive their weekly wages. "The packers all paid their men in checks, refusing all requests to pay in coin; and where in Packingtown could a man go to have his check cashed but to a saloon, where he could pay for the favor by spending a part of the money?" (15)

Many factors contributed to the potential for payroll scams during this period, and apparently Jurgis got caught up in one, for which he would subsequently be caught and sent to prison. "The paymaster sat in a little booth, with a pile of envelopes before him, and two policemen

Exhibit 9-19: "Pay-Day;" Artist: J.C. Leyendecker (1906); 30 Famous Paintings; Colliers; 1908; NOTE: Painting originally appeared on cover of Collier's Weekly in 1906

Exhibit 9-20: Packing House Workers in Pay Line; Photo by the Chicago American; The World Book; Doubleday, Page & Company; New York, New York; Volume XII; 1906; p. 7504

standing by. Jurgis went, according to directions, and gave the name of 'Michael O'Flaherty.' And received an envelope, which he took around the corner and delivered to Halloran, who was waiting for him in a saloon. Then he went again, and gave the name of 'Johann Schmidt,' and a third time, and gave the name of 'Serge Reminitsky.' Halloran had quite a list of imaginary workingmen, and Jurgis got an envelope for each one. For this work he (Jurgis) received five dollars, and was told that he might have it every week, so long as he kept quiet." (15)

Extract From "The Long Day" by Dorothy Richardson

Dorothy Richardson was one of the many farm girls who was forced to leave home to earn a living in New York City at the turn of the century and she shared some of her pay-related experiences in her 1905 book *"The Long Day."*

"At the stroke of the bell, at the clang of deep-mouthed gong, at the scream of siren whistle, the sluice-gates were lifted …..the atmosphere of holiday liberty was vibrant with expectation of Saturday-night abandon to fun and frolic…. for 'the ghost had walked' through the workaday world that day, and everybody had his 'envelope' in his pocket. It is a pleasant sensation to feel the still-cornered envelope tucked safely away in your vest pocket, or in the depths of your stockings…safe out of reach of the wily pickpocket who was lurking at every corner…" (16)

Extract From "The Pay-Roll Clerk" by Adelaide Lund

Lund's well-written and suspenseful short fictional story which originally appeared in the August 1917 issue of the *Atlantic Monthly* is being included here because it provides a realistic portrayal of a young woman (Emma) who was employed as a payroll clerk in an early twentieth century small manufacturing firm. The story provides an especially good account of the pay preparation process which included checking and rechecking the money to be disbursed to the workers later that day.

"The Blackwell weekly pay-roll money was delivered Saturday mornings, by messenger; after which the office-doors were locked until

the money was counted and placed in envelopes ready to pay out – thus, to quote Sam (Blackwell, the owner-manager) 'putting it up to those inside.' The money was counted and checked, after a painstaking method, by three persons: Emma's check was followed by Miss Glynn's, and again by Sam's thus eliminating all chances of error." (17)

The story is also being included because it addresses the theme of temptation versus honesty and integrity, with the latter two winning out more often than not. A brief summary of the story follows to illustrate the overall high level of integrity that has been characteristic of those in the profession over the years: (17)

Miss Emma Nevins, the senior (under-appreciated and underpaid) payroll clerk, takes (hides) $500 from the payroll in anticipation of an operation her doctor has told her is needed to save her sight. She leaves her employment to have the operation. Emma later confesses when she no longer needs the money and is no longer employed. In the meantime, her tough manager has in her absence learned to appreciate her years of good service and is about to invite her to come back when he receives a letter from her advising him that the $500 was hidden under the pay-table. Mr. Blackwell finds the missing dollars; rips Miss Nevin's letter to pieces and throws the pieces out the window; and then makes an adjusting entry with a notation by cash that reads "mislaid by S.B." (17)

Extract From "The Passing of the Pay-Car" by C.F. Carter

The following text is taken from a 1907 *American Magazine* article in which an old time railroad employee laments the passing of the old fashion payday earmarked by the sight of the pay-car and the sound of the coins. Imagine what it would have been like to be the paymaster on one of these payday runs!

"There, just coming around the curve, was a glittering vision of brass and varnish half hidden in a nimbus of smoke and dust… It was the Pay Car. ..There were nine in the little party and you knew by experience that the average time required to pay nine men was sixty seconds; also that Moriarty (the engineer) would have 'em rolling before the last man had scooped his allotted coin into this trembling palm. But in the presence of death or the paymaster one may live an eternity in sixty seconds....Great Mackerel! Just look at it! A metal coin rack crammed to the muzzle with three denominations of yellow boys, flanked with silver, and on the desk behind it a very large wooden tray on which were long columns of yellow coins. D'ye ever see anything so pretty in all your life? And all the time an exquisitely musical 'tinkle, tinkle, clink-clink' welled up from coin rack and counter in response to the calls of the assistant paymaster. Talk about Beethoven's symphonies! If it were not for that strong wire screen you could have touched that fascinating tray. For the infinitesimal fraction of a second a wicked thought flitted through your brain. Then you almost fainted as your roving eye stared down the barrel of a monstrous revolver. It was only in a rack, but it was within easy reach of the paymaster's hand and most eloquent for all that. Hurriedly your vagrant wits busied themselves with all the Sunday-school lessons you had learned. As your subconsciousness perceived that the head of the road's secret service department stood on the platform with his eyes intent on every man in the car at once, while the conductor stood on the ground outside very much alert, with his coat tail bulging suggestively, your bosom swelled with pride over the watchful care the company had exercised to bring its honest toilers their hard-earned money. A still greater rush of blood to your head caused you to gulp violently when your name was called. Mechanically you lifted your hand to touch the pen as the others had done, and turned to go. 'Here, come back and get your money.' When you came out of your trance you were standing in the middle of the track, your eyes wandering from some yellow objects in your hand to a nimbus of smoke and dust which was just tipping over the hill to the accompaniment of the diminuendo flutter of the Moriarty's exhaust. 'Why couldn't they have left us the Pay Car?'" (18)

TO BE FILLED IN BY COLLECTOR. | Form 1040. | TO BE FILLED IN BY INTERNAL REVENUE BUREAU.

List No. ....

.... District of ....

Date received ....

INCOME TAX.

THE PENALTY FOR FAILURE TO HAVE THIS RETURN IN THE HANDS OF THE COLLECTOR OF INTERNAL REVENUE ON OR BEFORE MARCH 1 IS $20 TO $1,000.
(SEE INSTRUCTIONS ON PAGE 4.)

File No. ....

Assessment List ....

Page .... Line ....

UNITED STATES IN ERNAL REVENUE.

RETURN OF ANNUAL NET INCOME OF INDIVIDUALS.
(As provided by Act of Congre , approved October 3, 1913.)

RETURN OF NET INCOME RECEIVED OR ACCRUED DURING THE YEAR ENDED DECEMBER 31, 191__
(FOR THE YEAR 1913, FROM ARCH 1, TO DECEMBER 31.)

Filed by (or for) .... (Full name of individual.) of .... (Street and No.)

in the City, Town, or Post Office of .... State of ....
(Fill in pages 2 and 3 bef making entries below.)

1. Gross Income (see page 2, line 12)		$
2. General Deductions (see page 3, line 7)		$
3. Net Income		$
Deductions and exemptions allowed in computing income subject to the normal tax of 1 per cent.		
4. Dividends and net earnings received or accrued, of corporations, etc., subject to like tax. (See page 2, line 11)	$	
5. Amount of income on which the normal tax has been deducted and withheld at the source. (See page 2, line 9, column A)		
6. Specific exemption of $3,000 or $4,000, as the case may be. (See Instructions 3 and 19)		
Total deductions and exemptions. (Items 4, 5, and 6)		$
7. Taxable Income on which the normal tax of 1 per cent is to be calculated. (See Instruction 3)		$

8. When the net income shown above on line 3 exceeds $20,000, the additional tax thereon must be calculated as per schedule below:

	INCOME.	TAX.
1 per cent on amount over $20,000 and not exceeding $50,000	$	$
2 " " 50,000 " " 75,000		
3 " " 75,000 " " 100,000		
4 " " 100,000 " " 250,000		
5 " " 250,000 " " 500,000		
6 " " 500,000		
Total additional or super tax		$
Total normal tax (1 per cent of amount entered on line 7)		$
Total tax liability		$

Exhibit 9-21: Form 1040; Income Tax Year 1913; Courtesy of Internal Revenue Service

Form 1040 Is Introduced in 1913

While not all Americans would be impacted, the first progressive income tax law did take effect during 1913 and the Form 1040 (Exhibit 9-21) was born. Not until World War II, however, would the income tax affect most wage earners, who earned too little to fall under the new law.

Reference Sources

1. The Rising of the Women; Tax, Meredith; Monthly Review Press; New York; 1980; pp. 27-29

2. Beyond the Typewriter; Strom, Sharon Hartman; University of Illinois Press; Urbana and Chicago; 1992; p. 19

3. Women, War, and Work; Greenwald, Maurine; Greenwood Press; Westport, CT; 1979; pp. 13-14, 116

4. Managers and Workers; Nelson, Daniel; The University Press; Madison, WI; 1975; pp. 61, 148-156

5. Computers, Office Machines, and the New Information Technology; Heyel, Carl; The Macmillan Company; Collier-Macmillan Limited; London; 1968; p. 21

6. "Saving Time in Paying Men"; Treat, Jedediah; System; Volume 26; July 1914; pp. 89-91

7. "How to Avoid Mistakes in Paying Workers;" System; Volume 21; March 1912; p. 303

8. "Providing Change for the Payroll;" System; Volume 21; June 1912; p. 657

9. "Short Cuts in Business - To Get the Pay Roll Through on Time;" System; Volume 19; February 1911; p. 205

10. Three cheers for the unemployed – government and unemployment before the New Deal; Sautter, Udo; Cambridge University Press; Cambridge, MA; 1991; p.14

11. "Establishing the Science of Personnel Management"; Industrial Management; December 15, 1920; Volume 60; pp. 10-11

12. We Americans; The National Geographic Society; Washington, D.C.; 1975; pp. 240-241

13. The Rising of the Women; Tax, Meredith; Monthly Review Press; New York; 1980; p. 554

14. J.C. Leyendecker; Shau, Michael; Watson-Guptill Publishing; New York; 1974; pp. 7-8

15. The Jungle; Sinclair, Upton; Doubleday, Page & Company; New York; 1906; pp. 35-36, 104-105; 304

16. Women at Work; O'Neill, William L., Editor; Quadrangle Books; Chicago; 1972

17. "The Pay-Roll Clerk"; Lund, Adelaide; Atlantic Monthly; August 1917; pp. 251-9

18. "The Passing of the Pay Car"; Carter, C.F.; American Magazine; Volume 64; 1907; pp. 267-270

CHAPTER 10:
World War I Paymasters and Pay Processes

Paymasters and Pay Processes in War-Related Industries — Payday at the Du Pont Smokeless Powder Plant

Wartime United States was a very busy one as epitomized by the following description of the Du Pont "Old Hickory Plant" in 1917:

"Plant and town shared the name 'Old Hickory,' and were built near Nashville, Tennessee. Seven miles of railroad had to be laid to take building materials to the site. Production of sulfuric acid began 67 days after groundbreaking, nitric acid 9 days later, guncotton, the raw material of smokeless powder, two weeks after that. The first finished powder was granulated 116 days after the breaking of ground for the plant, 121 days ahead of contract agreement. It took a total of 30,000 men and women to operate the plant, recruited everywhere." (1)

Imagine what the pay process must have been like given the sheer number of workers and the fact that employees were being hired in a relatively brief time span and for so many different kinds of jobs! The feeling of a Du Pont payday is captured in this great photo (Exhibit 10-1) "On This Day 12,500 War Workers Lined Up at the Paymaster's Booths to Get Their Weekly Pay." (1)

Army Pay Call

While civilians and soldiers alike were responding to the call of their country, military finance organizations (like the Army Finance Corps) were also responding to the war efforts in many different ways including preparations for the delivery of a much larger payroll.

Prior to 1914, Army soldiers were called to payday via the sound of the drum. Beginning in 1914, the drum was replaced with the march played by the field trumpet (Exhibit 10-2). (2)

Exhibit 10-2: Military Pay Day March; Bugle Signals, Calls & Marches; Canty, Captain Daniel J.; Oliver Ditson Company; Theodore Presser Company; Bryn Mawr, Pennsylvania; 1916; p. 31

"Receipt of pay was contingent upon two things. First, he had to be present at the monthly muster – a ceremonial roll call dating back to the times when in Europe a regiment was the property of an individual who received the pay in bulk and might therefore have interest in padding the payrolls. Next, our soldier, to the merry notes of "Pay Call" – one of the first calls he learned – lined up in dress uniform, side arms and white gloves, the right one neatly folded in his belt. When his name was called, he stepped smartly up to a blanket-covered table, saluted and received his pay from the paymaster, over whose shoulder breathed the first sergeant and the company commander to identify him, Then, carefully herded back to his company office in the barracks, he underwent the painful process of subtraction, to pay his accrued debts to the post exchange and the company tailor and barber – all carefully listed by the company clerk on a large collection sheet. If he was a Regular, he gave up twelve and one-half cents each month for the Soldiers' Home in Washington. There might be an additional subtraction, too, from his now rapidly melting thirteen dollars – illegal this, but widely prevalent. For there was always in a company some individual usurer, ready and eager to lend his impecunious comrades and requiring in return only what barracks slang termed 'the soldier's one per cent' – a dollar a month for each ten dollars advanced!" (3)

This "pay call" ceremony continued until around the time of World War II when the pay media transitioned from cash to check.

AMERICAN TELEPHONE AND TELEGRAPH COMPANY

TELEPHONE AND TELEGRAPH BUILDING

195 BROADWAY

New York, May 24, 1917.

TO ALL EMPLOYEES:

Any employee of the Company who desires to purchase through the Company any of the "Liberty Loan" 3½% Government Bonds and to pay for them in installments, by deduction from his pay, may do so on the following basis:

For each $50.00 bond subscribed for, the Company will deduct from the employee's pay as follows:

(1) Where the employee is paid weekly, $1.00 each week for fifty successive weeks, beginning with the week ending June 16, 1917;

(2) Where the employee is paid monthly, $5.00 each month for the months of June, 1917, and May, 1918, and $4.00 each intervening month.

The Company will retain the interest to be collected from the Government on each bond for the six months ending December 15, 1917, and will deliver the bonds on the completion of the installment payments. When delivered, each bond will have attached thereto the coupon for six months' interest due June 15, 1918, and all subsequent coupons. The interest represented by the June, 1918, coupon will substantially represent 3½% on each installment from date of payment.

Any employee may subscribe on this basis for bonds in any amount in multiples of $50.00, but not exceeding in the aggregate the amount of his annual pay.

Purchase of Liberty Bonds Through Payroll Deduction Plans

With the advancement of labor saving devices, a number of companies began to introduce the use of payroll deductions for various purposes including the purchase of Liberty Loan Government Bonds (Exhibit 10-3) during World War I to support the war effort.

More Soldiers and Fewer Workers Create Workforce Shortage

Finding and keeping workers during this period was an ongoing challenge and companies were turning to consultants to solve this costly problem as this 1917 Independence Bureau advertisement (Exhibit 10-4) in *"Factory Management and Maintenance"* illustrates.

Automation and Technology to The Rescue With Labor Saving Devices

With a shortage of male workers, industry hired more and more women and began to utilize as many labor saving devices as fast as such products came on the market. The Addressograph Corporation, like most other manufacturers of the period with machinery to sell, spoke to these issues in their 1917 advertisements. (Exhibit 10-5).

Addressograph, Felt & Tarrant, International Time Recorder and Marchant Calculating Machine companies (Exhibits 10-6 through 10-9) also placed advertisements in *System* during 1917 that reference new functionality and address contemporary concerns by stressing the time saving advantages of their products.

Perhaps two of the most interesting payroll labor saving devices of this period were the "Payteller" by the Porter-Cable Machine Company (Exhibit 10-10) and the Meilicke Calculator by the Meilicke Company (Exhibit 10-11). Both of these

Exhibit 10-4: In Again – Out Again!;" Independence Bureau; Factory Management & Maintenance; Volume 53; September 1917; p. 27

Exhibit 10-5: "As Your Employees March Away this Short-Cut will help fill their places;" Addressograph; System; Volume 32; August 1917; p. 230

tools provided the user with "permanently computed payrolls" and were marketed as automated tools and as advancements over earlier forms of wage calculation tables.

Wartime Tax Reporting – Vendors Design and Market Year-End Wage Reporting Tools

Triggered by new wartime tax laws, the paymaster of this period was required to keep an individual card or record for each employee, on which he entered the weekly earnings as soon as he had

Do Your Payroll Clerical Work With Addressograph Speed

WHETHER your list of employes runs into the thousands or only a hundred, there is an equipment that will fit into your system and give you Addressograph speed in handling your payroll.

Once a month, twice a month, or four times a month your payday means rush, worry, errors, and frequently overtime, to get it ready. You always manage to get it finished by the set hour, but the exhausting effort and the big job of copying names, numbers, and rates on your payroll sheets and other forms takes time and holds you back.

Now then, if all this listing of names, occupations, numbers, and rates could be taken care of by a simple device, it would eliminate that extra payroll clerical work which requires so much time. And this is exactly what the Addressograph will do.

Along with this relief, you get Addressograph speed. That means at least 15 times faster than the same work could be done with pen or typewriter. For instance, names, numbers, occupations, and

rates would be listed on payroll sheets at the rate of 60 to 100 a minute.

No mistakes can be made in filling in your payroll forms with the Addressograph —time cards, pay envelopes, checks, receipts. It is automatic. And being automatic, it is absolutely accurate.

In Waterville, Conn., is the H. L. Welch Knit Underwear Company, having only 90 employes and using the Addressograph to advantage. Names of concerns having 150, 300, 500, 8,000, and 25,000 employes, using this equipment in a similar capacity, will be furnished on request.

You, too, can effect a saving and get absolute accuracy in your payroll work by using Addressograph equipment made to fit right into your present system. The coupon below will bring the information you want, without obligation.

Addressograph
PRINTS FROM TYPE

made up the payroll. At the end of a year, those cards were added and a slip of paper, containing the total of his last year's wages, was put into each employee's pay envelope as early as possible in the month of January, for the purpose of furnishing him with the required figures for his income tax report." (4)

Stopping the rush on payroll work

One of the things that has to be out on time is the payroll. There is a big rush usually to get it figured up in time to meet the line at the window on payday. And always the figures must be accurate or it means no end of trouble.

THERE used to be a lot of such work in the offices of the American Multigraph Co., Cleveland, on pay-days. But they stopped that. There is not enough to worry about any more. And the reason is a battery of Comptometers.

In the words of Mr. T. H. White, the Chief Accountant of the Company, this is what happened:

"There is 75% less rush on payroll work since machines have taken over the greater part of the labor connected with it.

"Three Comptometers are used exclusively in our offices to figure extensions and time on payroll and cost calculations. Because the machines have been worked in gradually on a constantly increasing payroll, it is hard to say just how much labor is saved; but it is plain that with the old hand method the number of workers in our payroll department would need to be half again as large—a considerable expense item in monthly salaries.

"Then there is the big advantage of mechanical accuracy over even the best of mental figuring, for bookkeepers do get tired and make mistakes, while Comptometers never suffer from brain fag.

"With a few suggestions from the Comptometer people our girls easily picked up the operation of the machine, and have developed a speed which dispatches the ever-growing volume of work without additional strain."

In these war times, with help so scarce and production demands so heavy, there's real food for thought in this experience of the American Multigraph Co.

Perhaps you have been wondering how you are going to keep the office work going when your force is still further diminished. The Comptometer will solve the problem of your figure work.

Felt & Tarrant Manufacturing Co.
1733 N. Paulina St., Chicago

CONTROLLED-KEY

Comptometer
ADDING AND CALCULATING MACHINE

A Business Necessity

This New International Dial is the latest type of Payroll Recorder —every feature fully automatic

Time represents money. It should be checked up and accounted for the same as money.

Time, today, is more important to business than at any other period in the World's history, and the

International Time Recorder

becomes more than a useful article; it is a business necessity.

The International line of time recording devices include card recorders, dial recorders, cost recorders, electric time keeping systems, autograph recorders, elapsed time machines, recording door locks, key recorders, etc. They are made in 260 different styles and sizes, in both electric and spring driven models, to fill every possible time requirement.

Prices from $50 upwards.

Write Department 28 for complete information

International Time Recording Company of New York
ENDICOTT, N. Y.

Offices in all Principal Cities

LONDON OFFICE
57 City Road, Finsbury, London, E.C. Eng.

CANADIAN OFFICE
270 Dundas Street, Toronto, Ont.

PARIS OFFICE
Avenue de la Republique, Paris, France.

Companies like Burroughs began during this period to design and market products similar to the Burroughs' No. 146 Employees' Wage and Tax Return Poster (Exhibit 10-12) to help companies better meet their growing year-end reporting needs.

Images of Paymasters and Pay Processes of the Day

Not all operations were as large as those of Du Pont. In this period, bookkeeping departments (Exhibit 10-13) in medium size companies were often responsible for portions of the payroll process and "bosses" in smaller size firms often performed the role of the paymaster as illustrated here (Exhibit 10-14).

Company Newsletters - an Early Vehicle for Communicating Payroll Information

Almost as soon as companies began distributing newsletters to their employees, paymasters began to send messages through this means as illustrated in this article on "How to Get Your

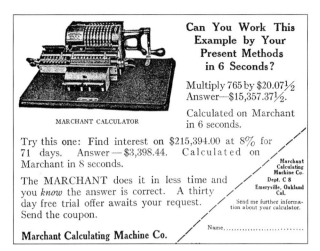

Can You Work This Example by Your Present Methods in 6 Seconds?

Multiply 765 by $20.07½
Answer—$15,357.37½.

Calculated on Marchant in 6 seconds.

Try this one: Find interest on $215,394.00 at 8% for 71 days. Answer—$3,398.44. Calculated on Marchant in 8 seconds.

The MARCHANT does it in less time and you *know* the answer is correct. A thirty day free trial offer awaits your request. Send the coupon.

Marchant Calculating Machine Co.

Marchant Calculating Machine Co. Dept. C 8 Emeryville, Oakland Cal.

Send me further information about your calculator.

Name..............................

The Product— INSTANTLY!

28½ RATE PER HOUR
41¼ TOTAL HOURS

NOT by the slow, tedious, subject-to-verification process of mental multiplication, but by the *instantaneous*, absolutely accurate figures of

THE PAYTELLER
PERMANENTLY COMPUTED PAYROLLS

A machine that indicates the amount due in every man's pay envelope the instant it is wanted. Gives the products of payrolls and distributes job costs in far less time than the most expert clerk can deduct them by pencil and pad.

A twist of the wrist, and you have the product of the most involved payroll fractions—whatever the rate per hour or the hours worked may be. Not a machine that *computes* products, but one that has 18,340 *computed* products.

Figure rolls celluloid covered. Indestructible. Portable. Compact—occupies little space. A wonderful time-saver, error-eradicator, labor-reducer.

Send for descriptive folder, "The Instant Paymaster"

DEALERS, AGENTS—Wherever there are payrolls to be prepared and job costs to be accurately distributed, there is a ready sale for the Instant Paymaster. We offer splendid territory and profits. Write for our proposition TODAY.

THE PORTER-CABLE MACHINE CO., Syracuse, New York

Meilicke Pay Roll Calculator

Pays for Itself In One Month

Note how Cards drop into **PERFECT REFERENCE POSITION** The Hinge Does It!

Send Coupon NOW for Money-Back Trial Offer

This wage calculating device—it is *not a book*—speeds up office routine. It eliminates the wasted time of solving and re-solving the same old problems.

Instead of mentally figuring each man's wage the operator lets his fingers find the figures. The most inexperienced clerk can do it. The results will be prompt and accurate.

For Universal Use

Large institutions and small concerns can make the saving afforded by the Meilicke Pay Roll Calculator. The American Railway Express Company has over 7000 in use. They are saving from 20% to 40% of the cost of any other system or device ever used. Such a saving will pay for the Calculator in one month.

Many Features

This device is flexible, loose-leaf. Cards can be replaced, added, or taken out at will. You buy just the cards you need instead of a lot of dead material. Made in many sizes and for various purposes.

The slanted rack, upright cards, celluloid reinforced tabs, all plainly in sight, help to produce the astonishing ease and efficiency with which this device is operated.

Prices from $18.00 up. Mailing the coupon properly filled out entitles you to our free trial offer which permits you to try this device in your office ten days without risking a cent.

Send coupon to

Meilicke Calculator Co.
354 North Clark St. Chicago

Send This Today!

Meilicke Calculator Co.
354 N. Clark St., Chicago
Tell me more about the Meilicke Pay Roll Calculator and how I can obtain a ten days' trial without risking a cent. Send price list and descriptions so I can let you know exactly which style I wish to try.

Name _____
Address _____
Firm Name _____
Title _____

Exhibit 10-9: "Can You Work This Example by Your Present Methods in 6 Seconds?" Marchant Calculating Machine Co; System; Volume 32; October 1917; p. 643

Exhibit 10-11: Meilicke Pay Roll Calculator; Meilicke Calculator Co; System; Volume 34; October 1918; p. 1187

Exhibit 10-10: "The Payteller Permanently Computed Payrolls;" Porter-Cable Machine Co.; System; Volume 32; July 1917; p. 110

ments are to receive their pay on the days indicated in the schedule printed below. Mr. Coleman has been a member of the cost department for a good many years where he has had charge of the payroll, and is now right at home in his new office. Employees will be paid off in the departments where they are working. A messenger will notify the foreman five minutes before arrival of the paymaster. Foreman will have his men line up in numerical order. Employee will hand timekeeper his pass, who will punch proper number and hand back to employee with his pay. All inquiries concerning pay should be made on the day following pay day at the paymaster's office in the employment department between two and three o'clock P.M. or between 9 and 10 o'clock Saturday morning. Employees not receiving their pay at the regular time can do so at the paymaster's office at the same hours given above." (5)

American Cities Take Leadership Role in Improving the Payroll Process

Not only companies, but large American cities and municipalities were also concerned with cost and efficiency, and many of them imple-

Pay" appearing in the January 1917 issue of *The Norton Spirit.* The article provides a glimpse of both the organizational structure of the company (i.e., the close relationship of payroll and the cost department) and the pay distribution process.

"A new system of paying off has been established with P.M. Coleman as paymaster, who now has an office in the basement of the Administration Building. Under this new system, every day in the week except Monday and Saturday is a pay day and the various depart-

Exhibit 10-12: "A Simple Way to Record Wages for Taxation – A Burroughs Machine (no. 146) Makes It Easy;" Burroughs; System; Volume 33, April 1918; pp. 582-3

A Simple Way to Record Wages for Taxation

NAME Andrew Ross DEPT. 5

ADDRESS 2467 West Fifth St. OCCUPATION gen. lab.

DATE EMPLOYED Jan 1, 1917 DATE LEFT

MONTH PAY DAY	AMOUNT	MONTH PAY DAY	AMOUNT
JAN 6	13.24	SEP 1	15.00
JAN 13	14.19	SEP 8	17.70
JAN 20	16.00	SEP 15	18.56
JAN 27	14.98	SEP 22	15.23
FEB 3	20.55	SEP 29	15.14
FEB 10	17.45	OCT 6	14.98
FEB 17	16.50	OCT 13	13.44
FEB 24	15.36	OCT 20	17.50
MAR 3	17.12	OCT 27	17.45
MAR 10	19.57	NOV 3	17.31
MAR 17	16.10	NOV 10	18.74
MAR 24	15.60	NOV 17	17.37
MAR 31	17.55	NOV 24	19.78
APR 7	17.30	DEC 1	20.56
APR 14	16.76	DEC 8	19.44
APR 21	8.45	DEC 15	18.23
APR 28	19.72	DEC 22	18.84
MAY 5	16.38	DEC 29	21.35
MAY 12	18.70		
MAY 19	17.24		871.58
MAY 26	15.65		
JUN 2	16.50		
JUN 9	18.00		
JUN 16	18.00		
JUN 23	17.75		
JUN 30	17.50		
JUL 7	16.35		
JUL 14	14.56		
JUL 21	8.37		
JUL 28	17.25		
AUG 4	19.12		
AUG 11	17.45		
AUG 18	17.36		
AUG 25	13.34		

EMPLOYEES WAGE AND TAX RETURN RECORD

Concerns which use the Burroughs Employees' Wage and Tax Return Poster do not find the Government's requirements a hardship.

The form reproduced at the left shows a simple, easily-made, easily-maintained record which makes compilation of the returns speedy and trouble-proof.

Look at the Machine-Made Form

Most of the concerns which have adopted the Burroughs way of making this figure-work automatic, use a card or a ledger-leaf similar in principle to the one shown at the left. When payrolls are made up, entries are made on separate cards for each employee—which is a simple and rapid process on the Burroughs. The card is inserted in the machine, and as the date prints automatically it is only necessary to depress such keys as register the amount of the payment. The process takes longer to describe than to perform; almost any clerk can make entries so rapidly that the time it takes to keep the cards (or sheets) complete and correct is negligible—in comparison with the time it takes to make up reports at the end of the year by going back to complicated sources to get every employee's total.

The simplicity and flexibility of this method make it adaptable to any sort of business, and to any payroll system that may be in use.

Full information about what can be expected of the method and machine in your business will be gladly supplied — without obligation on your part, of course.

A Burroughs Machine (No. 146) Makes It Easy

The Government requires from every employer an annual report of amount paid to each individual employee who earns $800 or more.

There's a Burroughs machine—the No. 146 Employees' Wage and Tax Return Poster—which furnishes the simplest, easiest, most economical way of meeting that requirement.

It eliminates all digging into complicated records for tax return data; and the collating and checking of dozens—or scores—of sheets for each total wanted.

It keeps a complete and correct record of all the facts—and all in one place. When the year-end comes, the work is ready, the figures right at hand.

Best of all, perhaps, it requires no working-out of a special system to meet the requirements of your particular business; it fits in anywhere. It uses either cards or ledger leaves, and it is so simple to operate that any of your clerks can keep the work always up to date, always right, always neat and legible and rapidly-performed.

But the usefulness of the machine to your business doesn't stop with its work as an Employees' Wage and Tax Return Poster. It does ledger posting, too, and statement-making, and other figure-work.

Next year's report to the Government will be easy (even though returns are demanded for every one of your employees) if you put a Burroughs Employees' Wage and Tax Return Poster on the work now. And you can count as an "extra" the betterment to your business which the other uses of a Burroughs machine always bring to any business, large or small.

Over 100 Burroughs Models

The wide range of Burroughs Models includes a Burroughs for any business—large or small.

Consult your banker or telephone book for the address of the nearest of the 189 Burroughs offices in the United States and Canada.

Burroughs offices are also maintained in other principal cities of the world.

FIGURING AND BOOKKEEPING MACHINES PREVENT COSTLY ERRORS—SAVE VALUABLE TIME

Burroughs   PRICED AS LOW AS $125

Exhibit 10-13: Bookkeeping Department of Heald Corporation (1918); The Heald Herald; Volume 1, No. 7; February 1918; p. 10; Courtesy of Collections of the Worcester Historical Museum, Worcester, Massachusetts

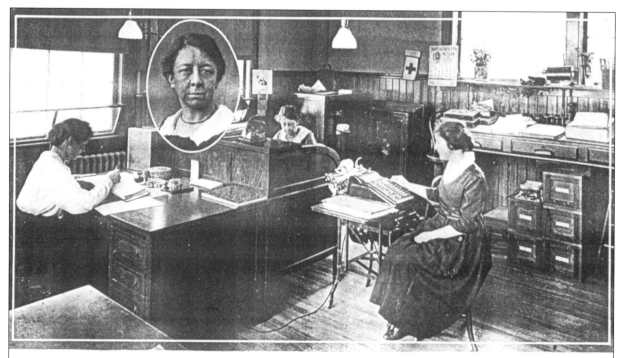

BOOKKEEPING DEPARTMENT

MRS. MABEL R. VAUGHN, ASSISTANT TREASURER (INSERT)

MRS. MILDRED ABBOTT

MISS BERNICE JACKSON

Exhibit 10-14: The Boss/Owner as Paymaster (1918); System; Volume 33; April 1918; p. 539

On this last point, the author writes that "the work of preparing payrolls, even when all unnecessary duplications have been eliminated, is a problem requiring a large amount of clerical work. In many cities much of this clerical work has been eliminated by the use of mechanical devices. Machines are now available for printing payrolls, both before and after the computations have been made, for securing totals and subtotals, for writing and signing the pay checks, for addressing envelopes, etc. The actual saving in dollars and cents which is thus possible is enormous, as has been proved in large cities and corporations. Cities whose payrolls carry from four to five hundred or more names might be well to interest themselves in the possibility of applying machines to their payroll problem." (6)

mented innovative solutions to improve their pay processes during this period. The following two articles were published in 1917. Extracts from these articles not only describe the pay environment of the second decade of the twentieth century but also present innovative solutions to the prevailing operational problems and challenges faced by both private and public payrolls of the day. In addition, these articles give supporting evidence to the statement that the groundwork for all future payrolls of the twentieth century were laid by 1920. Subsequent to this period, new laws would come into existence and new tools would be invented, but the basic process would already be in place.

"Municipality Payrolls – Their Preparation, Certification, Audit and Payment" by G.M. MacAdam

"Approximately fifty per cent of the money raised by taxation for the operation and maintenance of the average municipality is disbursed by the means of payroll. Yet in spite of this fact, it is undoubtedly true that as little constructive consideration is given to payroll problems as to any other phases of municipal accounting, with the result that inadequate municipal payroll systems are the rule rather than the exception." (6)

MacAdam, in the balance of the article, presents the keys to efficient municipal payrolls. His list includes the importance of a central payroll office, formal time records, the use of actual versus estimated hours, certification of every payroll, pre- and post-payroll audits, payment by check, shouldering initial criticisms from employees that often come with change, and the use of mechanical devices. (6)

New York City Payroll - "These Plans Saved $65,000 a Year"

"The city has moved a long way in the last 3 years in its methods of paying its employees. It has done three things. It has extended very generally the use of checks, and has correspondingly reduced the number of payments in cash. It has devised a new form of check which serves all the practical purposes of cash. It has developed a system of making checks by machinery, so that, as far as the entries on them are concerned, they are scarcely touched by hand from the moment they come from the printer as blank forms until they reach the pockets of employees." (7)

"The money benefit to the city in paying by check is easy to see. In considerable measure the same benefit would apply to other employers of large groups of laborers. We now pay 1,941 street cleaners by check every week – almost as many men as were paid by check throughout the city service in 1914. Street cleaners are paid at a rate which averages about 34 cents an hour. Paying them by cash used to take from 1 to 2 hours out of the working week, because no man wanted to be late for the paymaster's car, and in bad weather the paymaster could not help being late. So, for those 1,941 men it cost the city in lost time $659.94 for each hour used in paying them. The annual loss, represented in time spent away from the broom and shovel, was not far from $50,000." (7)

"These men are now paid when they come in from work – by check and on their own time.

Exhibit 10-15: "These Plans Saved $65,000 a Year – They'll Know Him When He Cashes His Check;" Morgan, Shepard A.; System; Volume 32; November 1917; p. 738

THEY'LL KNOW HIM WHEN HE CASHES HIS CHECK

Each employee signs his name on the face of his pay check when he receives it. Later, when he cashes the check, his endorsement and this signature must correspond and this serves as his identification. A sample check is shown just above

Exhibit 10-16: "These Plans Saved $65,000 a Year - Where Machines Do the Work of Men;" Morgan, Shepard. A.; System; Volume 32; November 1917; p. 738

Payday used to leave its traces in the streets – pavements not cleaned, cans not emptied, refuse not removed. Now payday, as far as the appearance of the streets goes, is like any other day." (7)

"The change from the cash to the check plan of paying laboring forces could not have been effected except for the peculiar type of check the city uses. The feature of the check that makes its application possible in the labor service is a self-identifying device which insures the holder the power to collect every cent of its face

value. According to instructions which the comptroller rigidly enforces, the employee signs his name in a space provided at the lower left-hand corner of the check at the moment he receives it, and before he signs the payroll. He must sign his name in the presence of the payroll clerk (Exhibit 10-15), who is obliged to certify to that effect at the foot of each payroll sheet." (7)

"More than 200 banks in the five boroughs agreed to cash these checks on presentation, provided the signature line was filled in. Thus the par value of the city's pay checks was immediately established. Hundreds of storekeepers throughout the city accept them without discount, a practice very different from what used to obtain under the old style of checks." (7)

"There are one or two other features of the new check which reduced operating costs. Along the top and on the left-hand margin of the check appear two rows of numerals. These are notched out in the central payroll division of the bureau of audit (a division coordinate with but separate from the pay division) to designate the payroll period, starting from the first of the year. The number of the payroll period is identical with the number of the account in the bank. The numbers at the top are units; those at the left tens. The black-face letter at the right of the check is the code letter of the bank. In a box at the left appear a row of letters, each representing the code designation of a bank. The printer perforates the checks on a given bank in the space opposite the identifying letter; thus, a notch in the space marked "2" at the top of the check, a notch in the space marked "5" at the left of the check and a perforation opposite the letter 'W,' indicates that the check is drawn against account 'W-52,' and it is recognized as having been drawn on the Brooklyn branch of the Corn Exchange Bank, which handles all weekly checks, and is for the last payday of the year. The notches and perforations serve an accounting purpose. Holding a bundle of checks to the light will show whether any strangers are among them. The notches, furthermore, make a furrow along the sides of a stack of checks and automatically guard against charging this month's checks against last month's account." (7)

"The central payroll division (Exhibit 10-16) is about 60% machine shop. It has the aspect of a munitions plant. The checks are written on a machine. They are added on a battery of specially designed adding machines. They are numbered serially and dated on an automatic machine. Then they are sent down a shaft, where they are signed by machine." (7)

"One man signed nearly all of the 1,800,000 checks which the city issued last year, sometimes as many as 30,000 in a single day. He signed away nearly $100,000,000, and no check was for more than $625. His machine is the only one of its kind save one which the city holds in reserve lest its employees have to get along without a payday." (7)

Less Work on Pay Day

In order to save time and expense, the card shown here (Exhibit 10-17) was devised by some employers during this period. "One card is allotted to each employee. It is made out by the Treasurer's department at the beginning of the year, or whenever a man enters the service. Each employee is given a number, and this is entered on his payroll card, in addition to his name, occupation and the rate of pay which he receives. The card is filed according to number, with an alphabetical cross reference file. The payroll number is filled in every pay day, and the period stamped in with a rubber stamp, followed by the amount of wages. The employee signs his name in the final column, thus acknowledging the receipt of the money due him." (8)

No.				
Name		Occupation		
Received from				
A. H. Gleason & Co.				
In full of all services			Rate	
Pay-roll No.	From	To	Amount	Signature

Large Cash Payrolls Create Growing Security Threat

While some employers by this date had recognized the value of paying their employees by check, many continued to pay in cash and for that reason, the threat of payroll robberies continued to represent a very real danger to those who acted as paymasters or were involved in transporting or protecting cash payrolls while en route.

Here again, products were being developed to protect employer payrolls. "Pay-cars" were manufactured for companies who needed vehicles to disburse funds at different work site locations. These "pay-cars" (Exhibit 10-18) were advertised as "bandit-proof." *Scientific American* reports "A motor truck with a specially designed body containing all the conveniences of an office and protected against highway bandits, is used by the Chicago Surface Railway Lines to carry the pay envelopes of thousands of its employees to car barns and other widely scattered districts. In some cases the truck merely transports paymasters and large sums of money from one barn to another. In others, trips of several miles are made into the country to pay off line and track men and gangs engaged in special construction work, such as the building of new bridges, tunnels, buildings and general track improvements. The truck has accommodations for four paymasters, a chauffeur and a guard, all of whom go heavily armed. The paymasters are provided with swivel chairs and work at tables which hang on hinges and may be dropped down when not in use. The table in the center of the office is used for making up payrolls while the truck is en route and within easy reach on either side are shelves for money trays. The windows are protected by iron bars and connected with an alarm system. In paying direct from the truck the chief paymaster sits at the extreme end of the office, takes the pay envelopes form the shelf and passes them out to the workmen through a wicket in a window on his left. While the truck is traveling through the streets all money and other valuables are carried in a special steel vault built in the body of the truck behind the rear seat." (9)

Exhibit 10-18: "The Motor-Driven Commercial Vehicle – The Bandit Proof Pay-Car;" Scientific American; Volume 116; June 16, 1917; pp. 18-19

Exhibit 10-17: Pay Day Record Keeping (1915); "Less Work on Pay Day;" System; Volume 27; January 1915; p. 91

Protect Your Payroll

W HAT chance has your paymaster against waiting thugs on dark stair-ways, alleys, and corners of your factory, or on the lonely, dangerous road he travels with your payroll?

What chance has your messenger against the clever criminal bands infesting banks, operating unhindered and unhampered in open streets?

What chance has your cashier alone in his cage against desperate, despair-driven degenerates?

Give each a Savage 10-shot Automatic Pistol, and you will give him a perfect arsenal of defense. Without practice he can aim and shoot like an expert.

Aims as easy as pointing your finger. Covers your man in a flash. Per-fectly danger-proof. A touch tells whether loaded or empty. Shoots one shot with each trigger pull. Shoots from 2 to 4 more shots than any other auto-matic—that means 20% to 40% more protection.

Take the precaution before it is too late. Go to your dealer's and let him explain the Savage, or send for our interesting free booklet.

SAVAGE ARMS COMPANY, 3712 SAVAGE AVENUE, UTICA, N. Y.

VALUABLE BOOKLET FREE!

Aims as easy as pointing your finger

10 Shots Quick

Every firm needs Savage business protection—it is far more necessary than check protection, fire protection, or any other form of protection.

If you have never considered it before, let us send you our interesting booklets. A request on your business letterhead will bring full information and explain why the Savage offers the most positive and safest protection.

THE *10 Shots Quick* SAVAGE AUTOMATIC

"The Savage Automatic" was marketed by the Savage Arms Company to "Protect Your Payroll" and as illustrated (Exhibit 10-19) assured poten-tial customers that "aiming was as easy as point-ing your finger."

Concerns Over Fraud Increase With Larger Check Volumes

Banks and those employers converting to or contemplating payment by check were also finding that there were new and different kinds of problems with this payment method, like those associated with the risk of fraud. (Exhibit 10-20) Products, like the Fesler & Evans "Check Writer," (Exhibit 10-21) helped provide greater security for both employers and banks.

AT THE BANK.

Clerk—" You must get someone to iden-tify you. Someone who knows that you are Michael Clancy."

Clancy—" Fwat 's th' matter wid yez? Don't yez suppose Oi know who Oi am ?"

Check Writing —That Protects Only $20.00 Why Pay More?

At Last— the Efficient Check Protector At a Reasonable Price Business has needed the efficient, reasonably priced check protector. $20 now buys the best check protector and writer on the market. No need to pay more—and at this price you simply can-not afford to be without check protection—cannot afford to lay your checks open to the work of expert check raisers. $20 invested now will prevent possible losses of hundreds of dollars—and in addition save hours of time in your office. Investi-gate—mail the coupon for details.

FESLER & EVANS Check Protector and Writer

is the only *high-grade* machine sold at anywhere near its price—makes mechanical protection so economical that even the smallest business cannot afford to be without it. Con-venient—speedy in operation—sure in results. Simply set the keys—and one quick movement of the lever and the *exact amount* is legibly and permanently imprinted on the desired part of the check.

"Inside Facts" On Request Simply mail the coupon and we will send "Inside Facts" on check protection. Do not delay—one raised check may cost you hundreds of dollars. Mail the coupon at once and get protection.

Hedman Mfg. Company
227 West Erie St., Chicago, Ill.

Salesmen Wanted
Here is a big oppor-tunity for live-wire salesmen—sales come easily and every machine placed is a boost for other sales. Write or wire us for par-ticu-lars.

Hedman Mfg. Company 227 W. Erie St. Chicago, Ill.

Send me "Inside Facts" on $20 F & E Check Protector and Writer.

Name_____
Firm_____
Address_____

PAY $20 AND 50 CTS.

Please mention SYSTEM when writing to advertisers

Reference Sources

1. Du Pont – the Autobiography of an American Enterprise; E.I. Du Pont de Nemours & Company; Wilmington, DE; Charles Scribner's Sons; New York; 1952; pp. 76-77

2. Bugle Signals, Calls & Marches; Canty, Captain Daniel J.; Oliver Ditson Company; Theodore Presser Company; Bryn Mawr, PA; 1916; p. 31

3. The Compact History of the United States Army; Dupuy, Col. R. Ernest; Hawthorn Books, Inc.; New York; 1956; p. 189

4. "How Five Firms Keep Payroll Records Up to Date;" Industrial Management; June 1918; pp. 499-501

5. "How to Get Your Pay;" The Norton Spirit; January 1917; Courtesy of Collections of the Worcester (Mass.) Historical Museum

6. "Payrolls – Their Preparation, Certification, Audit, and Payment"; MacAdam, G.M.; The American City; October 1917; Volume 17; No 4; pp. 344-347

7. "These Plans Saved $65,000 a Year"; Morgan, Shepard A.; System; Volume 32; November 1917; pp. 738-739

8. "Less Work on Pay Day;" System; Volume 27; January 1915; p. 91

9. "The Motor-Driven Commercial Vehicle;" Scientific American; June 16, 1917; Volume 116; pp. 18-19

CHAPTER 11:
The Post-World War I Years

The period following World War I was one of change. Companies continued to design and implement new organizational structures to better manage their businesses. They continued to deploy scientific management techniques and utilize more and more mechanical solutions to achieve higher levels of efficiency and accuracy and lower operating costs. It was also a period in which the problems of large cash payrolls became very evident and the search for alternative solutions began.

AN EMPLOYEE AHEAD OF HIS TIME –

"If I were an employer, I would mail my employees' pay checks to their homes. The advantages to this plan – besides the usual advantages of paying by check – are that it saves time for bookkeepers, cashiers, and employees; it prevents employees from congregating needlessly together; and gives the home folks a 'check' on the wages."

D. D. Nelson
System, May 1920

Contemporary Company Organizational Structures

The book *Office Management: Its Principles and Practice* by Lee Galloway was in its sixth edition by 1923. In it, the organizational structure for a large New England manufacturing concern with over 16,000 employees was presented as a model for other large companies. (1)

Within the model there were the commercial and cost departments that in turn were further

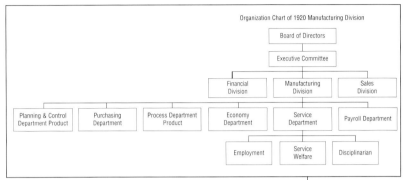

Organization Chart of 1920 Manufacturing Division

sub-divided into sections under the control of a comptroller, a chief accountant, and an auditor. The comptroller had supervision over the accounts and finance. The chief accountant had direct charge of daily operations and supervision of personnel and of accounts and accounting methods. The auditor was given general charge of accounting inspection, including the auditing of payrolls. (1)

Under this model, the paymaster and payroll clerks reported through the cashier's section within the chief accountant's organization. Although part of the same section, the paymaster and payroll clerks were segregated for control purposes. The payroll clerks made up the payroll and the paymaster placed the money in employee envelopes and disbursed the pay. (1)

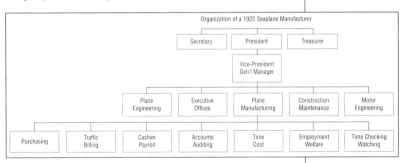

Organization of a 1922 Seaplane Manufacturer

Shown here are two other organizational charts (Exhibits 11-1 & 11-2) of the period reflecting the positioning and reporting lines of the payroll, timekeeping and cost departments.

Scientific Management Taken Very Seriously

The commitment to scientific methodologies continued unabated after the war years with

Exhibit 11-1: Extract From Organization Chart of Manufacturing Division; Industrial Management; Volume LIX, No.4; April 1920; p. 302

Exhibit 11-2: Extract From Organization of a Manufacturer of Seaplanes for the U.S. Government; Management: The Principles Which Underlie Modern Industrial Administration; Business Training Corporation, New York and Chicago; 1922

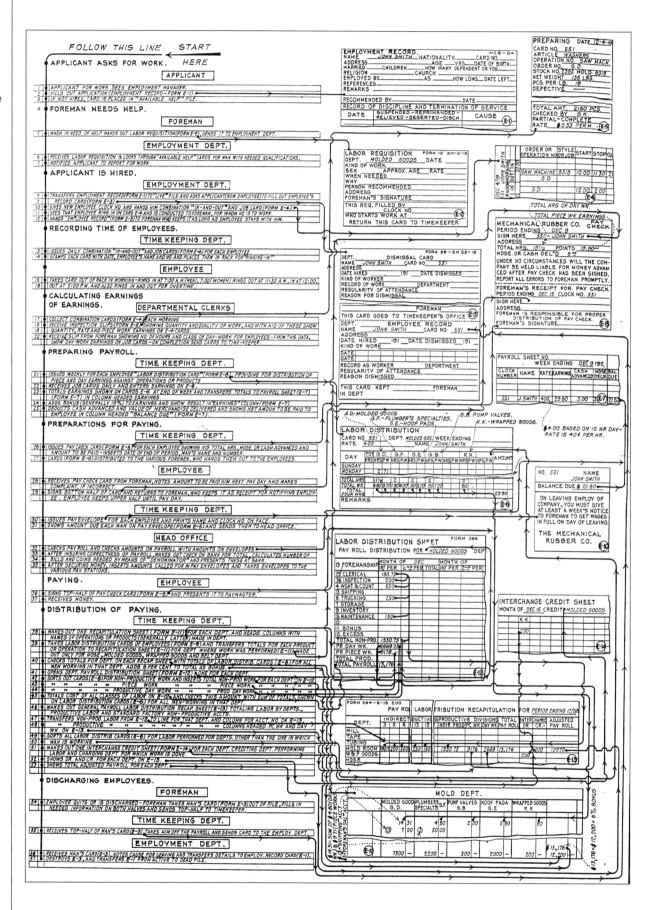

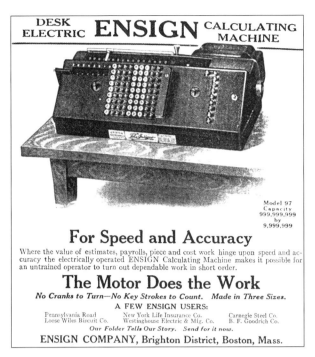

DESK ELECTRIC ENSIGN CALCULATING MACHINE

Model 97
Capacity
999,999,999
by
9,999,999

For Speed and Accuracy

Where the value of estimates, payrolls, piece and cost work hinge upon speed and accuracy the electrically operated ENSIGN Calculating Machine makes it possible for an untrained operator to turn out dependable work in short order.

The Motor Does the Work

No Cranks to Turn—No Key Strokes to Count.   Made in Three Sizes.
A FEW ENSIGN USERS:

Pennsylvania Road
Loose Wiles Biscuit Co.

New York Life Insurance Co.
Westinghouse Electric & Mfg. Co.

Carnegie Steel Co.
B. F. Goodrich Co.

Our Folder Tells Our Story. Send for it now.
ENSIGN COMPANY, Brighton District, Boston, Mass.

such methods becoming more and more sophisticated as illustrated in this highly detailed flow chart (Exhibit 11-3) displaying the end to end payroll process at a U.S. Rubber Company plant in 1920. Flow charts, such as this, were used as management, control, training and development tools. (2)

Vendor Products Emphasize Time, Labor, and Cost Control Advantages

The emphasis by employers on time, labor, and cost controls continued and vendors responded with new generations of adding, cal-

It's Surprising How Much You Can Do With an Addressograph—

No other office dev
From card index pla
which you copy name
"Addressograph-ed" 15

culating, and addressing machines, time recording devices, and anti-check fraud equipment (Exhibits 11-4 through 11-10), along with an ever-increasing array of new products and services.

Forms became an important element of process improvement as were paper-related products that helped companies organize paper, such as illustrated in this advertisement for filing systems by Yawman and Erbe Manufacturing Company (Exhibit 11-11).

Putting the Payroll on an Automatic Basis

Products offered during this period reflect a growing sophistication. The following 1920 article describes a new machine called the International Payroll Machine, introduced by the International Money Machine Company (Exhibit 11-12), that takes over where the adding machine leaves off.

"A product of this age of office efficiency which has proved its worth is a machine which adds making out the payroll to the long list of business details now accomplished with mechanical ease. For years one of the most trying tasks for every company with a large number of employees has been making up the weekly or monthly payroll." (3)

"Now comes a machine that solves all of the paymaster's problems at once. It operates like a standard adding machine in so far as it adds and lists the payroll, giving the grand total and sub-totals. But it does not stop there. The next step it performs is to denominate the payroll, that is, to indicate exactly how many twenties, tens,

Exhibit 11-4: Ensign Desk Electric Calculating Machine; Ensign Company; System; Volume 37; January 1920

Exhibit 11-6: "It's Surprising How Much You Can Do With an Addressograph;" Addressograph Company; System; Volume 37; January 1920; p. 113

Exhibit 11-5: Monroe Calculating Machine; Monroe Calculating Machine Company; System, Volume 37; January 1920; p. 157

Exhibit 11-7:
International Dial
Recorder;
International Time
Recording Company;
System; Volume 45;
February 1924; p.
239; Reprinted by
permission of
Simplex

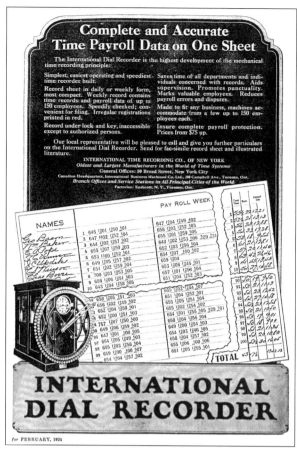

Turn the Light on Your Business

Good Cost Records are like a flood of light illuminating every corner of your factory. Until you have them you cannot *see* what you are doing, nor can you direct wisely either your Production or your Sales policies.

Stromberg Job Time Recorders

Exhibit 11-8:
Stromberg Job Time
Recorders;
Stromberg Electric
Company; Industrial
Management; Volume
59; June 1920; p.
167

Exhibit 11-9: The
New Sentinel System;
Hall-Welter Company;
System; Volume 37;
January 1920; p. 138

fives, ones, half dollars, quarters, dimes, nickels, and cents must be drawn to pay correctly. This is so long and tedious a job that many cashiers and paymasters simply approximate these denominations, carry an extra change account and balance the cash when the payroll is finished. This entails extra bookkeeping and the possibility of having to hold up the entire payroll to send out for more coins if those of any denomination are exhausted." (3)

"This remarkable machine goes still further. When the money is on hand the scheduling device is replaced by a coin tray into which all coins, gold or silver, are placed. The operator then runs off each payroll item on a keyboard similar to the standard adding machine keyboard. Each time the operator lists an item and pulls the handle the machine automatically counts out the correct amount of coin and drops it into the employee's envelope, at the same time making out a permanent printed record of the amount put into each envelope. In using paper money instead of gold coin the procedure is slightly different but the results are identical. The payroll is thereby apportioned in a fraction of the time otherwise necessary and there is a printed record of the total amount put into each envelope. This record is perhaps the most important individual feature of the machine." (3)

Exhibit 11-10: Todd
2-Color System;
Todd Protectograph
Co.; System; Volume
41; May 1922; p.
507; Reprinted by
permission of the
Unisys Corporation

Positive Prevention
Backed by Insurance

TODD 2-COLOR SYSTEM

"Under the old system, if an employee claimed that his pay was short (Exhibit 11-13) it was practically impossible to check his claim once he had opened his envelope. Even though the cash had balanced after making out the payroll it was possible that some other employee

Make this test in your filing department

Direct Name Filing System

might have been overpaid a similar amount. With the International Payroll Machine all such claims can be readily adjusted because the paymaster knows from his printed record exactly how much was put in each envelope." (3)

Pay Envelope Begins to Evolve Into Pay Statement With New Purpose

During this same timeframe, the traditional blank employee pay envelope with no more than employee number, pay date, and pay amount indicated on the outside of the envelope began to evolve into a more detailed pay statement. While still acting as an envelope to hold coin, paper currency, or in a growing number of cases a check, the outside of the envelope was now beginning to serve other purposes by providing more information from the employer to the employee regarding the payment being made as illustrated in this sample form (Exhibit 11-14). (1)

Henry Ford Speaks to the Value Of Multiple Pay Days

For manufacturing plants with a large number of workers, Henry Ford saw the value of creating multiple pay days to replace the traditional single pay day to pay all employees. On this matter, he said "We have not for years been able to have a single pay day because of the general inconvenience it would cause, not only to ourselves and to our workmen, but to the

ONE   TWO
THREE   FOUR

The International Payroll Machine
WHAT IT DOES

1. Adds and lists the payroll, using whatever method you have found most satisfactory. There is no need to change your system to suit the machine.

2. Denominates the payroll. When the total has been obtained, the coin-o-meter shows instantly the exact denominations in which this money must be drawn to pay each item correctly. How many twenties, tens, fives, etc., right down to the last cent.

3. Counts change into pay envelopes, keeping a permanent printed record of the total amount in each envelope. Absolute protection against mistakes.

4. Balances Cash. When the payroll is correctly made up, the cash is exhausted, giving an automatic cash balance. If it does not balance, the mistake will show on the printed tape and can be corrected in a moment.

THOUSANDS of International Payroll Machines are saving time and money all over the country. After using two machines for over three years the John B. Stetson Co. writes: "We are still more than satisfied with the service rendered us by the International Money Machine and would not care to go back to our old way of putting up money."

The G. & J. Tire Co., after four years of experience with an International Payroll Machine, still consider it "One of the most valuable additions to our office equipment."

If you employ 200 persons or over you should investigate the International Payroll Machine. Interesting descriptive matter will be forwarded on request.

International
MONEY MACHINE COMPANY
Reading, Pa.

District Offices:
New York City, N.Y.   Cleveland, Ohio
Rochester, N.Y.   Detroit, Mich.
Syracuse, N.Y.   Chicago, Ill.
Newark, N.J.   Washington, D.C.
Boston, Mass.   Charleston, W. Va.
New Haven, Conn.   Bluefield, W. Va.
Philadelphia, Pa.   San Francisco, Cal.
Pittsburgh, Pa.   Los Angeles, Cal.
Cincinnati, Ohio   Toronto, Canada
Havana, Cuba

The International Visible Adding and listing machine has many exceptional and exclusive features.
ASK FOR PARTICULARS

COUPON   8, 7
International Money Machine Co., Reading, Pa.
Please send me without obligation on my part, full particulars of
☐ The International Payroll Machine.   ☐ The International Adding Machine.

community in general. To pay out some millions of dollars on a certain day each week would have made it necessary for the stores to carry idle stock against the payday rush; it would

PAYMASTER

"Here! My pay is wrong"

Could this happen in your business?

Exhibit 11-11: "Make this test in your filing department;" Y & E Filing Equipment; Yawman and Erbe Manufacturing Company; Industrial Management; Volume 61; January 15, 1921; p. 26

Exhibit 11-12: "The International Payroll Machine – What It Does;" International Money Machine Company; System; Volume 37; May 1920; p. 1059

Exhibit 11-13: "Here! My pay is wrong;" System; Volume 36; November 1919; p. 948

Exhibit 11-14: Early Pay Statement & Envelope; Office Management Its Principles and Practices; Galloway, Lee; The Ronald Press Company; New York, New York; 6th printing; 1923. NOTE: This exhibit has been recreated for purposes of legibility.

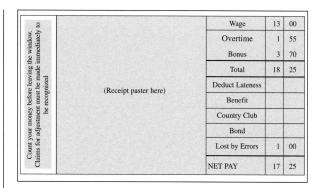

Wage	13	00
Overtime	1	55
Bonus	3	70
Total	18	25
Deduct Lateness		
Benefit		
Country Club		
Bond		
Lost by Errors	1	00
NET PAY	17	25

(Count your money before leaving the window. Claims for adjustment must be made immediately to be recognized)

(Receipt paster here)

have been an invitation to crooks of all kinds to gather around on the one day when everyone had money, and it would have made local banking exceedingly difficult. On our own part, it would have made necessary a large payroll force, and even at the best, the men would have lost hours waiting for their pay. So now we pay in groups. Almost every hour of the day is pay day somewhere in the plants." (4)

Paymasters in the Arts, Science And Literature

"Where Every Day Is Pay Day" By James H. Collins

An extract from the following article appearing in the August 2, 1924 issue of *The Saturday Evening Post* provides a wonderful view of the changing role of the paymaster and pay process and gives a vivid account of the possible beginnings of many contemporary payroll practices: (5)

Payday at the Factory Shop

"Rumors begin to run around the shop in whispers. Will the ghost walk? Has the Old Man been unable to raise the pay roll? What relief when, just before twelve, the Old Man himself comes in and hands the bookkeeper a roll of bills and a bag of coin. Instead of drawing at the bank this morning, he has made collections from customers. The old bookkeeper takes out a little packet of manila envelopes, counts the right amount into each one and passes them around among the relieved employees......That's one kind of pay day, and there are a good many enterprises of this magnitude still in the world." (5)

The Ghost Has Become an Auditor

"Pay day has grown, like everything else, with the expansion of business organizations, and is now quite a complicated affair, calling for quantity production." (5)

"The ghost has become a corporation auditor, looking after the pay envelope of 50,000 or 100,000 employees scattered all over creation. Work is done, time clocks are punched, tickets are made out and put into a slot, machines whir at distant general offices, and the pay envelope arrives in an armored automobile guarded by men with rifles. It seems mechanical, as though the thrill had been taken out of pay day." (5)

Every Day Is Payday

"To the auditor, every day is pay day. If there are 60,000 employees on the company's payroll, instead of working like the devil one day a week to give them all their money, he has a force of 100 workers on the job steadily, paying off about 10,000 every day. But while every day is pay day for the auditor, and the making up and passing out of manila envelopes a year-round job, that gentleman is most scrupulous about seeing that some particular day is pay day to everybody on his vast pay roll, and he has one haunting fear – that on the day appointed for paying Bill Jones or Molly Kelly the ghost will not materialize." (5)

Importance of Punctuality

"'Keeping faith with employees and being on the spot with the pay envelope at the regular day and hour is the uppermost thought in every corporation auditor's mind' said an office-appliance salesman who specializes in the installation of pay-roll machinery and systems. 'It is so all over the country, and the bigger the corporation, the more anxious its auditor will be about regularity. People who work in the pay-roll division of a corporation are prepared at any moment to double their efforts and stay all night if necessary to dispatch a pay roll that has fallen behind the time-table.'" (5)

"So while the modern corporation auditor does his work with machinery, and handles hundreds of separate pay rolls and thousands of pay envelopes every day in the week, the particular pay day and pay hour for Bill Jones or Molly Kelly is to him as sacred as the Puritan Sabbath, and he counts it a sin if the hour arrives and he isn't there with the pay envelope and the thrill." (5)

Machinery Is Essential for Large Payrolls

"Without machinery, pay day would be a mighty expensive proposition for the corporation with thousands of employees. Up to about 150 employees, it is possible to pay by the hand method of the old-fashioned bookkeeper (Exhibit 11-15), figuring each worker's time and counting the correct amount into his envelope. But after that, say the appliance men, it is a job for machinery, because literally thousands of clerks would be needed to make the complicated calculations necessary in dispatching a big pay roll.'" (5)

"'An illustration of what it costs to make up a big pay roll by hand is found in the adjustment of a dispute,' said a corporate treasurer. 'Not long ago we had a case in which an employee reported his envelope fifty cents short. We figured that it cost more than ten dollars to adjust the amount, counting the employee's time, the clerical work and the searching and making of records. On that account we not only use machines for every possible operation but the machinery is backed with all the accuracy we can secure - through scientific methods.'" (5)

Overview of the Payroll Process

"Everything begins with the time clock, the time ticket and the timekeeper....To know where and how to get the most efficient use of time is the great problem of business. The unloved time clock and time ticket, besides being the very foundation of payday, yield a great many facts useful in management." (5)

"So while he is doing work, the employee is also creating the records that show work, helped by the time clock. A recent wrinkle is requiring his signature on the time card. It has been found that, though people will obligingly

Exhibit 11-15:
Illustration extracted from "Calculator Contrasts – New and Old;" System; Volume 39; April 1920; pp. 770-771

ring an absent fellow employee in or out on the time clock, and think it no great harm, they balk at signing another's name." (5)

"The next pay-roll operation is extending time from the time ticket and making up the pay roll proper. In some cases this is done on the job, and in others the time tickets are forwarded to the pay-roll department at headquarters. The tendency is toward centralization of records, with a real live human ghost to hand out the envelopes and make local adjustments if there is anything wrong. 'Extending time' means figuring the number of hours worked during the week, the wages, overtime, piecework, premiums and so forth, to arrive at the actual amount that is to go into the pay envelope. With 50,000 or 60,000 employees working on several different pay plans, this would involve a world of figuring were it not for wage tables that show at a glance the exact amount due for a given number of hours at any wage rate and the special pay-roll machines that do much of the work without the setting of pencil to paper." (5)

"The addressing machine is a very important device in pay-roll operations. It prints Molly's name and certain facts about her on the pay sheet, on the pay ticket, on the pay envelope itself – cabalistic letters and figures which show where Molly works, her wages and pay plan with certain other facts. Usually this printing of sheets and tickets follows the extension of time, and then the pay roll starts through the works. The addressing machine department keeps close track of Molly, making a stencil for her when she is hired, another every time she goes from one department to another or has her pay raised. A good-sized corporation, with 40,000 or 50,000 employees, needs several thousand new

Exhibit 11-16:
"Savings Plan in Full
Force;" Long Lines;
April 1926; p. 26;
Property of AT&T
Archives. Reprinted
with permission of
AT&T

stencils every week to keep track of pay-roll changes, and all the information on the successive stencils made out for Molly Kelly are filed away under her name, making up a complete history of her connection with the company, a sort of Who's Who of employees that has many uses." (5)

"The pay envelope is now ready to be filled. It bears Molly Kelly's name and organization address. The amount due her has been carefully checked. At that point certain invisible hands begin helping themselves to Molly's money before it is counted out." (5)

The Origin of Payroll Deduction Savings Plans

"First, Poor Richard reaches in and takes the money Molly wants to save. When everybody was buying Liberty Bonds on the installment plan during the war, corporations had to set up machinery to make the deductions. Many a worker discovered that they could save money, and wanted the thing continued after his final Victory Bond had been paid for. Corporation officials like those at AT&T (Exhibit 11-16), discovered that saving on those lines was a good thing for the company, making employees independent in money emergencies, killing much of the worry and fear that go with money trouble and creating a better spirit all around. So the Liberty Bond bureau was turned into a savings bureau." (5)

Exhibit 11-17: The
Stock Subscription
Plan; The American
Woolen Company
Employees Booster;
American Woolen
Company; Volume 7;
No. 2; August 1922;
Courtesy of
Immigrant C.M.
Archives, Lawrence,
Massachusetts

"Molly Kelly decides to save two dollars a week. She makes out a slip authorizing the paymaster to deduct that amount and deposit it to her credit. The savings bureau makes the deduction and puts the money in the savings bank." (5)

Early Forms of Payroll Employee Stock Purchase Plans

"After the savings bureau finishes with Molly Kelly's pay envelope, it may pass along to a stock-deduction department, where installment payments on purchases of the company's capital stock are taken out. Many corporations (Exhibit 11-17) now sell stock to employees at a price below the outside market, spreading the payment over a year or more so they will be moderate. After Molly Kelly's order for a share of stock has been signed, she pays for it automatically, this department doing all the work." (5)

Description of Federal and State Income Tax Withholding Procedures

"Now her envelope is ready to be passed along to Molly herself, unless the taxgatherer is going to get a crack at it. If she earns enough to pay Federal or state income taxes nothing may be taken out; she deals with Uncle Sam or the state income-tax department direct next spring, making out the well-hated blanks and turning them in with the money." (5)

But here is a situation that exists in New York State, and may very well spread to other localities if state income taxes are extended. "Molly lives in New Jersey and works in New York, where she is paid. Being unmarried, and supporting no dependents, she is entitled to an exemption of $1,000. At the beginning of the year she must make a statement showing her status and exemption. This is filed with the company's income-tax bureau. Molly gets all her wages up to $1,000, a point that may be reached somewhere along in September or October, according to her earnings, or again early in the year if she is paid a substantial salary. When the exemption has been reached the bureau deducts the percentage tax due on the rest of her income that year, amounting to one per cent up to $10,000." (5)

Auditor Routines for Confirming Payroll Accuracy

"There is nothing more to take out. The time has come to put something in – actually, these various deductors and subtractors helped themselves to Molly's money on paper, figuring the net income due her, checking and rechecking one another, while the thin little manila envelope bearing her name lay waiting flat and empty. Now the time has come to put some money in, and there are one or two clever little wrinkles connected with that." (5)

"Anybody who handles considerable sums of cash daily will tell you that it is not easy to come out even. The personal equation enters in here, just as it does in astronomical observations, and you wind up the day with so much over or under. It may be only a nickel or a dime but absolute accuracy in the counting and handling of money is difficult to attain." (5)

"So when a certain pay roll is ready, the auditor provides a check upon the girl who fills the envelopes. She is given a pay roll for, say 127 people, totaling $4,815.99. He gives her more money than will be needed – may be $10 or $20. Or some odd sum like $17.62. The girl does not know the correct total of the pay roll she is handling. With piles of bills on one side and her change-making machine for coins on the other, she puts the amount opposite each person's name on the pay roll into that person's envelope. Then the envelopes and the surplus cash are turned in and checked. If she is over or

under there must be a discrepancy in somebody's envelope and it is hunted up and corrected. This is not in any sense a check upon the girl's honesty, of course – simply a check upon the possible stray coin or bill." (5)

"When you pay 50,000 people weekly, probably three-fourths of them in cash there is likewise the possibility of coming out over or under. Three parts of a pay roll are checked against one another for accuracy – the time-clock or time-card amount, the pay-roll-sheet and the total cash taken from the bank." (5)

"If some employee got a half dollar too little he will probably report the shortage bringing it to light. But if he got a half dollar too much he is a half dollar ahead, or maybe he didn't count his money carefully. Finding that lost coin would be an expensive job, even if it could be done. So the auditor and his immediate assistants usually maintain an over-and-under pot to balance their cash. Each chips in twenty-five or fifty cents of his own money weekly. If it is found, after everybody has been paid, that there is money over, it goes into the pot; while if a shortage appears, it is made good out of the pot." (5)

The Birth of Armed Security Services for Payroll Deliveries

"Finally, the ghost is ready to perambulate. Its route may be devious as well as secret, and the farther it walks, the safer from bandits. Of the tens of millions of dollars a day paid to people in the factories, stores, utility organizations, offices and other establishments, a very large proportion circulates in large amounts. Cash payment is general and the use of checks exceptional for wages in large cities. Practically all this cash must be transported in a lump sum from the bank to the paymasters' office. From there it is forwarded in large sums to branch offices and stations, and carried out to construction and repair workers in distant places." (5)

"Pay-roll robberies and murders have made it necessary for the corporation paymaster to devise protective measures. Where the company is large enough, and pay rolls are being transported every day, it may have its own armored car and armed guards. For the concern that pays on a certain day in the week there is now outside armored-car service by which money is

Exhibit 11-18: "A Good Little Plan for Payday; Amalgamated Metals Company; Ladd, G.W.B.; System; Volume 38; July 1920; p. 50

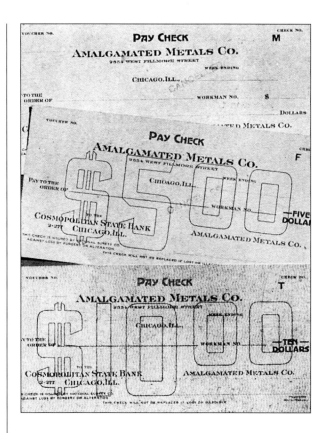

brought from the bank to the factory under guard. The car belongs to a company that makes a business of rendering such service, the guards are in its employ, and hundreds of thousands of dollars in separate pay rolls are transported daily for different customers. In one Ohio factory a guarded steel car runs right through the plant stopping at each bay and laying down the pay envelopes to employees without interrupting their work." (5)

"The ghost vehicle is a formidable fort. The compartment in which money is transported is of armor steel capable of stopping bullets. It has slots through which rifle fire can be directed by the armed guards. The driver sits in a separate steel compartment with windows of bulletproof glass. Should bandits get into this compartment by any chance, they are still walled off from the money by a barrier of steel, and the guards in the money compartment can bring the car to a dead stop by controlling either the brakes or the ignition. On top of that, secrecy is used for protection." (5)

"'Our daily pay rolls foot up considerably more than $100,000,' said the paymaster of one big corporation. 'So we keep our own armored car busy. I do not myself know its hours of going or coming, nor what particular part of the city it is working in, nor would I know what route it is taking to reach a certain part of the city.'" (5)

"'This money is in individual pay envelopes. Our guards see that it is safely delivered to a branch, where the local paymaster is waiting to receive it. The moment it comes into his hands he begins distribution, and in a few moments it is so widely scattered in individual pockets that bandits would have to line up a whole force to make any kind of haul.'" (5)

Early Arguments for and Against Payment by Check

"The floating workman is becoming more and more a problem to the paymaster. Take the troubleshooters, meter readers, installation and connection gangs of public-utility corporations that are scattered over a great city, or out over the highways of the suburbs or country. Very often nowadays such employees report by telephone in the morning instead of coming in person to a certain office or branch, and are assigned to jobs. They go from job to job through the day, calling in for the next assignment as it is finished, and may not be where the paymaster can reach them. It is a loss of time to the company to have them come in for their pay envelopes. Men on construction jobs are still farther afield. The paymaster must find ways of reaching them all, however, and the farther afield, the more the danger of transporting money. So the armored car runs out to lonesome places, ideal for banditry were there no such protection." (5)

" 'But why carry around so much cash in these days of check payments?' you ask. From the standpoint of the paymaster, the universal use of checks would be grand. No more cash to count and carry, no more armored cars or sharp shooting guards. But from the wage earner's standpoint it doesn't look so good, and in matters like this the paymaster meets the wishes of the wage earner as though he were a customer. 'We want,' said the auditor of one large corporation, 'service to the public and loyalty to the company. In meeting their wishes in certain matters we are serving them and making our own loyalty a tangible thing.'" (5)

To overcome large check problems, some companies like the Amalgamated Metals Company limited their checks to smaller increments (Exhibit 11-18). While this practice facilitated cashing, the administrative effort of issuing multiple checks to employees was increased.

Westinghouse Electric & Mfg. Co.
PAYMASTER

The bearer, with order, has been interviewed by this department.

Quit slip sent through Yes No ______ 191__
Check collected - - Yes No
Tool account balanced Yes No
Amount due for tools $______
Wages payable - - ---- ←-date

Dept. ______
Check No. ______
Date ______
Form 6010-A

EMPLOYMENT DEPT.,
Per ______

PAYMASTER

"Formerly the saloonkeeper cashed pay checks, but that was far from being ideal. Today, the grocer, butcher and other tradesmen will often oblige their customers as bankers, but the latter distinctly dislike letting merchants know what they earn. Where employees live or work near a bank they can take checks there; but there are difficulties of identification and objections to workmen lining up at the paying teller's window. The banker himself has no prejudice against the honest toiler, but when forty or fifty of him come in, perhaps in digging clothes and with strong pipes, he blocks regular depositors – the objections are theirs. The banker's chief objection is that corporations paying by check switch some of the work and expense of their pay roll to his organization. The use of check is growing, however, and workers in towns not too large for people to know one another prefer them. But the vast amounts of cash necessary in paying off are used because no successful substitute has yet been found." (5)

The Power of the Paymaster

"The paymaster has it in his power to bring sweetness and light to a work force; heading off trouble and turnover. On that account, he usually works hand in glove with the personnel man who looks after the welfare of employees – not the paternalistic stuff, but welfare in the dictionary sense, the state of faring well, well-being, prosperity. Faithfulness in paying on the appointed day, accuracy in figuring wages, giving people the kind of money they can spend without inconvenience, promptly adjusting disputes about pay – these make for true welfare." (5)

EMPLOYEE'S RECORD —19 1921

NAME Leon F. Beasdamas

ADDRESS

MARRIED? | IF UNMARRIED, HEAD OF A FAMILY?

DATES

HIRED | LEFT | HIRED | LEFT

TOTAL EARNED DURING YEAR $______
(DETAILS ON REVERSE SIDE)

DUMAS & CO., LOWELL - FORM 81 - 80248

Wk. Endg.	Earned	Wk. Endg.	Earned 576 50	Wk. Endg.	Earned 1055 70	Wk. Endg.	Earned 1584 90
Jan. 8	37 80	Apr. 16	37 80	July 23	37 80	Oct. 29	37 80
15	37 80	23	37 80	30	37 80	Nov. 5	37 80
22	37 80	30	37 80	Aug. 6	37 80	12	37 80
29	37 80	May 7	37 80	13	37 80	" 19	37 80
Feb. 5	37 80	14	37 80	20	37 80	26	33 60
12	37 80	21	37 80	27	37 80	Dec. 3	33 60
19	37 80	28	37 80	Sept. 3	37 80	10	33 60
26	35 [illegible]	June 4	37 80	10	37 80	17	33 60
Mar. 5	37 80	11	37 80	17	37 80	24	33 60
12	37 80	18	37 80	24	37 80	31	33 60
19	37 80	25	37 80	Oct. 1	37 80		1937 70
26	37 80	July 2	37 80	8	37 80		
Apr. 2	37 80	9	37 80	15	37 80		

Personnel Departments and Directors Are Added to Company Rosters

By the end of this period, most companies with welfare departments and welfare secretaries had replaced them with personnel departments and personnel directors.

The need for a close working relationship between personnel and payroll had now been recognized by most companies. Procedures developed during this period often reflected involvement by both groups in certain worker related matters as illustrated in this termination form used by Westinghouse Electric & Manufacturing Company. (6) (Exhibit 11-19) and in this standard Employee's Record Form used by many companies of the day (Exhibit 11-20).

Exhibit 11-19: "How Five Firms Keep Payroll Records Up to Date;" Merriam, George B.; Bower, John C.; Westinghouse Electric & Manufacturing Company; Industrial Management; June 1918; p. 500

Exhibit 11-20: Employee's Record Card (1921); Uxbridge Mills; Courtesy of American Textile History Museum, Lowell, Massachusetts

Exhibit 11-21: "We Found This a Better Way – Shortening the Pay-Day Rush at Youngstown Sheet and Tube Company;" System; Volume 47; April 1925; p. 473

Exhibit 11-22: Extraction from Westinghouse Electric Motors and Controllers Advertisement; System, Volume 37; February 1920; p. 329

On the Lighter Side – Company Uses "Pay-Pan" to Shorten Payday Rush

As reported in an article titled "We Found This a Better Way," the Youngstown Sheet and Tube Company apparently found a "mobile" (Exhibit 11-21) way to shorten the payday rush by going to the worker instead of the worker lining up at the traditional "pay window" (Exhibit 11-22).

Reference Sources

1. The World of the Office Worker; Crozier, Michel (translated by David Landau); The University of Chicago Press; Chicago; 1965; pp. 422-423, 431, & 607

2. "Graphic Planning of Payroll Procedure"; Bober, W.C.; Industrial Management; 1920; Volume LX, No. 5; pp. 5 –6

3. "Putting Payroll on an Automatic Basis"; Scientific American; September 18, 1920; Volume 123

4. Today and Tomorrow; Ford, Henry; Crowther, Samuel; Doubleday, Page & Company; Garden City, N.J.; 1926; p. 137

5. "Where Every Day is Pay Day – and the Ghost Walks in an Armored Car"; Collins, James H.; The Saturday Evening Post; August 2, 1924; Volume 197; pp. 18-19, 72, & 76

6. "How Five Firms Keep Payroll Records Up to Date"; Industrial Management; June, 1918; pp. 499-501

CHAPTER 12:
The Great Depression

Over Fifteen Million American Workers Lose Their Jobs

More than 15 million Americans lost their jobs and many more millions all of their life savings between the 1929 stock market crash and the mid-1930s. At a time when there was no unemployment insurance and very few pension plans, the outlook for American workers and their families was bleak at best, with no short-term remedies outside of charity and welfare on the horizon.

Jobs Were Scarce and Workers Often Went Payless

In a period that was short on cash and high on unemployment, workers often had to wait to be paid as illustrated in this August 1935 scene of Cambridge, Massachusetts Electric Railway Association workers playing cards (Exhibit 12-1). Earlier in the day, these payless workers had massed in front of the Administrator's Cambridge office demanding to be paid. The Administrator and his paymaster stood helpless awaiting the arrival of funds from Boston. While these workers were employed but payless, many more were unemployed and job openings when announced brought out large numbers of job seekers.

The Thirty-Hour Workweek and The Debate Over a Minimum Hourly Wage

Some thought that the 30-hour workweek might provide a means to put more workers back on the payroll, like the Kellogg Company of Battle Creek, Michigan, which implemented a five-day six-hour workweek in December 1930. Here Kellogg Company men and women workers line up (in separate lines) to be paid by the paymaster (Exhibit 12-2). Others thought that the overhead costs would increase (including those related to payroll) and drive product

Exhibit 12-1: ERA Workers, Payless Since Last Thursday (8/26/1935); Courtesy of Boston Public Library, Print Department, Boston Herald-Traveler Collection (Photo # 07127)

Exhibit 12-2: Pay Day of Men and Women on 30 Hour Week at Kellogg Company; "Are You Ready for a Shorter Day?"; Rositzke, R.H.; Factory Management and Maintenance Journal; Volume 91; June 1933; pp. 211-213; Courtesy of Kellogg Company

In The *Offices, Too,* This is *An Age* of *Machinery*

Exhibit 12-3: Card Sorting and Tabulating Machines; "In the Offices, Too, This is an Age of Machinery;" The Norton Spirit; April 1928; pp. 3-5; Courtesy of Collections of the Worcester Historical Society, Worcester, Massachusetts

Exhibit 12-4: Western Union Simplex Printer; "In the Offices, Too, This is an Age of Machinery," The Norton Spirit; April 1928; pp. 3-5; Courtesy of Collections of the Worcester Historical Society, Worcester, Massachusetts

prices too high. Still others thought the 30-hour workweek would result in overproduction. Many agreed that there would have to be a national minimum wage to avoid unfair competition, but the debate did not end until 1938 with the passage of the Fair Labor Standards Act along with other major social reforms.

The Payroll Office Environment Of the Late Twenties and Early Thirties

In spite of or because of the adverse conditions of the Depression Era, new labor saving devices continued to appear in the finance, accounting, and administrative offices of U.S. companies. In addition to those devices already considered standard office machinery (like the typewriter, telephone, comptometer, adding machine, letter opener, and sealer and stamper), many companies were now benefiting from even more sophisticated "mechanical clerks" like the card sorting and tabulating machines illustrated here (Exhibit 12-3). (1)

While tabulating technology was invented in the late nineteenth century by Herman Hollerith and utilized in processing the 1890 U.S. Census, and while insurance companies were among the first in the twentieth century to pilot and benefit from this technology, it was not until the process was perfected and offered at an affordable price that companies began to use the technology on a large scale. Refinements of the basic technology, including the ability to sort alphabetically and provide printed listings of output, took well over a decade alone to perfect but were in place by the end of the 1920s.

The card sorting machinery could take a stack of cards and sort them in whatever manner the operator wanted; according to employee number, name, or into any other grouping. The card sorter was operated by holes punched in the cards. The cards were sorted into various compartments as they were run through the sorter. The sorting device could process upwards of 350 cards a minute. The tabulator was a companion device to the sorter that performed various specified calculations on the pre-sorted cards. (1)

For example, in calculating the payroll with the use of the sorter and tabulator, the operator was now able, in one operation, to "instantaneously" calculate the number of workers, number of hours, and amount of money to be paid to each worker. (1)

The payroll organization of this period was made much more accurate and efficient through the use of these machines. Capability and performance had now advanced far beyond those of the days of the "pencil and paper" methods. (1)

Further capabilities were added by Western Union (in the late twenties) with their new Simplex Printers (Exhibit 12-4) and by Bell Telephone (in the early thirties) with their new teletypewriter services (Exhibit 12-5), which provided businesses with the ability to send and receive written messages as typed by the message originator. It is highly probable that during this period, some businesses may have

The New Western Union Simplex Printer recently installed in the Telegraph Room

NOW...
a new teletypewriter service

Teletypewriter exchanges, similar to telephone exchanges, now make it possible for any subscriber to this service to typewrite by wire instantly to any other subscriber, whether he be around the corner or across the continent. Subscribers can type back and forth by wire for short or long periods, just as they now talk by telephone.

Messages, inquiries, reports—typed in your office—are instantly and accurately reproduced on any other subscriber's teletypewriter. Identical typewritten copies, made by both sending and receiving machines, are available for permanent records.

This new service differs from private line teletypewriter service in that any subscriber may ask for any other subscriber and be connected immediately. The cost is low.

Teletypewriter Service provides two-way communication.
Speed of connection is as fast as telephone service.
A typewritten record, one or more copies, is produced simultaneously by both sending and receiving machines.
Material transmitted may be recorded on forms if desired.
Teletypewriters are like ordinary typewriters in appearance.
Teletypewriters can be operated by any one who can operate a typewriter.
You can use Teletypewriter Service any time you need it.
A most economical form of record communication.

FOR FURTHER INFORMATION JUST CALL **YOUR BELL TELEPHONE BUSINESS OFFICE**

begun to apply these capabilities to the payroll function, perhaps for remote time reporting?

Payroll Banditry Reaches Record Proportions

Quotation:

"A Good Paymaster Needs No Security"

Cervantes, *Don Quixote*, 1620

NOTE: This quotation may have been true in 1620 but certainly was no longer valid in first half of the twentieth century!

It is no surprise, given the economic condition of the country, that payroll robberies, although occurring throughout U.S. history, reached record proportions in the late twenties and early thirties.

In the first six months of 1930 alone there were over 200 reported cases of payroll robberies in which at least 20 persons were killed and more than 32 injured. In addition, over $1 million was lost to robbers in these crimes. (2) Many notable criminals of the day, including "Pretty Boy" Floyd, had pulled off one or more payroll robberies. (3)

In Memory of a Shoe Factory Paymaster - Frederick A. Parmenter

Without a doubt, the most famous payroll robbery and murder (Exhibit 12-6) is the Sacco-Vanzetti case, which actually occurred in 1920. The case received international attention when the media began to report the case and the public began to take sides, with many feeling that Nicola Sacco and Bartolomeo Vanzetti were unjustly accused because of their foreign backgrounds and radical anarchist beliefs. The two were convicted and then executed seven years later. (4)

Exhibit 12-5: "Now ...a new teletypewriter service;" The Saturday Evening Post; Volume 204; No. 27; January 2, 1932; p. 30; Property of AT&T Archives. Reprinted with permission of AT&T.

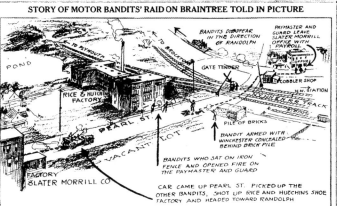

BOSTON HERALD [EXTR

FRIDAY MORNING, APRIL 16, 1920—TWENTY-FOUR PAGES   · · ·   TWO

MOTOR BANDITS MURDER GUARD, WOUND PAYMASTER DASH AWAY WITH $18,0

STORY OF MOTOR BANDITS' RAID ON BRAINTREE TOLD IN PICTURE

Without commenting on the guilt or innocence of the accused (a debate that continues to this day), it does seem to be appropriate to pay tribute to the victims of this crime – Frederick A. Parmenter and Alessandro Berardelli, who were killed in the process of performing their payroll-related jobs.

Frederick A. Parmenter, the paymaster for the Slater and Morrill Shoe Company of South Braintree, Massachusetts, and his payroll guard Alessandro Berardelli were shot and killed at 3 P.M. on April 15, 1920 while returning to the factory from the bank with the weekly payroll of approximately $16,000. (4)

Each Thursday, the payroll for the factory arrived on the 9:18 A.M. train from Boston. As usual, the American Express agent met and

Exhibit 12-6: "Motor Bandits Murder Guard, Wound Paymaster, Dash Away with $18,000;" microfilm copy; The Boston Herald; April 16, 1920; p. front page

accompanied the payroll back to his office. The agent then delivered the payroll to the Slater and Morrill payroll office upstairs in the same building as that occupied by American Express. There the paymistress filled the pay envelopes and repacked and locked the payroll in two steel boxes. By three o'clock, the payroll was ready to go to the factory, located across the railroad track a short distance away. The money was normally carried by the paymaster and an armed escort. Sometimes the two drove to the factory with the payroll and other times they walked. On April 15 they walked alone, each carrying one of the steel boxes. (5)

Without making these payroll professionals into heroes, the death of Frederick A. Parmenter and Alessandro Berardelli do remind us that paymasters and payroll guards of the past did have to assume an additional element of risk that most contemporary payroll professionals do not have to shoulder and cannot fully appreciate. In a very real sense the death of these two gentlemen and all other persons killed or hurt during a payroll robbery in the first three decades of the twentieth century have contributed to making the process safer for future generations.

While change would come slowly and such crimes would continue through the thirties and forties (Exhibits 12-7 & 12-8), a national debate was now underway to find solutions to the problem.

Armored Cars – A Partial Solution

Given the severity of the situation, companies and banks were looking for greater security and vendors were responding with a whole series of products and services to prevent crimes of this nature including robber-proof safes and bullet-proof glass. However, the most important product and service being offered were the armored car and the armored car security service.

By 1931, company and bank use of armored cars to move payrolls was commonplace, especially in and around large cities. Such services were provided largely by three companies; the Armored Service Corporation, the United States Distribution Corporation, and the Brink's Express Company. Some banks, companies, and cities (Exhibits 12-9 & 12-10) operated their own armored-car services. As of 1931, there were over 550 armored cars in service generating over $3.9 million in revenue. During the first 10 years of service, according to a report by the National Commission on Law Observance and Enforcement, the use of armored cars had proven to be an effective deterrent to payroll robberies. (6)

Profile of the Brink's Express Company

The Brink's Express Company was actually started in 1859 in Chicago as a general delivery service following the success of Henry Wells, William G. Fargo, and others. It was not until 1891 that Brink's made its first payroll delivery to the Western Electric Company. Motorized deliveries began in 1904. In 1905, Brink's began to provide similar services to the Chicago Ornamental Iron Company. By 1907, the Brink's Board of Directors had recognized the opportunity and had authorized company management to pursue this business. Soon, Hart, Schaffner & Marx, the Florsheim Shoe Company and other companies entered into formal payroll delivery

Exhibit 12-9: New York City Armored Payroll Truck; "The Payroll Check Plan;" Downing, John R.; American Bankers Association Journal; Volume XIX; January 1927; Reprinted by permission of the City of New York and the American Bankers Association Journal

and distribution service (Exhibit 12-11) contracts with Brink's. Others followed. (7)

When Brink's first began offering these services, security was not the problem it would later become. A Brink's man picking up money would often just wrap it in a newspaper and put in under the seat of the wagon. Where larger sums were involved, a rifle would be kept inconspicuously under the seat. But things

began to change in the second decade. (7)

Initially, Brink's had to convince companies of the risk of having company employees carry cash payrolls through the streets and of some of the weaknesses of utilizing local policemen to escort company payrolls. (7)

The increasing number of payroll robberies certainly helped to convince companies of the danger. The first payroll robbery in Brink's history occurred in 1917. During the following decade, there were four robbery attempts in total, the last of which included the use of dynamite. Each time Brink's further tightened its procedures. (7)

Brink's began to use armored cars in 1923. These first vehicles were produced of boiler plate steel with wooden floors. By 1927, Brink's had a fleet of fully armored cars in use and by the early thirties, hardened aluminum was replacing the heavier steel models. (7)

Exhibit 12-10: Payroll Delivery (1935); Courtesy of Archives, City of Baltimore

ON THE LIGHTER SIDE – The importance of timing when planning a pay roll robbery

On November 4, 1928, several would-be payroll robbers appeared at the National Bronze Art Metal Works in St. Louis, Missouri. Everything had been planned in advance. Well, everything except one small detail - Payday was the day before!

Data taken from the Statement of Payroll Robberies Committed from September 1928 to March 1929 from the Report to the National Crime Commission by Raymond Moley, Chairman of the Pay Roll Robbery Committee (1930)

Exhibit 12-11: Brink Payroll Services; Moving Money; Crissey, Forrest; Brink's Express Company; 1929; p. 33; Courtesy of Brink's Incorporated

111

Early Initiatives on Check Versus Cash Payments

Many corporations, along with members of the banking community and various labor and industry associations, were working very hard to solve the theft problem and were not sitting idly by while payrolls were being robbed and paymasters and payroll guards shot.

Publications during this time period indicate that most large employers with large cash payrolls were very concerned about the problem. Many companies, such as United States Steel, Pennsylvania Railroad, and International Harvester Company, had already converted some or all of their workforce to payment by check with such changes often encouraged by a recent experience with an attempted or successful robbery at one of their plants or offices.

Throughout the 1920s and 1930s those with vested interests were evaluating the causes and recommending possible solutions. Many surveys were conducted, like those published by the Research Department of the Illinois Chamber of Commerce, the American Electric Railway Association, the Gray Institute Association (for the iron foundry industry), the Policy Holders' Service Bureau of the Metropolitan Life Insurance Company, and the American Bankers Association.

These surveys and subsequent published reports on their findings served as important educational tools that would eventually lead to common solutions to the problems created by cash payrolls.

Extracts and summaries from several of the above cited surveys provide important insights into the problems of the day and the thinking of employers, bankers, and employees regarding the controversial issue of payment by check versus cash.

The American Bankers Association and Their Payroll Check Plan (1927)

John R. Downing, Vice President of Citizens Union National Bank of Louisville, Kentucky and President of the American Bankers Association, Clearing House Section, presented an objective view of the situation following a survey conducted of some 400 member banks. (8)

Based on survey results (Exhibit 12-12), most bankers were generally supportive of payment by check although they were concerned about check bearer identification issues and the possible risk of forged endorsements. They were also concerned about the added administrative burden and expense that such a change would place upon banks. (8)

Mr. Downing concluded, in his survey report, that "the question resolves itself largely into a contest for favor between the greater safety of the payroll check and the convenience to the workers of obtaining their wages in cash." (8)

"The resistance of employees to the pay check has taken the form in some parts of the country of direct action by the labor unions. In many instances objections have been raised on account of the inconvenience attached to converting the check into money and the time lost in going to the bank. In most cases, however, the banks advise that when the proposition has been put to the men in the proper way they have invariably accepted the check plan voluntarily." (8)

Questionnaire on Payroll Checks

1. "Do you make up payroll envelopes for your customers? If so, do you charge a fee?"
   226—No. 38—Yes. 26—Free of charge. 12—Small fee.
2. "Do you deliver payrolls free of charge?"
   231—No. 22—Yes, two at customers' risk.
3. If so, do you use armored trucks? If not, what protection do you provide for your messengers?
   Many banks use armored trucks, but only seven banks, which actually deliver payrolls, use this safeguard. Several banks use armed guards to protect messengers.
4. Is there in your city a payroll delivery service privately operated? Do you pay for this service or do your customers?
   136 banks—No. 78 banks—Yes. Customer almost invariably pays cost of service.
5. With proper safeguards and an assurance of reasonable compensation by balances and otherwise, would you favor the use of payroll checks by your customers?
   By far large majority answering favor use of payroll checks. 25 banks—No.
6. Has your Clearing House Association adopted any rules or regulations affecting the use of payroll checks? Or delivery of payrolls and collection of deposits by banks?
   150 banks—No. 14—Yes.
7. Would you favor and support by your patronage insurance against loss to your bank on payroll checks through forgery, assuming that special insurance against such a loss can be secured?
   147—Yes. 38—Insurance now carried covers such losses. 24—If not too expensive.
8. Have you special arrangements with your customers who use payroll checks for your mutual protection?
   Most do not. In ten cases, customer relieves bank of responsibility.
9. Has any resistance to the use of payroll checks in your city on the part of employees been brought to your attention, and what, if any, objections have been made to it?
   187—No resistance. Chief objections—difficulty of identification, inconvenience and time required in cashing checks.
10. Do you provide a special window for cashing payroll checks?
    206—No. 37—Yes.
11. What precautions do you take as to identification of payee?
    159—Usual precautions. 25—Positive identification. 10—Identification waived by agreement with customers.
12. Do you carry payroll check accounts on a separate ledger?
    208—No. 9—Yes. 7—Carry separate ledger sheet for each firm doing payroll check business.
13. Would you cooperate in any effort the Clearing House Section, American Bankers Association, might undertake to standardize banking practice with respect to the use of payroll checks?
    Yes, almost unanimously.

"To offset these advantages, it is generally agreed that the check plan makes more work in the office, means a larger number of persons coming into the bank and longer waiting lines at the tellers' windows, and tends to lengthen the banking hours. In some cases banks have been forced to obtain enlarged quarters to take care of the demands thus created. It is well for the banker to ponder over the possibility of having to acquire more space if he handles an increasing number of payroll check accounts." (8)

"A number of banks have special windows for the express purpose of cashing pay checks, while a few assign special windows on certain days or during rush periods." (8)

"While we are not prepared at this time to make definite recommendations, it is quite evident that the more widespread adoption of the payroll check plan would cut down the risks that are now run in transporting large sums of currency about the streets." (8)

The American Electric Railway Association (1928)

Industry journals and newsletters, like the one published by this railway association, also helped to educate and influence their readers. According to its own survey, by 1928 the payment of wages by check among electric and steam railroad companies was already quite common. (9)

The Association reports that early attempts to convert employees at the Chicago Rapid Transit Company had actually begun around 1918. While the attempt failed to a large extent, it did result in the conversion of Transit agents and porters on the condition that they could cash their checks against company cash receipts at stations along the lines. (9)

The Monthly Labor Review (1929)

In regards to the position of organized labor, the *Monthly Labor Review* reported that an examination of the trade agreements in the files of the Bureau of Labor Statistics reflected that

most agreements of the day stipulated that all wages must be paid in cash. One even required the payment of wages in United States gold. Others included wording that would permit fines for any employee accepting payment by check. However, most also included language that would permit payment by check under certain conditions. (10)

The Illinois Chamber of Commerce Conducts Survey (1929)

The *Factory and Industrial Management* Journal dated October 1929 reported the results of a survey conducted by the Research Department of the Illinois Chamber of Commerce of Chicago area employers, bankers, and employees on their reasons for and against payment by check (Exhibit 12-13). These types of surveys helped to change attitudes and address areas of resistance. According to this survey, 73% of the 329 responding companies had already transitioned some or all of their work force to checks. (11)

The National Crime Commission Report Triggers Country-wide Debate (1930)

In 1930 the National Crime Commission appointed a Subcommittee to investigate the pay-roll robbery issue.

Payment by Check From the Employees' Standpoint

Reasons For	Reasons Against
1. When check is lost or stolen, payment can be stopped and another check issued; if cash is lost, nothing can be done.	1. When payroll bearer checks are issued and lost or stolen, new checks are not issued, until time limit has expired and they have not been cashed by anyone else.
2. Holdup risk decreased.	2. Undesirability of having income known by people cashing checks.
3. Employee having bank account can save time by mailing check for deposit and paying bills by check.	3. Identification difficulty.
4. No embarrassment in proving that pay was short.	4. When banks are not convenient, difficulty of getting checks cashed without making purchases.
5. Encourages saving.	5. Sometimes have to pay for getting checks cashed.
6. Bank account provides good training for keeping business-like records of receipts and expenditures.	6. Makes it necessary to go to same place of business in order to cash checks, and to make purchases.
7. Check can be mailed as per employee's instruction when work carries him away from main office.	7. Many banks lack adequate facilities for cashing checks on pay day.
8. Requests for loan from fellow employees not as frequent when paid by check.	8. Wage earners prefer cash

From the Standpoint of the Employer

Reasons For	Reasons Against
1. Danger of holdup, with loss of life and money, eliminated.	1. Time required to check paid vouchers, which is not required under cash system.
2. Better records—easier to check errors.	2. Opposition of employees.
3. Eliminates burglary and holdup insurance.	3. Danger of checks being raised.
4. Canceled check is receipt.	4. Time required to make and sign checks.
5. Branch plants payroll paid from main offices.	5. Cost of equipment to pay by check.

From the Bank's Standpoint

Reasons For	Reasons Against
1. Means of getting new savings accounts.	1. Congestion at peak times in tellers' windows.
2. Large balances are carried by customers having payroll accounts.	2. More bookkeeping work for banks.
3. Sometimes possible to make special charge for this service to customer.	3. Necessary to install special facilities in some cases
4. Helps in the safety movement.	4. Possible losses by improper identification.

Exhibit 12-13: Payment by Check From the Employees' Standpoint; "Payrolls – Check or Cash;" Factory and Industrial Management; Volume 78; October 1929; p. 818; Courtesy of State of Illinois Chamber of Commerce

The Sub-Committee consisted of over 20 leaders from education, banking, industry, labor, legal and law enforcement. The Sub-Committee reviewed all aspects of the problem including details regarding recent payroll robberies and considered all potential solutions before sending its findings and recommendations to the National Crime Commission.

The National Crime Commission Sub-Committee, referred to as the Pay Roll Robbery Committee, under the chairmanship of Professor Raymond. C. Moley of Columbia University, concluded that "The prizes are too tempting and the daring of professional criminals too great. It is obvious that pay-roll robberies are directly invited by the practice of carrying cash. This is quite obviously the root from which pay-roll banditry springs and flourishes. The use of armored cars very considerably reduces the danger of pay-roll robberies. This protection, however, is expensive. Employers are apparently willing to pay by check if they can secure adequate protection against the danger of forgeries, and against difficulties in making the checks themselves. There is every evidence that opposition to payment by check is declining, and that organized labor, and labor in general, is quite willing to cooperate in every reasonable way in bringing about a termination of the old system of payment in cash under suitable conditions." (12)

Following the Sub-Committee's report, newspapers and then the public lined up on one side or the other, or in some instances straddled the fence.

On one side, those in favor, like the *Indianapolis Star*, reported that "The remedy is so simple and effective that there should be no hesitation about its adoption." While on the other side, many felt like the *Syracuse Post Standard*, that "The whole business is a strange commentary upon the lack of law enforcement in the busy heart of our cities." (2)

Eventually consensus was reached and the transition to the check-based payroll system as the primary method of payment was embraced by employers, bankers, and employees alike.

Payroll Disbursement Processes Begin to Change

As a result of payroll robberies and the attention given to the problem at all levels, a number of changes in the process were introduced, especially as related to the disbursement of payrolls to employees:

Origin of On-Site Company Check Cashing Services

It was in the late 1920s, while the transition from cash to check was taking place, that the practice of on-site check cashing services was introduced. In order to obtain authorization from the state department of labor to pay by check, some states, like New Jersey, granted permission to companies with the understanding that such companies would cash employees' checks so far as funds were available. To protect the employer, dollar limits were printed on the face of the specially designed checks and the employee had to confirm his identity by signing his name on the space provided on each payroll check. Because maximum dollar limits were set low, employees often received multiple paychecks per pay period. (9)

First Evidence of Partial Outsourcing of Payrolls

By the late 1920s, the practice of outsourcing the disbursement of payrolls to third-party service providers (sometimes banks) was prevalent, again prompted by company concerns over the security and safety of large cash payrolls.

According to the findings of the 1929 Illinois Chamber of Commerce check versus cash survey, 85% of the companies paying by cash had "turned the responsibility over to a company (like Brink's) that makes a business of handling payrolls, cashing the check, putting the money in the envelopes, and paying the employee." (11)

Under this method, the company prepared the pay envelopes (with employee name and amount to be paid, etc.) and delivered them to the armored car service provider along with a check for the amount of the payroll. The service provider would then cash the check, fill the pay envelopes, and deliver them to the client's factory or business location where they would distribute them to workers from permanent armored booths, pre-selected guarded locations, or movable payroll trays carried or rolled through the plant or office. (7)

Reference Sources

1. "In the Offices, Too, This is the Age of Machinery;" The Norton Spirit; April 1928; pp. 3-5; Courtesy of Worcester Historical Society, Worcester, Massachusetts

2. "To Check Payroll Banditry"; The Literary Digest; August 30, 1930; Volume 106; p. 42

3. "Pretty Boy Floyd's Visit to the Gateway City"; Webb, Michael; http://qns.com/~dcordry/Floyd.html

4. Sacco-Vanzetti Case; wysiwyg://http://infoplease.com/ce5/CEO45270.html

5. The Sacco-Vanzetti Case, 1920-1927; Dickinson, Alice; Franklin Watts, Inc.; New York; 1972; pp. 13-15

6. "Report on the Cost of Crime;" National Commission on Law Observance and Enforcement; No.12; United States Government Printing Department; Washington; 1931

7. Moving Money (1859 – 1929); Crissey, Forrest; Brink's Express Company;   Chicago, IL

8. "The Payroll Check Plan;" Downing, John R.; American Bankers Association Journal; January 1927; Volume XIX; pp. 491 - 492; 544-545

9. "Pay by Check System Makes Strides in the Industry"; American Electric Railway Association (AERA); September 1928; Volume XIX; No. 9

10. "Payment of Wages by Check"; Monthly Labor Review; September, 1929; Volume 29; pp. 532-535

11. "Payrolls – Check or Cash?"; Factory and Industrial Management; October 1929; Volume 78; p. 818

12. Document: "Report submitted to the National Crime Commission by Raymond Moley, Chairman of the Committee on Pay-Roll Robberies"; Columbia University, New York; c 1930; Library of Congress

CHAPTER 13:
The Franklin Delano Roosevelt Era

Few periods in American history have been faced with more problems than those of the Franklin Delano Roosevelt Administration. The U.S. faced and survived the devastating impact of both a major economic depression and a world war within a relatively brief period of time.

And yet, in terms of economic impact and social change, it was a period of tremendous progress and growth. The paymaster (and his/her employer) as well as the worker (Exhibit 13-1) would be significantly impacted for generations to come by the decisions made and actions taken during the Roosevelt era. At the same time, payroll personnel played an active role in implementing and subsequently maintaining the many changes created during the Roosevelt Administration.

The "New Deals"

The "New Deals" platform which President Roosevelt ran on in 1932 and was re-elected on in 1936 focused on relief, recovery, reform, and social security.

Relief and recovery efforts focused on pulling the country out of the economic crisis while reform initiatives focused on prevention and improvement in the form of tighter regulations. From these reforms came the Securities and

Exchange Commission to control the sale of securities, the Robinson–Patman Act to prevent price discrimination, the Walsh-Healey Act to require government contractors to adhere to approved labor standards, and the Fair Labor Standards Act to regulate hours and wages and address child labor concerns.

The Social Security Act

Perhaps the most far reaching of the "New Deal" initiatives were the changes achieved under the National Social Security Act signed into law by President Roosevelt (Exhibit 13-2) in

1935. Roosevelt referred to this program as "History's Most Ambitious Welfare Plan" and noted "Today a hope of many years' standing is fulfilled…. We can never insure one hundred per cent of the population against one hundred per cent of the hazards and vicissitudes of life, but we have tried to frame a law which will give some measure of protection to the average citizen and to his family against the loss of the job and against poverty-ridden old age." (1)

Passage of the Act hadn't been easy. While it was considered good news for workers in American industry, many businesses felt other-

Exhibit 13-1: Photo of Paymaster Window; "Does Jim Blank Rate a Raise?"; Kress, A. L.; Factory Management and Maintenance; Volume 97; January to December, 1939; p. 65

Exhibit 13-2: President Roosevelt Signs the Social Security Act on August 14, 1935; Courtesy of Franklin D. Roosevelt Library

wise. They questioned the government's ability to make it work. "The section dealing with unemployment insurance benefits seemed particularly obscure. No one appeared to know just whom it would affect. Businessmen felt that they might be swamped under a sea of red tape which keeping its necessary records would involve. Some condemned the act as socialistic, a mere extension of government meddling with business. Others frankly said that they believed the government was offering benefits which private companies could not match." (1)

While President Roosevelt felt that Senate passage was "the best news coming out of Capitol Hill in many a long day," the opposition would challenge the constitutionality of the Act and Social Security would be implemented long before this issue was finally resolved.

Plans for implementation proceeded. Businesses (Exhibit 13-3) were asked to bury the campaign hatchet and reserve criticism of the Social Security Act long enough to cooperate in registering 26,000,000 wage earners eligible for the old-age pension annuity. (2)

A Path Not Taken – Use of the Stamp System

Other countries with social programs already in place were using stamp systems. Under the stamp system, every employee would have a stamp book. Employers would purchase stamps from post offices and affix stamps to the book in behalf of the employee. Larger employers would use metered machines. When a book was filled, the employer would send the book to Social Security. When terminated, employees would take a partially completed book with them and surrender it to their new employer. This system, even though initially supported by the Social Security Board, was ultimately rejected in favor of the centralized enrollment and record keeping approach.

The Formative Years of Social Security, Arthur J. Altmeyer, University of Wisconsin Press, Madison, WI, 1966; p. 66

By late 1936, Social Security was moving rapidly into the enforcement phase with employers and their unions, personnel departments, and payroll organizations playing a major role, in addition to the U.S. Postal Service, in the distri-

bution, completion, and return of employees' applications (Forms SS-5). Every employee included in the program had to fill out a Social Security "blank" as illustrated in this photo of clerks at a Cambridge Tobacconist (Exhibit 13-4). Communication and education were paramount to the success of this program, and the government used every medium possible to promote the program and educate the population (Exhibit 13-5). (2)

Social Security Cards were issued at various locations throughout the country. Here (Exhibit 13-6), women clerks in Boston are typing Social Security Cards.

However, the greater effort on the part of companies and their payroll organizations was related to new record keeping requirements. Beginning January 1, 1937, employers (Exhibit 13-7) would need to track and report (to the government and to workers) much more information than had ever been required before. (2)

For each worker, employers would have to report employee name, address, social security number, occupation, total amount of compensation, amount of compensation subject to social security tax, and amount of social security tax withheld, along with any other taxes withheld

Exhibit 13-5: "Join the March to Old Age Security" (1936); www.ssa.gov; Courtesy of Social Security Administration

Exhibit 13-6: Typing Social Security Cards in Boston (1938); Courtesy of Boston Public Library, Print Department, Boston Herald-Traveler Collection

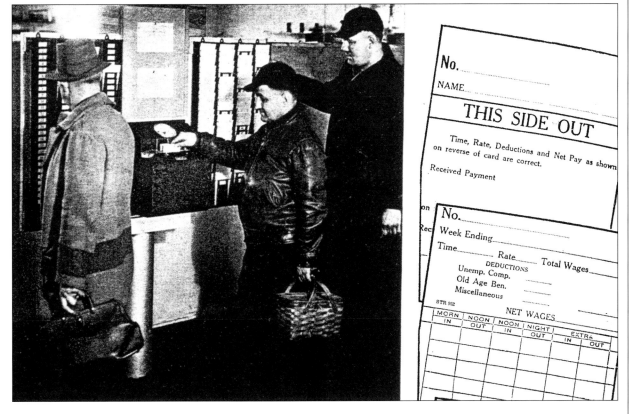

Exhibit 13-7; "Social Security Records;" Urquhart, Lewis K; Factory Management and Maintenance; Volume 95; No. 1; December 1937; pp. 370-381

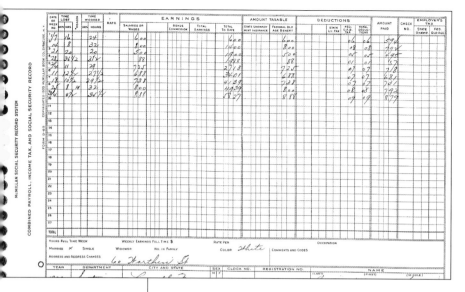

Exhibit 13-8: Payroll Register with O.A.B. Column (1939); Merrimack Utility Company; Item MS113 5.3; Courtesy of American Textile History Museum, Lowell, Massachusetts

Exhibit 13-9: Women Working on Verifying Machines for Wage Records, Baltimore (1939); Courtesy of Boston Public Library, Print Department, Boston Herald-Traveler Collection

(such as state unemployment taxes). In addition, employers would be held accountable for accurate records and for reporting any adjustments. For many companies, with or without mechanical solutions already in place, the effort was monumental, especially given the brief period required to implement the capability. Smaller companies continued to rely on manual processes and customized record keeping forms as shown here (Exhibit 13-8). (2)

Payroll played a key role in the implementation of this massive collaborative effort between industry and government and can justifiably be proud of its contribution. The Social Security Administration's historian, Larry DeWitt, provid-

ed the following comments to describe the magnitude of this joint effort:

"The start of Social Security's payroll reporting in January 1937 required the issuance of Social Security Numbers to 26 million American workers; the assignment of 3.5 million Employer Identification Numbers; the development of a centralized system of record keeping that included a Visible Index listing the name and number of every covered worker and taking up 24,000 square feet of floor space – all in an era before the advent of computers. In fact, the weight of the paper records involved was so massive that no building in Washington had floors sturdy enough to hold it and the records had to be housed in an old Coca-Cola factory in Baltimore. The Candler Building, on Baltimore's waterfront, was thus transformed from a dusty, largely-unused, factory building into the site of one of the most intense government activities of the New Deal era, as thousands of fresh recruits flowed into Baltimore from all over the nation to assist in the establishment of the payroll records." Thousands of SSA employees were hired to verify wage records (Exhibit 13-9) and others to perform accounting related duties (Exhibit 13-10). "It was described in news accounts of the time as 'the largest bookkeeping operation in the history of the world.' While this may have been a bit of hyperbole, it did accurately express the scope and spirit of the undertaking." (3)

In 1937 following the implementation of the Social Security Act, the Supreme Court declared the Act constitutional and by 1939, amendments to the Act had been made to provide "More Security for the American Family" (Exhibit 13-11) as the program was expanded beyond individual worker benefits into family income security benefits.

An Early Debate Over Pay Envelope Messages

Pay envelopes were seen by employers and others, including both political parties, as a great communication tool. In the national elections just prior to the start-up of Social Security, the Republican National Committee convinced a number of business leaders to include the following message in employee pay envelopes:

Early Accounting Operations

A scene from SSA's early accounting operations in Baltimore circa 1936. The issuing of Social Security numbers and the creation of earnings records on all Americans covered by Social Security was the largest bookkeeping operation in the history of the world.

More Security -- 1939

MORE SECURITY FOR THE AMERICAN FAMILY

THE SOCIAL SECURITY ACT AS AMENDED OFFERS GREATER OLD-AGE INSURANCE PROTECTION TO PEOPLE NOW NEARING RETIREMENT AGE.

FOR INFORMATION WRITE OR CALL AT THE NEAREST FIELD OFFICE OF THE

SOCIAL SECURITY BOARD

This poster announces the passage of the 1939 Social Security Amendments. These important amendments transformed Social Security from a retirement program for individual workers, into a family income security program--providing retirement, survivors and dependents benefits.

Exhibit 13-10: Early SSA Accounting Operations (1936); www.ssa.gov; Courtesy of Social Security Administration

Exhibit 13-11: More Security for the American Family (1939); www.ssa.gov; Courtesy of Social Security Administration

Pay Envelope Message

"Effective January 1937, we are compelled by a Roosevelt "New Deal" law to make a one-percent deduction from your wages and turn it over to the government. Finally this may go as high as four percent. You might get this money back in future years...but only if Congress decides to make the appropriation for that purpose. There is NO guarantee. Decide, before November 3 – election day – whether or not you wish to take these chances."

The New Republic November 4, 1936, p. 6

President Roosevelt and many others were quick to call this tactic unfair and deceitful. These kinds of misuses of the pay envelope have led many companies to limit the use of pay envelope communications. (4)

The Fair Labor Standards Act

The history of payroll cannot be told without some reference to the Fair Labor Standards Act (FLSA), which has been so important to millions of workers and their employers.

The Wage and Hour Law was made effective on October 24, 1938 and was the country's first federal law governing wages of workers in interstate commerce. It provided for minimum hourly wages of not less than 25 cents for the first year, 30 cents for the next six years, and increases to 40 cents thereafter. In addition, maximum hours per week were set at 44 hours for the first year, 42 for the second and 40 thereafter, with overtime permitted at time-and-one-half the employee's regular rate of pay. (5)

As with the Social Security Act, the Fair Labor Standards Act would be tested in court and it would take over three years before the Supreme Court would affirm the constitutionality of the Act and make the FLSA the law of the land.

The role of the payroll organization in FLSA compliance since 1938 has largely been in the area of record keeping, retention and retrieval in response to Wage and Hour Division requests and claims. In addition, when employers have been found in violation of the FLSA, their payroll organizations have been responsible for issuing back payments and correcting pay calculation formulas and procedures to ensure future compliance. In 1940, the United States Supreme Court confirmed the right of the Wage and Hour Division to make routine inspections of employer payroll records under the Act, including its right to access to all employee records and not just those records under dispute.

Wage-Hour Division Orders Increased Pay for 70,000 Tobacco Workers

"Seventy thousand workers in various branches of the tobacco industry will receive higher pay under the terms of a series of wage orders signed by L. Melcafe Walling, administrator of the Federal wage-hour law."

The Labor News, July 17, 1942

Laws on Pay Frequency

While the Fair Labor Standards Act does not address how often employees must be paid, it is interesting to note that as early as 1892 there was legislation approved at the state level on the frequency of wage payments and that by 1938 most states had enacted laws to address pay frequency issues. In 1936, the International Association of Government Labor Officials proposed a standard state wage cycle of semimonthly while recognizing the need for some flexibility:

"Unless pay days come at frequent intervals, their value to the employees is diminished because the employees will have drawn their money in advance, at a discount, and when pay days do occur there are no cash settlements to be made. In actual practice the spacing of pay days, and the length of hold-over, varies somewhat among reputable concerns. Some employers pay weekly, others every 2 weeks, some semimonthly. Employers of large numbers of piece workers find it difficult or impossible to settle up to, and including, the day of payment. The suggested language is especially designed

to eliminate the undesirable practice of withholding wages for unreasonably long periods of time. While at the same time permitting the employer some latitude in arranging his pay days and in making up his pay roll." (6) To this day, states control laws regarding pay frequency.

1937 Philadelphia Payoff Survey – Chamber of Commerce Results

53% of all employees were being paid weekly, 35% semimonthly, 4% biweekly, and 7% monthly.

The most popular payday was Friday, Wednesday ranking next, followed by Thursday, Saturday, Tuesday, and Monday.

51% of all employees were paid by check and 49% by cash.

"All About the Payoff," *Business Week*, March 27, 1937; p. 25

World War II

Time Clocks and Workers Go on Overtime

As the worker in this Baldwin Locomotive Works Company Advertisement (Exhibit 13-12) says, "My time's not my own anymore. It hasn't been since we made up our minds to win this fight. Every hour I can put in belongs to Joe Murphy's boy in Africa, to young Danny Green in New Guinea, and to their buddies."

Payroll organizations in most U.S. companies during World War II were also working overtime along with factory and office workers to keep pace with the increased volumes resulting from round-the-clock operations. Shown here (Exhibit 13-12A), mechanical workers line up on payday to receive their paychecks at the Esso Refinery in Baton Rouge, Louisiana during a week in December 1943.

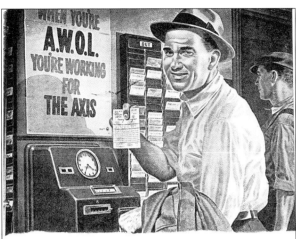

Exhibit 13-12: War Time Clock Punching (1943); Baldwin Locomotive Works; Newsweek; Volume 21; No. 15; April 12, 1943; p. 34 (facing page); Courtesy of BLH Electronics, Inc.

Exhibit 13-12A: Mechanical Crew at the Baton Rouge Esso Refinery in Line for Pay Checks; December 1943; Courtesy of National Archives, Washington, D.C.

"Girl" Paymasters Step Forward

As a result of shortages in male workers, many women assumed paymaster roles during World War II as shown in this photo of Lillian Wilson (Exhibit 13-13) of the paymaster's department at Arlington Mills. The caption under the article reads as follows: "Girl Paymasters now are taking the place of men in the Arlington Mills. Here is attractive Lillian Wilson from the paymaster's department paying off in the Top Mill, Bradford Combing Department. Thaddeus S. Kimball, one of our guards, accompanies her. He is shown on the right. First to receive his pay envelope is John Vickers, section hand, a veteran of both World War I and World War II." Lillian certainly presents a confident image of a professional paymaster as she looks head on at the camera. Note the pay tray and push cart which were used to distribute plant payrolls during this period.

Soldier's Individual Pay Record

Soldiers of this period were issued individual pocket-sized pay books (Exhibit 13-14) that included all data necessary for the issuance of pay including name, serial number, grade, years of service, insurance premium amounts, and emergency contact. Each time pay was to be issued, the soldier would present this book. The book would record date of pay issuance, deductions taken, net pay, voucher number and disbursing officer's signature. With the frequent movement of soldiers and in the absence of supporting technology, these books provided a means for recording and controlling payments to military personnel that was not otherwise possible.

Exhibit 13-13: "Girl Paymasters Taking the Place of Men in the Arlington Mills;" Arlington Mills News and Views; July 1943; p. 5; Courtesy of American Textile History Museum, Lowell, Massachusetts

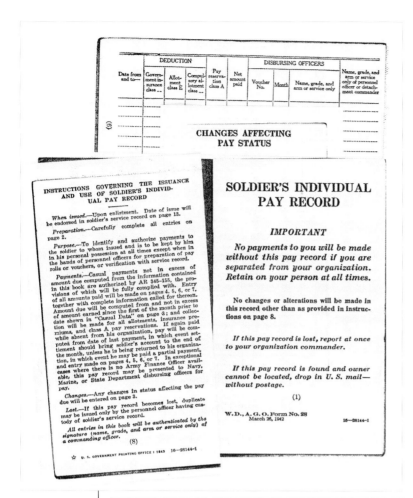

Funding the War Efforts - The Sale of Defense Bonds via Payroll Deductions

Paymasters played an important role in selling Defense Bonds and collecting money to fuel war efforts. Although a number of companies such as AT&T had already introduced bond purchase payroll deduction options during World War I, it wasn't until the second world war that both the need and the technical capability enabled large numbers of American companies to participate.

In 1941, Treasury Secretary Morgenthau authorized a pilot payroll deduction program to promote the purchase of lagging Defense Bond sales. A number of large corporations including Armour, AT&T, Bowery Savings Bank, General Electric, International Harvester, Kraft Cheese, Metropolitan Life, New York Life, Riggs National Bank of Washington, Standard Oil of New Jersey, and U.S. Rubber participated in the program and helped prove the viability of the process (Exhibit 13-15).

With the viability of the program proven, greater focus was then placed on the purchase of bonds through payroll deductions. Marketing campaigns were developed and goals set, and labor unions, company leaders, and payroll

Savings Bonds Payroll Deduction Plan Has 20,000 Participants As First Year Ends

More than 20,000 telephone employees are buying United States Savings Bonds through the System payroll deduction plan, now a little more than a year old. In the country at large more than 1,500,000 people have bought Savings Bonds with a maturity value of nearly two billion dollars. No other security is held by so many owners.

The bonds fit personal thrift programs in various ways. For instance, they will provide retirement income, or funds for children's education. Here is how the plan may be worked to provide future income at regular intervals:

Arrange under the pay-roll deduction plan to buy a bond as often as you can. It takes $18.75 to buy a bond which will be worth $25 in ten years. After that time, as your bonds mature, you will have a continuous flow of income. This income you may either reinvest in new bonds or use for any purpose you wish.

If anything happens to prevent your carrying through such a program, you will not have to sacrifice any of the money you have put in. Any bond you have owned for 60 days may be redeemed for what you paid for it, plus some interest if you have had it more than a year. If you happen not to live, your bonds will go to your beneficiary, if you have named one, or otherwise to your estate.

Of course, completion of such a program as is outlined above depends upon the Government continuing to sell Savings Bonds. No one can give absolute assurance of this, but the plan has been so satisfactory that it will probably be continued in some form indefinitely. If not, there is still no good reason for not investing in Savings Bonds while they are available.

Any regular employee may arrange to purchase Savings Bonds under the pay-roll deduction plan by filling out Form D464, a copy of which may be obtained from your supervisor.

Exhibit 13-17: Extract from Barlett-Snow Advertisement; "100% War Bond Buyers"; Business Week; October 10, 1942; Courtesy of Bethlehem Corporation

Exhibit 13-18: View of Paymaster Window – "This is My Fight Too!"; The Labor News; Volume 38, No. 45; January 7, 1944; p. 16; Courtesy of Collections of Worcester Historical Museum, Worcester, Massachusetts

organizations signed up to meet the aggressive sales goals.

By 1942, the U.S. Treasury had set payroll deduction sales goals of $500,000,000 a month, and in 1943 the greatest drive for dollars in the history of the world was conducted. Paymasters like the one shown in this 1943 campaign (Exhibit 13-16) doubled their bond selling responsibilities.

Companies like Bartlett-Snow (Exhibit 13-17) promoted their products and patriotism by publishing their employee bond purchase participation rates, while literally everyone from Gypsy Rose Lee to this young unknown female worker standing in front of the paymaster's cage (Exhibit 13-18) provided an endless series of testimonials to convince the non-participating company or employee to enroll or to convince those already participating to buy more.

Many company newsletters like the one published by Arlington Mills (Exhibit 13-19) announced the implementation of new payroll bond purchase deduction programs for their employees.

According to Van Zeck, the current Commissioner of Public Debt, "Payroll professionals made an enormous contribution to the financing of World War II. Their support fueled the growth of the payroll savings plan which accounted for half of all Series E bonds sold. By 1945, more than 27 million Americans were buying bonds through the payroll savings plan. Payroll savings sales assured the Treasury of a steady stream of cash averaging more than $500 million each month. The creativity and imagination of payroll professionals set in motion what remains to this day one of the most popular ways for millions of Americans to invest in U.S. Savings Bonds." (3)

Exhibit 13-19: "Mill to Start Pay-Roll Allotment Plan;" News and Views; Arlington Mills; Volume 1, No. 9; April 1942; p. 5; Courtesy of American Textile History Museum, Lowell, Massachusetts

▲ Mill to Start Pay-Roll Allotment Plan ▲

Bonds May be Purchased Through a Deduction From Weekly Pay —

Many Requests Prompt Mill to Install System

At the request of many employees and with the cooperation of the Defense Savings Staff, the Arlington Mills is establishing on April 1 a Weekly Pay-Roll Deduction Plan for the purchase of United States Savings Bonds by employees. Under this Plan, employees may now purchase Defense Savings Bonds conveniently at the Mill by merely asking the Company to deduct $1.25 from their pay each week until the Bond is paid for. The Bond will then be issued to you at

$1.25, or any multiple of $1.25, out of your pay each week and credit it toward the purchase of a Defense Bond. Your Overseer will have a supply of Authorization Cards which should be filled in by you and returned to him.

Fill Out Card Carefully

Please note particularly when filling out the Authorization Card that any co-owner's or beneficiary's name and address should be written in. The Paymaster will start making the deductions on the first weekly pay after he receives the properly completed Card.

FOR DEFENSE

plete their plans and allow the Clubs to run their course. This new Plan does not permit inclusion of the Clubs now in existence. When these Clubs are finished the members may switch to the new Plan.

A committee, representing different parts of the Mill, has been studying various systems and will act as the guiding body of this new Plan. This committee comprises: Adolph Wenzel of the Treasurer's Department; Horace Herlihy of the Employment Office; Joseph Brearley, Mending Dept.; Catherine McGreevy, No. 28 Mill; Alice Gale, No. 3 Mill; Christy Rubio, Top Mill; and Nellie Fikor, Weaving Department.

Bonds May be Bought for Cash

It should be added at this point that

The Birth of the Federal "Pay-As-You-Go" Income Tax Program

Funding war time efforts while keeping basic civilian infrastructures operational was no easy task, and the U.S. Treasury was stretched to the limits making the environment and timing ripe for expansion of the federal income tax program.

Exhibit 13-20: Beardsley Ruml Before Boston Chamber of Commerce (1943); Courtesy of Boston Public Library, Print Department, Boston Herald-Traveler Collection

Today's federal income tax withholding program was conceived during World War II out of proposals for a "pay-as-you-go" plan offered by Beardsley Ruml (Exhibit 13-20), who at the time was the chairman of the Federal Reserve Bank of New York. His proposal actually included wiping out the 1942 debt ($7.5 billion dollars) and starting fresh in 1943. His "skip-a-year-and-pay-as-you-go" income tax plan was supported by most everyone including corporations and taxpayers and made him a national hero at the time. (3)

Donald Lubbick, former Assistant Secretary of Tax Policy for the U.S. Treasury, would agree. According to Mr. Lubbick, "At the onset of World War II the United States moved to a universal application of the income tax as the principal source of revenue to finance government operations. The key to its success was the Ruml plan that put the collection of tax on a pay as you go basis. Vital to that system was universal withholding on wages. History has demonstrated that tax compliance rates approaching 100% can only be achieved through that means." (3)

According to the *IRS Historical Fact Book*, "To raise revenues, Congress dropped the threshold for payment of income taxes to the lowest level ever, bringing over 50 million new taxpayers into the system for the first time. To educate these new taxpayers, the Bureau of Internal Revenue launched a major educational campaign. This resulted in widespread acceptance of the income tax into virtually all American households for the first time." (7)

Under the new law, on July 1, 1943 employers began to deduct 20% of all wages and salaries above the specified exemption levels. Employers began depositing funds collected on a monthly basis and filed the first return with the Treasury (Form W-1) on October 31, 1943 for the months of July, August, and September. On January 31, 1944, employers issued to their employees the new W-2 Forms, replacing the old 1099 Forms and the newer Victory Tax (V-2) Statements and filed the first W-3 Form, reconciling total collections with statements provided to employees. (3)

It should be noted that only 50% of the actual 1942 debt was actually forgiven. Employees with earnings in excess of the new exemption levels were obligated to pay the balance in two equal installments, the first half on March 15, 1944 and the second half on March 15, 1945. (3)

The introduction of the "pay-as-you-go" plan, while providing a necessary source of revenue for the government at this critical time in U.S. history, also resulted in more taxes for more workers. In addition, the change required new forms, new tables, and new and more complex processes for both the employee and the employer. (3)

For some employees, the new plan required the filing of estimated earnings and tax liabilities and payment of quarterly installments for the current year and for all employees the new process began with Form W-4 (Exhibit 13-21). (3)

Employers and their payroll organizations had to put new withholding systems and processes in place quickly. According to data provided by

Exhibit 13-21: Form W-4 (1943); Business Week; June 19, 1943; p. 120

FORM W-4 U. S. TREASURY DEPARTMENT INTERNAL REVENUE SERVICE	**EMPLOYEE'S WITHHOLDING EXEMPTION CERTIFICATE** (Collection of Income Tax at Source on Wages)

Name _____
(Print full name)

Address _____   Social
(Print home address)   Security
                                            No. _____

I. Check the box in the line below which applies to *you* on the date this form is filled in:
- Married person living with husband or wife but claiming none of the personal exemption_____ (1) ☐
- Married person living with husband or wife but claiming half of the personal exemption_____ (2) ☐
- Single person (not head of a family) or married person not living with husband or wife (not head of a family)_ (3) ☐
- Married person living with husband or wife and claiming all of the personal exemption (spouse claiming none of the exemption)_____ (4) ☐
- Head of a family (a single person or married person not living with husband or wife who exercises family control and supports closely connected dependent relative(s) in one household)_____ (5) ☐

II. Number of dependents **receiving chief support from you** who are either under 18 years of age or incapable of self support because mentally or physically defective._____ _____

I declare that the entries made herein are a true and complete statement as of the date indicated, pursuant to the Internal Revenue Code and the regulations issued under authority thereof.

Date _____ 194___   _____ (Signature)

Exhibit 13-22: Income Tax Cartoon; H.F. Hill; News and Views; Arlington Mills; Volume 1; No. 7; January 1942; Courtesy of American Textile History Museum, Lowell, Massachusetts

Exhibit 13-23: "Form 1040 or FRAMIS ON THE APDAY;" Parker, Dan; Artist: Hoff, Sidney; Colliers; Volume 113; No. 1; Jan-Mar 11, 1944; pp.14+

Exhibit 13-24: Income Tax Returns (3/14/1944); The Philadelphia Inquirer; Reproduced by permission of Urban Archives, Temple University, Philadelphia Pennsylvania

Exhibit 13-25: "Every Business an Income Tax Expert;" Newsweek (Anthony Rollo & John Horn), February 28, 1944; Newsweek, Inc. All rights reserved. Reprinted by permission.

the IRS, revenue from the new income tax withholding program soared from $686 million in 1943 to $7.8 billion in 1944 and $10.2 billion 1945. (3)

From this time forward, employers and their payroll organizations became partners with the IRS and assumed a much expanded role as income tax withholding, payment and reporting agents in behalf of the federal government. (3)

Paymasters in the Arts, Science And Literature

While some Americans looked at the new federal income tax as an "insurance policy" to help win the war against Germany and Japan, others felt that the plan was unfair to certain wage earners and referred to it as the "pay-as-you-go-and-come" tax plan. The majority understood and supported its need but were confused by the more complicated formulas and forms, especially those large numbers of first-time tax filers (many of them women). Some lost sleep over it as portrayed in this cartoon (Exhbit 13-22), others like "Mushky Jackson and the Boys" congregated (Exhibit 13-23) to figure it all out together, while still others rushed to the local

income tax office for help (Exhibit 13-24). Others saw the opportunity to make a quick dollar, and small businesses (Exhibit 13-25) quickly became "tax experts and consultants."

127

H&R Block

While H&R Block was established in 1946 as United Business Company, it would not be until 1955 that the company would assume its current name and begin to specialize in income tax return preparation.

Norman Rockwell Captures the Mood of the New Taxpayer

One of America's most beloved illustrators and artists, Norman Rockwell, captured the mood of the country in this painting (Exhibit 13-26) that appeared on the cover of the March 17, 1945 *Saturday Evening Post*. Editors included the following note on the cover: "If there is one time of the year when a man wishes he didn't make so much money, this is it. Most of the year, he can and does get along with six or seven children. On March 15, if at no other time, he may wish he had sixteen or seventeen pairs of little feet pattering up and down the stairs at home. Norman Rockwell's man has been at work, we judge, about seven hours already, and obviously is planning to make a night of it. The coffeepot has been brought up as a mobile reserve. The clutter of papers you

will recognize as the trail left by a man who is frantically beating the woods to find exemptions. The cat, as untroubled as only cats can be, is sleeping the sleep of the innocent. His name is Morgenthau." (8)

A Change in Personal Tax Filing Deadlines

In the 1940s, the deadline for personal income tax filing was March 15. In 1955, the date was changed to April 15 effective for tax year 1954. By extending the personal income tax filing deadline by 30 days, the IRS was able to separate corporate and other types of returns from personal income tax returns and thereby equalize the workload.

Commissioner's 1955 Report - IRS Media Relations

Making It All Work – The Technology of the Period

The demands of industry and government during this period required more from workers and technology than ever before.

By this time, technology had advanced significantly and was being used on a very large scale, not only by the public and corporate sectors, but also by the average citizen at large. The telephone industry, for example, was celebrating its 25th anniversary of coast to coast service and was now supported by over 170,000 operators (Exhibit 13-27).

Exhibit 13-26: Income Tax Filing Time; Artist: Norman Rockwell; The Saturday Evening Post; The Curtis Publishing Company, Licensing Division; Volume 217; No. 38; p. front cover; Printed by permission of the Norman Rockwell Family Trust; Copyright 1945, The Norman Rockwell Family Trust

Exhibit 13-27: "170,000 Women Employed as Operators;" The Saturday Evening Post; March 5, 1938; p. 103; Property of AT&T Archives. Reprinted by permission of AT&T.

If your company employs 3,000 or more individuals, and they are purchasing War Bonds through payroll deductions, let us tell you how this special Elliott Machine is issuing bonds for the employees of the New York Central Railroad, New York Telephone Company, Railway Express Agency, Inc., Prudential Life Insurance Company, Lever Brothers Company and many others.

Write now on your company letterhead for free Elliott Portfolio regarding this problem.

THE ELLIOTT ADDRESSING MACHINE CO.
151 Albany Street, Cambridge, Mass.

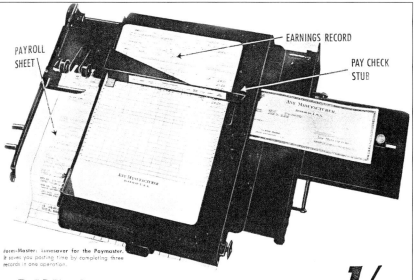

PAYROLL SHEET

EARNINGS RECORD

PAY CHECK STUB

Form-Master: Timesaver for the Paymaster. It saves you posting time by completing three records in one operation.

PAYROLL POSTING TIME CUT ½

Whether you have 15 employees on your payroll or 1500, the new Todd Form-Master can save you time and money. With this simple mechanical device, any clerk can learn quickly to hand-post check stubs, earnings records and payroll sheets *in one operation,* at the rate of 100 to 160 postings an hour. ¶ Form-Master is portable ... gives you clear and complete payroll records from which Social Security and other governmental reports may be prepared accurately, quickly and economically. It lessens errors ... speeds posting and proving and provides wage and deduction receipts for your employees. ¶ Write for the Todd Form-Master folder and samples of forms that can effect additional savings for you.

THE TODD COMPANY, INC.
ROCHESTER, N. Y.

Gentlemen: Please send us information on the Todd Form-Master and samples of forms as suggested in your advertisement in the September 14 issue of Business Week.

COMPANY NAME _____

ADDRESS _____

CITY _____ STATE _____

BY _____

Exhibit 13-28: Elliott Addressing Bond Issuing Machines; Business Week; October 17, 1942

Exhibit 13 29: "Payroll Posting Time Cut ½;" Todd Company, Inc.; Business Week; September 14, 1940; p. 73; Courtesy of Unisys Corporation

While payroll organizations supporting smaller companies of 40 to 80 workers could continue to produce their payrolls and maintain their records manually, their work was often facilitated by the use of customized forms or machines like the Todd Form-Master (Exhibit 13-29) that permitted the payroll employee to post records to multiple pay records at one time by hand.

However, for larger companies, the payroll office environment was more often designed around the use of technology. Company payrolls depended on this technology to handle the increased volumes and perform their more complicated functions in the post "New Deal" and federal "pay-as-you-go" income tax environment. Payroll organizations and their management were more and more involved in evaluating, selecting, and using this technology.

In turn, vendors created products to better meet the needs of the times like this Elliott Addressing Machine (Exhibit 13-28) designed to specifically help companies handle the heavy increase in Defense Bond purchases.

Medium to larger sized employers were, out of necessity, often on the leading edge of these advances in technology. A typical profile of the technology (referred to as machines) being used by such employers, their employees and payroll organizations during this period might look something like the following:

The assembly of payroll data for punch card systems normally would begin with the stamping of job tickets by the worker in the shop. Typical job and time tickets are shown here

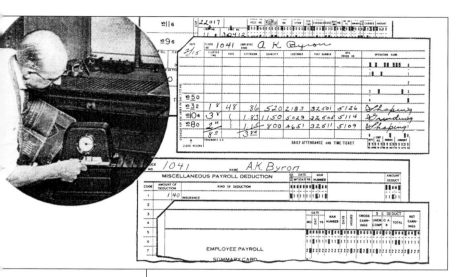

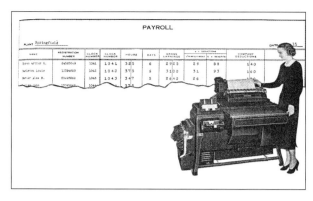

Exhibits 13-30 through 13-35: "Social Security Records;" Urquhart, Lewis K; Factory Management and Maintenance; Volume 95; No. 1; March 1937; pp. 370-381

(Exhibit 13-30) along with payroll deduction cards and summary cards that are automatically punched. A permanent set of cards is used over and over again for standard deductions. (9)

Individual summary cards are then combined with those of other workers and processed through an electric accounting machine to produce the plant payroll sheets as illustrated here (Exhibits 13-31 & 13-32). Electric accounting machines permitted operators to print payroll sheets, earning records, and pay checks simultaneously. The electric accounting machine performed all calculations and printed all data and totals in proper columns. (9)

Alternative products such as the dial time recorder (Exhibit 13-33) could be used to automatically post time data directly from the employee onto a payroll ledger sheet. (9)

The use of addressing machines enabled payroll organizations to avoid a lot of labor intensive work including all handwritten entries of redundant data. Stencils were prepared for all constant payroll data such as clock number,

name, and rate and could also include such information as gross earnings, applicable deductions and net pay. The use of "masks" permitted the operator to control what data on the stencil would appear on each form. This illustration

(Exhibit 13-34) shows the operator and the stencil along with the posting of payroll data on various types of pay forms. Instead of stencils, some addressing machines used metal plates. Ten key electric accounting machines (Exhibit 13-35) permitted operators to enter both alphabetical and numeric characters.

Growing Importance of Forms And Forms Processing Equipment – Moore Business Forms

The forms and forms processing machine industry grew rapidly in response to growing transaction volumes, process complexity and

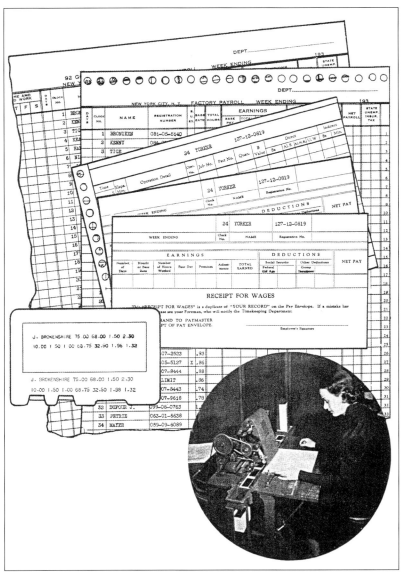

technology. One such company that illustrates the growth of this industry on which payroll and so many other businesses would rely heavily was Moore Business Forms.

Moore began business back in 1861 when its founder, Samuel Moore, acquired the rights to produce a multi-ply paper and carbon paper sales book from its inventor, Carter. In one writing, the salesman was able to take an order and produce simultaneously one copy for the customer and one copy for order administration under the motto "let one writing serve many purposes." (10)

Although a Canadian, Samuel Moore quickly realized the potential market in the United States. In 1886 Moore Business Forms (doing business at the time under the name of Carter & Company in honor of the inventor of the sales book) opened its first manufacturing plant in Niagara Falls, New York under the name of the American Sales Book Company. (10)

By 1925, the company had realized the need for forms processing equip-

ment and formally became a manufacturer of such machines. During this timeframe, web-fed lithography was introduced and permitted high speed mass production and more precise product standardization. (10)

By 1936 the company had reached such a level of success that the U.S. government turned to it for the production and delivery of the first 40 million Social Security application forms and cards (Exhibit 13-36). (10)

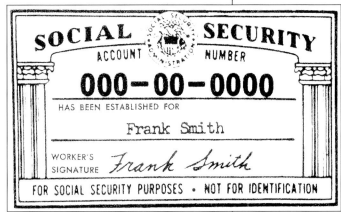

Exhibit 13-36: Social Security Card; Courtesy of Social Security Administration

131

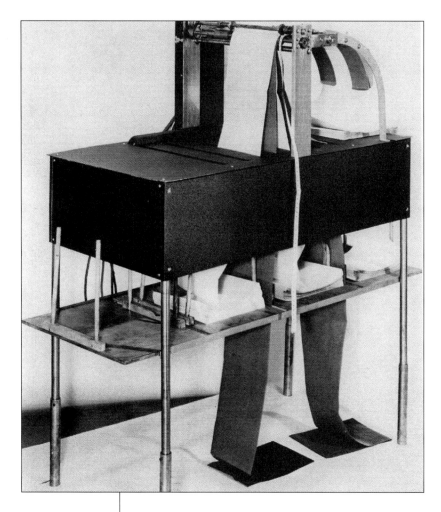

Moore has maintained heavy investments in research and product development throughout its history, and by the mid-1940s had introduced a wide range of such products including form decollators, imprinters, and detachers (Exhibits 13-37 through 13-40) to meet the growing forms processing needs of its customers. Often times, this meant developing products that would work with the printers developed by other companies, like this Moore Remaliner mounted to a Remington Rand No. 3-100 Sector Machine (Exhibit 13-41). (10)

Examples of Employer Pay Processes of the Period

The City of Rochester, New York And Growing Numbers of Deductions

In the early 1940s, employers began to realize that beyond providing employees with a statement of mandatory withholding information (Federal Income Tax, Social Security, etc.) for each pay period, it was also desirable to give their employees a pay check that provided all their deduction information, which at this time included an average of six deductions. The City of Rochester reported the following types of deductions applicable to its employees during this time period: 1) pension; 2) pension loan repayment; 3) credit union deduction; 4) group health and accident insurance; 5) garnishment; 6) quarterly hospitalization insurance; and 7) annual Community Chest deduction. It also recognized that deductions for war bonds would soon be added to the list. (11)

Exhibit 13-37 through 13-41; Moore Decollator (c. 1941), Moore Forms Imprinter Model 433 (c. 1941), Moore 1025 Variable Form Detacher Breaking Large Multiple Form (7/3/1941), Moore 1033 Remaliner #3 and Moore Kemaliner mounted to Remington Rand No. 3-100 Sector Machine (c. 1944) respectively; Reprinted with permission by Moore North America, Inc.

For the above reasons, the City of Rochester Finance Department selected a combination of office machines that included an electric accounting machine from I.B.M. and various adding-listing and signing machines from Protectograph. (11)

Through the use of the electric accounting machines, the city was able to prepare: 1) the payroll in five copies, interleaved with one-time carbon paper; 2) pay checks, with bottom stubs and explanations of all deductions; and 3) individual earnings records for each employee showing by pay periods the gross pay, deductions, and the net payment. (11)

The Protectograph machines enabled the Treasurer to sign and balance the total numbers and amounts of checks with the total numbers and amounts submitted by Finance for signing. (11)

The City of Austin, Texas and Centralizing Payroll Operations

As companies continued to grow and mature through experience and improved management techniques, some began to realize that with technology, some functions, like payroll, could be centralized and in the process better controlled. In 1945, the City of Austin found that by using a pay-

roll accounting machine by Burroughs it was able "to maintain proper controls over all payrolls with the minimum of clerical help." (12)

The City of Bridgeport, Connecticut and the Use of Tabulating Robots to Lower Cost

The City of Bridgeport's Comptroller emphasizes the importance of "watching the nickels" and that during wartime controlling operating costs has been more important than at any other time in the city's history. The city pays approximately 2,600 employees and points out that legal requirements make municipal payrolls more complex. The Comptroller also notes that Uncle Sam is making the job harder as well with Social Security and federal income tax withholding requirements. The loss of qualified help has also been an issue. For these reasons, the city increasingly had to turn to the use of machines. (13)

To lower costs and gain efficiencies and controls, the city selected tabulating equipment from Remington Rand. Their installation included three automatic key punches, one sorter, one multi-control reproducing punch, one interpreter, one alphabetic tabulator, one numeric tabulator and one summary punch. (13)

Through the use of these machines, the Comptroller reports that "Payroll costs of the City of Bridgeport, Connecticut, covering all phases of costs in connection with the production of pay checks, including their inception and the setting up of records, reporting, auditing and other applications" is now 29.04 cents per check versus the national median of $1.00. (13)

Assuming the City of Bridgeport was typical of other municipalities and companies of the day, the following overview may provide some insights into the generic tabulator-based payroll process environment of the World War II period (13):

PREREQUISITE: A permanent personnel number is assigned to each employee. Once assigned, it is never changed.

STEP 1: Work Sheets with master employee information from the last pay period are sent to individual departments for manual corrections. These corrections when received will be used to generate pay for the current pay period.

STEP 2: Copies of the corrected worksheets are sent to the Civil Service Commission for certification or additional corrections.

STEP 3: The Civil Service Commission retains a copy of the approved worksheet and sends the original to the Comptroller's Office.

STEP 4: Cards are punched based on information on the corrected and approved worksheets.

STEP 5: Cards are then sorted according to personnel number.

STEP 6: Using the numeric tabulator and the summary punch, a single card is cut from all these cards and a listing is made which proves the accuracy of the punching to the accuracy of the initial corrected payroll worksheets. The summaries are cut and the proof run is made and checked. All preparation has now been completed and proved correct. The summary cards are then used to draw the checks and provide the disbursement records.

STEP 7: Vouchers are set up. The number of checks required is determined and a block of fanfold, pin-feed checks set aside.

STEP 8: Summary cards are processed through an alphabetic 100-sector tabulator and a payroll register is run.

STEP 9: One register copy is retained by the Comptroller and one is given to the Treasurer to assure, again, the accuracy of the figuring and the checks used.

STEP 10: The same cards are run again to produce the printed checks.

STEP 11: A set of these cards is then created and placed in the accounting file for future check reconciliation.

STEP 12: The register sheets are then bound and handed to a clerk who takes off the totals from the registers and sets up a control by totals to tie to monthly bookkeeper totals on the monthly statements.

STEP 13: Summary cards are then used to run a listing by check number and every check is accounted for. The total amount of this listing provides the final control totals. Summary cards are then placed in sealed boxes and stored.

STEP 14: On a quarterly basis, summary cards are run and a single summary card created for the quarter which will be filed and then used at year end to produce W-2 forms. (13)

The Ford Motor Company and Pay Disbursement Practices

In 1938, Ford Motor Company was paying over 100,000 men and had developed a very structured process for paying its workers.

Workers were paid every two weeks in groups of 10,000 so every day was payday for some employees. For control purposes, groups were divided into sections of 150 workers. All workers knew exactly when they would be paid. Pay time was always at the end of the workday, regardless of shift. The "paying office" consisted of 40 men. Preparation of each payroll required about four hours. The clerks, working from approved timecards with hours and rates of pay used calculating machines to determine the amount of pay due each worker.

The amount of pay due each worker was then written on the pay envelope with the worker's name and number in preparation for filling. For control purposes, Ford Motor Company always ordered the least amount of currency and coins required to fill each pay envelope. For example, if an employee was due $87.60, the paying office would fill the envelope with one fifty dollar bill, one twenty dollar bill, one ten dollar bill, one five dollar bill, two single dollar bills, one fifty cent coin and one dime (not two nickels). In order to do this, the paying office had to calculate the exact denominations needed for each worker, section, and group as a total. From Ford's perspective, this practice provided a consistent approach and reduced the risk of errors while making it more convenient and safe for workers, who wouldn't be walking away from the plant with bulging pockets and become a target for vendors and thieves. Limiting sections to 150 men also facilitated the process of finding errors by the paying office. (14)

On the Lighter Side - Paymaster Urges Employees to Call for Pay Envelopes

"The paymaster's window will be open from 12 to 1 o'clock from now on for employees to transact business during the noon hour. There seems to exist in the minds of some employees the idea that by leaving a pay at the paymaster's office, regardless of the length of time, it keeps their names on the payroll. This is not so and has no connection whatsoever with the service record of any employee."

Arlington Mills News and Views, Volume IV, No. 2 (June 1944); Courtesy of the American Textile History Museum, Lowell, Massachusetts

Held Electric Accounting Company – Early Payroll Service Provider

> **Paid by Machine**
> Chicago accounting firm provides full, automatic payroll service to industrial employers - everything but the money.
>
> *Business Week* (March 11, 1944)

On March 11, 1944, *Business Week* reported on the establishment of one of the earliest payroll service providers, Held Electric Accounting Company and one of its first clients, the Midland Die & Engraving Company of Chicago. (15)

To start the program, Midland provided all the basic employee information including employee name, department, clock number, Social Security number, rate per hour or unit, tax exemption amount, and itemized regular deductions (such as war bond purchases).

Held put the records up on punch cards. Each week Held provides Midland with a sheaf of payroll authorization forms with employee information imprinted on the forms. Midland fills in hours worked (or units completed) along with any employee data changes and returns the completed forms to Held. Within twenty-four hours upon receipt, Held produces and returns employee checks (Exhibit 13-42) to Midland. In addition, Held prepares ledger accounts and deduction statements and prepares reports for federal and state governments, all for a flat fee of 20 cents a check. (15)

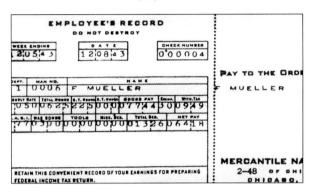

Exhibit 13-42: "Paid by Machine;" Held Electric Accounting Company; Business Week; March 11, 1944; p. 42

The founder, Harold W. Held, indicates that he has developed a technique for running multiple payrolls for different companies in one process using electric computing-tabulating-recording machines. With a target of employers with less than 500 employees, Held believes he can get the cost per check down to 10 cents a check through higher volumes. (15)

Reference Sources

1. "Social Security: U.S. Lays Down Law for Payment of Unemployment Insurance Premiums;" *Newsweek*; Volume 7; March 21, 1936; pp. 36+

2. "For Employers: SS-4;" *Business Week*; November 14, 1936; p. 22

3. "The Major Payroll Milestones of the Twentieth Century;" Haug, Leonard A.; *PayTech*; American Payroll Association; January/February 2000

4. "Falsehoods on Pay Envelopes;" *The New Republic*; November 4, 1936; p. 6

5. "The Wage and Hour Law;" Morrow, L.C.; Editor; Factory Management & Maintenance; Volume 96; January to December 1938

6. "Laws Requiring Payment of Wages at Specified Times; *Monthly Labor Review*; Volume 47; December 1938; pp. 1297-8

7. IRS Historical Fact Book: A Chronology – 1646 to 1992; Department of Treasury, Internal Revenue Service

8. "This Week's Cover;" *The Saturday Evening Post*; Volume 217; No 38; The Curtis Publishing Company; Philadelphia, PA. March 17, 1945; p. 1 Facing Cover

9. "Social Security Records;" Urquhart, Lewis K.; Associate Editor; *Factory Management & Maintenance*; Volume 95; No. 1; December 1937; pp. S370-S380

10. "The Moore Story;" Parsons, Dudley L.; Sudarsky, Peter; Moore Corporation Limited; Toronto, Canada; 1957

11. "Making City Pay Checks Talk;" Ereth, Fred, Deputy Comptroller, City of Rochester, N.Y.; The American City; Volume LVII, No 8; August 1942; pp. 43-44

12. "Centralized Payroll Equipment Writes Three Records in One Operation;" Seaholm, Walter E., Director of Utilities, Austin, Texas; *The American City*; Volume 60; December 1945; p. 92

13. "Tabulating Robots Produce Letter Perfect City Payroll;" Rodman, Perry W.; City Comptroller; Bridgeport, Connecticut; *The American City*; Volume 60; May 1945; pp. 103+

14. "Where Two Nickels Are No Dime;" Norwood, Edwin P.; *World's Work*; Volume 60; January 1937; pp. 32-33, 107

15. "Paid by Machine;" *Business Week*; March 11, 1944; p. 42

CHAPTER 14:
The Post-World War II Years Through the Fifties

While social security and federal income tax withholding were firmly established by the mid to late forties, the function of payroll continued to grow more complex as payroll withholding expanded to include an increasing number of local and state taxes. In addition, fringe benefit-related programs were also growing and brought with them new responsibilities for the payroll organization.

While the payroll function continued to evolve, business machines kept pace and enabled payroll organizations to meet these new demands. By the late 1950s the computer industry had begun to transition from a strictly scientific client focus to a broader application of business uses including those within payroll.

The payroll service provider industry took root during this period as well and many companies began to turn to these professional "payoff" companies for the delivery of payroll services because of the increasing complexity and the expense of acquiring and maintaining new computer technology. All in all, it was an exciting period from which the modern day payroll organization would emerge.

The Entrance of African-American Women Into the Office Environment

Prior to this timeframe, opportunities for African-American women in industry were very limited and while beginning to increase in the 1950s (due in part to the post-World War II economy) the process was a slow one. It would be decades before African-American women would achieve greater equality in the workplace. Young professionals, like Hazel Gibson Bookman of Columbia, SC (Exhibit 14-1), found limited employment opportunities in the 1920s. Their efforts, however, helped to anchor the growing African-American middle class. Hazel Gibson Bookman started her career as a secretary for the National Benefits Life Insurance

Company. From 1953 to 1958, she worked as a bookkeeper for the Good Samaritan-Waverly Hospital. While her bookkeeping duties at the hospital may or may not have included payroll responsibilities, her career illustrates the advancement of African-American women, in general, within U.S. industry. From this timeframe forward, African-American women would play a larger role in all job categories, including those jobs within the payroll arena.

Exhibit 14-1: Hazel Gibson Bookman (c. late 1920s); Courtesy of the Estate of Richard Samuel Roberts and reprinted by permission of Bruccoli Clark Layman, Columbia, South Carolina

The Late Forties and Early Fifties Payroll Environment

Electric accounting machines had advanced considerably over the past decade and were in wide use by the beginning of the 1950s. The City of Norfolk, Virginia is shown here in 1951 (Exhibit 14-1A) performing payroll duties on one of these machines. These machines, along with more sophisticated forms and forms processing equipment, were fast becoming essential

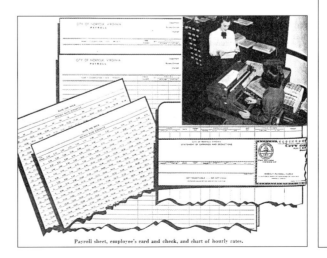

Payroll sheet, employee's card and check, and chart of hourly rates.

Exhibit 14-1A: "Machine-Written Central Payroll;" Nichol, R. T.; The American City; Volume 66; February 1951; pp. 90-91; Courtesy of the City of Norfolk, Virginia

Exhibit 14-2: "Picture of a Perfect Pay Day;" Marchant Calculators; Newsweek; June 9, 1947; p. 31; Reprinted by permission of Smith Corona Corporation

to every medium to large size payroll operation.

Marchant Calculators paints a picture of a beautiful payday for management, paymaster, and employees alike in this 1947 advertisement (Exhibit 14-2), while other companies, like I. Miller & Sons (Exhibit 14-3), declare the ease

Exhibit 14-3: "There's still a place for slow painstaking hand work...but not in your accounting department!;" National Cash Register; Newsweek; April 21, 1947; p. 55; Courtesy of the NCR Corporate Archives at the Montgomery County Historical Society, Dayton, Ohio

with which they produce their payrolls using the National Payroll Machines.

The Growing Impact of Fringe Benefits

In the late forties, many companies, led by those in the pulp and paper industry, began to realize the growing financial impact of company-paid fringe benefits. By 1948, fringe payments were becoming a significant addition to annual worker income and a great concern to many employers. As an example, in addition to the legally required payments for social security and compulsory and other payroll deductions, many pulp and paper mills (followed by other industries) during this period were paying for hospitalization insurance, surgical insurance, sick-accident insurance, life insurance, and paid vacations and holidays. Over the coming decades some of these costs would be shared with company employees through more payroll deductions, and payroll deduction administration would ultimately become a larger and more significant part of payroll work. (1)

The Beginning of Local Income Tax Withholding by Payroll

On March 1, 1946, Toledo, Ohio became the second city to approve a local income tax program through employer payroll withholding. The ordinance was passed as part of a five-year recovery program following both the Depression and the end of World War II. Like many other large cities plagued by financial woes and on the verge of bankruptcy, Toledo was seeking to establish fiscal soundness, act on postwar investment plans, and extend the authority of home rule. Opponents, led by the Congress of Industrial Organizations (CIO), forced a referendum in April, but the tax was upheld by Toledo citizens. (2)

Under the Toledo plan, employers were required to deduct the tax (1%) from employees' salaries and wages as they were already doing for federal income and social security taxes. Employers were required to remit the withheld amounts to the City of Toledo on a quarterly basis. (2)

Through this city tax, Toledo was able to raise $9,000,000 in just the first two years. From this added revenue, Toledo was able to meet its obligations, amass funds for long-deferred capital improvements, improve schools, and increase municipal worker wages. (2)

The City of Philadelphia was actually the first city to pass a local income tax in 1940. The law survived many suits including one challenging the right of the city to compel withholding by employers. (3)

The Toledo plan was actually modeled partially after the Philadelphia plan. (2) In the case of Philadelphia and Toledo, both were located in states in which there were no state income tax provisions at the time. (4)

Other cities to pass similar tax plans in the years immediately following the war included St. Louis and Columbus. The St. Louis plan was determined to be unconstitutional. Some states could not utilize the city income tax method due to demographics or they chose other solutions, like the City of Detroit, which opted for a share of the state's sales tax revenue. Over the years, thousands of local taxing agencies have implemented similar programs to those initially introduced by Philadelphia, Toledo, and Columbus.

State Revenue Departments Follow Suit - Slowly

For many of the same reasons, states in the post-World War II period also began to look at ways to increase their revenues. While some states had already implemented state income tax programs, few had yet mandated payroll withholding of such taxes. Over the next 50 years, some 41 states would impose mandatory withholding of income taxes by employers. Some states, like Indiana, implemented payroll withholding laws as early as 1947 while others like Connecticut would not impose such laws until 1991.

Professions in "Pay-Offs" Take Off!

While new, more sophisticated machines were now available and certainly helped employers to perform their payroll functions with greater accuracy, in less time and at a lower cost, many companies still had problems keeping pace with the inherent complexities of the post-World War II payroll environment.

While the concept was not new, the timing may not have been as right for professional payroll service providers before as it was in the post-World War II period, with large numbers of soldiers returning to civilian jobs.

Paymasters, Inc. Opens Its Doors For Business in 1947

In June 1947, W. Ralph Keen and Joseph T. King, both Columbia Aircraft Company executives, along with Howard E. Sternau, an attorney, began Paymasters, Inc., with offices in New York and Los Angeles. Their goal was to demonstrate to companies that payroll was no longer merely a matter of opening a cash drawer and filing a few forms with various agencies but was in fact a much more complicated and costly process that could better be done by specialists. (5)

For a flat charge per employee per pay period, Paymasters, Inc. would prepare employees' checks or cash vouchers and then deliver the unsigned checks to the company for signing and distribution or arrange for armored delivery of required funds to the company's pay-window at designated times. To accomplish this, companies needed to provide Paymasters, Inc. with the required information such as worker names, clock numbers, social security numbers, addresses, rates of pay, number of dependents, etc. (5)

According to Paymasters, Inc., most corporations were not aware of the "hidden" expenses in getting up a payroll. Man and machine hours along with overhead and the added time required to keep abreast of various governmental regulations made the cost per employee sizable. (5)

Paymasters, Inc. was able to convince a number of banks, automotive, transportation, construction, printing and food companies of the benefits of their services and soon many companies had "relieved themselves of the payroll headaches and dumped the task into the laps of this new service agency." (5)

Automatic Payrolls Incorporated —The Future ADP, Inc.—Begins Operations in 1949

Henry Taub, following college graduation, joined a small accounting firm and quickly saw

that some of his client companies were having problems preparing their payrolls. Social security and federal income tax withholdings through employer payrolls had only recently been implemented, and it was often difficult for companies to maintain the necessary supporting data to create the payrolls and perform the necessary reporting.

He acted on this idea by starting his own company in 1949 to provide payroll services to clients in the New York and New Jersey area under the name of Automatic Payrolls Incorporated (API). Although he started with little more than an adding machine, he realized the importance of the term "automatic" in conveying to potential clients a sense of progressiveness, efficiency, and affordability.

In its initial service offerings, API did not provide check signing services or place cash into employee pay envelopes. By 1953, both Henry's brother, Joe, and a friend, Frank R. Lautenberg, had joined the company. By 1957, annual revenues had increased to $150,000 but with only a small profit. At this point, API had installed an early version of IBM computers (Exhibit 14-4) and after working out a few problems ("that dammed near killed them," according to Henry

Taub), API learned how to effectively utilize the new technology.

From these humble beginnings, API would eventually become incorporated as Automatic Data Processing, acquire other payroll processing services, expand services beyond its initial payroll focus, and ultimately go on to become the largest payroll service provider in the world.

Continued Movement Toward Payment by Check

While some companies were still paying their workers in cash and using armored escorts and while payroll robberies were still occurring,

although less frequently, the momentum toward payment by check was now unstoppable. With machines now available to make the job of issuing pay checks easier and with worker acceptance of checks higher than ever, many companies converted their payroll systems to produce pay checks during this period.

One of those companies, Ford Motor Company, discontinued its long-term commitment to the slogan *"Every Day is Payday at Ford,"* a reference to its daily biweekly pay cycles, and to *"Two Nickels Are No Dime"* in reference to its policy to pay in the smallest number of cash denominations possible. Ford began in early 1950 to pay all of its 106,635 hourly workers by check every Friday. Ford was one of the last of the big auto manufacturers to discontinue its biweekly cash payrolls (Exhibit 14-5) in favor of weekly checks. Over the years, Ford had disbursed billions of dollars in cash to Ford employees. During the war years, a single payday often exceeded $1.5 million. (6)

partnership with National Cash Register, which worked with Ford to customize its National Payroll Machines to meet Ford's unique needs. At a cost of over $560,000, the machines (Exhibit 14-7) were referred to as "thinking machines" and did everything but endorse the checks. (6)

To facilitate check cashing, Ford made arrangements with local banks to provide free check cashing for all of its employees. It also utilized the services of Brink's Inc. mobile pay trucks to provide check cashing services for its workers outside of company property. (6)

While most companies would change to checks for the same reasons, many companies would transition their workers in phases.

How your PAYCHECK Gets to You.

The change was prompted by both the CIO (United Auto Workers) and the company itself. The United Auto Workers felt, since the beginning of World War II, that employee budgeting problems could be relieved with a weekly pay cycle. (6)

At the same time, the company felt that checks would reduce pay lines by eliminating the need for pay receipts. Ford also felt that by allowing foremen (Exhibit 14-6) to pay their men instead of impersonal paymasters, relationships between management and employees could be improved. (6)

The changeover was accomplished through a

A Railway Payroll Captured in Photos

In 1951, *"TIES,"* the employee newsletter of the Southern Railway System, ran a great article titled "How Your PAYCHECK Gets to You" (Exhibit 14-8) on its payroll process in part to educate employees and in part to recognize the members of the organization responsible for payroll for their good work. The article includ-

Exhibit 14-8: "How Your Paycheck Gets to You;" TIES – The Southern Railway System Magazine; January 1951; Courtesy of TIES

141

Exhibit 14-9 through 14-13: "How Your Paycheck Gets to You;" TIES – The Southern Railway System Magazine; January 1951; Courtesy of TIES

(Above) Miss L. M. Cothran, roadway and transportation timekeeper, verifying checkrolls from division offices. (Below) Mrs. C. O. Thompson, mechanical timekeeper, verifying the clocking on shop time cards.

(Above) J. T. Bradley operating the Burroughs machine used in train and enginemen's timekeeping. (Below) A. E. Stevens (left), and D. Thomas, Jr., posting retirement tax and income tax on payroll cards.

(In circle) B. F. Fields, Jr., operating one of the Class 2000 payroll machines.

(Above) P. L. Steele (left) and M. E. Long, working on payroll cards.

(Above) C. H. Bell (left) and C. H. Weems, Jr., sorting payroll and deduction cards for payroll machine.

(Above) Mrs. P. B. McDaniel (left) and Mrs. M. L. Dunn, sorting payroll and deduction cards before sending them to the payroll writing machine. The ice-pick-like tool lying on the desk is the sorting instrument and the holes and grooves on the card (see the one reproduced here) are the things that make the sorting possible. By starting at the right hand edge of the card and inserting the needle into each perforation, lifting all the cards caught and pulling them at the back of the stack being sorted, the sorter can arrange the payroll and deduction cards together in payroll number order. Thus the operator of the payroll writing machine has the necessary information for each payroll entry and paycheck in just the order that he needs.

(Above) E. Eargle (left) and Mrs. D. W. Martin, balancing payrolls against payroll cards.

Earnings and records section: (seated) B. W. Munroe, chief clerk; (standing, left to right) Mrs. S. H. Smathers, Mrs. S. D. Craft, Mrs. F. J. Hornbuckle, W. H. Trestham; R. N. Darvin, head clerk; and Mrs. M. F. Bowman.

Roadway and transportation section: (seated) J. N. Kaufman, head clerk; (standing, left to right) J. C. Baker, Mrs. J. F. James, R. B. Jenkins, Mrs. S. S. Ferguson, C. H. Miller, R. C. Smathers, Mrs. P. B. Olliff and Miss W. I. Swain.

Mechanical timekeeping: (seated) W. H. Wills, head clerk; (standing, left to right) L. W. Cox, Miss R. D. King, Mrs. P. W. Cooper, J. R. Benalf, Mrs. M. A. Richardson, Miss J. Allen, Miss I. C. Ward, B. C. Chattin and J. R. Boyette.

Machines section: (seated) Mrs. M. W. Turner, head clerk; (standing, left to right) G. M. Malone, A. E. Stephens, D. Thomas, Jr., Miss M. L. Tanner, Mrs. N. M. Dodd, W. V. Johnson, S. D. Kirkland and J. S. Knigler.

ed photos of all payroll members of the Atlanta office of the assistant auditor responsible for about two-thirds of the Railway's total payroll. The following photos and captions presented in chronological order provide a sense of organizational structure, delegation of responsibilities, payroll work processes and flows, and use of specific machines which were fairly similar to those used by other industries of the day. (Exhibits 14-9 through 14-13)

The Mid-Fifties Payroll Environment

The AFL-CIO Is Created

Labor unions have been an integral part of American history. The interaction between industry, government and unions has been instrumental in defining the framework under which Americans work and are paid. The payroll profession and the work performed by payroll personnel across the country reflect the ongoing impact of this interaction.

The AFL-CIO was established in 1955 by the merger of the American Federation of Labor and the Congress of Industrial Organizations. Under the foundation built by its first president, George Meany, the AFL-CIO would grow by the end of the 20th century to over 13 million members from over 68 national and international labor unions.

Electric Machines Are "In"

By the mid-fifties, many employers like the Morrison-Knudsen Company, the Phillips-Jones Corporation, and the Sun Oil Company were appearing in National Cash Register advertisements (Exhibit 14-14) providing testimonials on the payroll operational and cost saving advantages of National Accounting Machines. Others like the City of Somerville (Exhibit 14-15) shared their success in using the NCR 142 electric accounting machine to consolidate its payroll

While paychecks for one pay period are being signed and mailed out, the bureau is already busy on preparation for the next payroll. Some of this vital "advance work" is shown on this page: (top above) R. E. Carmichael (left) and S. A. Sailers mail out check rolls to the roadway and transportation departments for recording working hours. (Above left) Using the automatic addressograph machine, C. D. Stretch prints names and other pertinent information from the addressograph plate onto shop time cards for use in a subsequent pay period. (Above center) J. C. McGinley grooves the edges of the shop time cards so they can be sorted when returned to the bureau at the end of a pay period. (Above right) R. C. Denham packs the prepared time cards for shipment to master mechanics. (At right, left to right) W. D. Sexton, J. T. Jones, Jr., and Miss J. L. Fox shown securing employee personnel information from the "wheel files" of index cards. Every one of the 28,000 people paid from the Atlanta bureau has a card on file here.

(At left) J. T. Branton uses the addressograph plates to print roadway and transportation check rolls on the addressograph machine. (At right) Addressograph plates, too, are kept on file. Here, J. H. Davis turns down metal tabs on the tops of certain of the plates to indicate that the employees concerned have now left the service of the Southern.

Though these are the final steps in sending out paychecks, there's
a "let-down" afterward. By the time one set of checks goes out,
the payroll bureau is busy with preparations for the next.

"*National* Accounting Machines save us $75,000 a year...
return 100% of investment annually."

—SUN OIL COMPANY, *Pioneering in petroleum progress for 70 years*

National

operations with readers of *The American City.*
These ads and articles provide revealing insights
into both the technology and payroll processes
of the day, as does this "Equipment Facts" sheet
published by Moore Business Forms describing
the mechanics behind the Burroughs Sensimatic
Accounting Machine (Exhibit 14-16).

In addition to electric accounting machines,
many payroll organizations also were using
more advanced electric calculators like this
"Thinking Machine" from the Friden Calculating
Machine Company (Exhibit 14-17), as well as
electric typewriters like those made by IBM to
improve their payroll operations.

Teletype Machines and Early Piloting of Remote Check Printing

In 1955, the International Resistance
Company of Boone, North Carolina began using
teletype machines to transmit pay data and print

checks at two branch offices using continuous
interfolded marginal (trademark of Moore North
America, Inc.) punched check forms (Exhibit 14-
18) rather than preparing checks at the main
office and then mailing them to the branch
offices.

By 1957, other companies with remote operations began experimenting with the use of teletype machines to send data to remote work sites
for local printing of checks as summarized from
an article appearing in the June 29, 1957 issue
of *Business Week*:

To cut overhead on its shifting and far flung
construction sites, F.H. McGraw & Co., of
Hartford, began experimenting with remote control payrolls. Under this approach, the main
office prepares the weekly payroll for jobs over
1,300 miles away via a central computer.
Workers at the remote site enter time and cost
data directly into a Teletype which feeds the
computer in the main office. On payday, the
main office makes out the payroll and feeds the
data into the Teletype which then prints out
worker pay onto blank check stock at the
remote work site, thereby saving on the
expense of maintaining separate accounting and

Exhibit 14-16:
Burroughs
Sensimatic
Accounting Machine;
Booklet "Equipment
Facts;" Moore North
America, Inc.;
Reprinted courtesy of
Moore North
America, Inc. and
permission of Unisys
Corporation

Exhibit 14-17:
"Simplest of all ways
to Figure is on the
Friden;" Friden
Calculating Machine
Co., Inc.; Newsweek;
September 8, 1952;
p. 94; Reprinted by
permission of
Neopost, Inc.

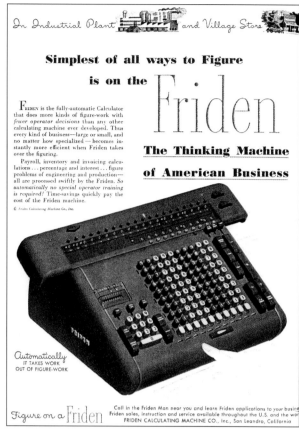

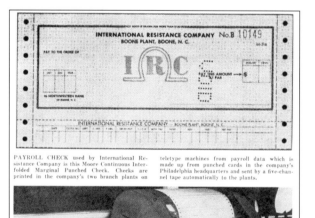

PAYROLL CHECK used by International Resistance Company is this Moore Continuous Interfolded Marginal Punched Check. Checks are printed in the company's two branch plants on teletype machines from payroll data which is made up from punched cards in the company's Philadelphia headquarters and sent by a five-channel tape automatically to the plants.

Exhibit 14-18:
"International
Resistance Company
Prints Payroll at
Remote Sites;"
Moore Sales News;
April 1955; p. 5;
Reprinted by permission of Moore North
America, Inc.

bookkeeping operations in far away sites where payroll resources are often hard to find. (7)

The Late Fifties Payroll Environment

The Transition of the Computer From Science to Business

There is no question that by the end of the decade, the computer was making its presence felt in the commercial world. Earlier in the decade, the computer was largely a tool for the scientific community and not a practical solution for business. By the end of the decade this had all changed.

The first commercially available computers were those introduced in the early fifties by the Remington Rand Corporation. This first computer was called the UNIVAC I (Universal Automatic Computer). By the end of the decade, many large employers like the City of New York (Exhibit 14-19) were using UNIVAC to produce their payrolls.

Remington Rand was not alone. IBM was rapidly producing computers for the business world and was changing mindsets with their well orchestrated advertisements that marketed their Model 702 Electronic Data Processing Machine as "A Giant Brain that's Strictly Business" (Exhibit 14-20) and their Model 650 as "The Electronic Workhorse of American Industry." (Exhibit 14-21)

By the end of the decade, competition in the computer industry was in full swing. Other companies such as Royal McBee, Bendix, Honeywell (Exhibit 14-22) and Philco (Exhibit 14-23) began producing and marketing their own computers. New companies like the Digital Equipment Corporation came into existence and competed by offering more affordable computer solutions for the business user. The business world, including payroll, would benefit from this competition.

Signs of the Times

Data processing organizations came into existence and high speed printers and new generation forms processing devices began printing (Exhibit 14-24), signing, separating, and inserting forms in pay envelopes faster than ever to keep pace with the speed of the new found tool – the computer.

The symbols of the period were the data key punch cards, readers and tapes (Exhibits 14-25 & 14-26), and access to technical knowledge and resources became of great importance to every payroll operating unit.

Modern Day Copier Introduced –

In 1959, Xerox introduced the first commercial copier – payroll along with the rest of the world would soon become big users of copiers.

A "Giant Brain"
that's Strictly Business

IBM's new 702 Electronic Data Processing Machine brings to the accounting and record-keeping problems of business the speed and capacity of giant scientific computers.

It can absorb millions of facts and figures on its magnetic tapes (shown here), process this vast quantity of data, and turn out the results in the form you need. Payrolls, billing, manufacturing and inventory control, cost allocation, manpower scheduling, fiscal accounting—all the complex operations of modern business—are performed at high speed.

This is business automation at its highest development.

International Business Machines
590 Madison Avenue, New York 22, N. Y.

IBM World's Leading Producer of
Electronic Accounting Machines

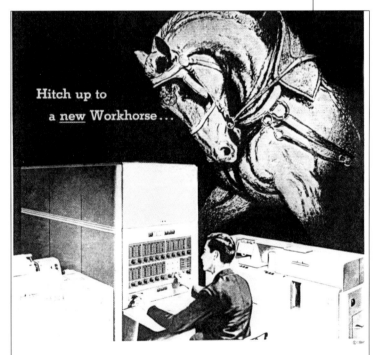

Hitch up to
a new **Workhorse**...

THE IBM 650—"ELECTRONIC WORKHORSE" OF AMERICAN INDUSTRY!

From the production lines of American industry have come many outstanding products—products whose performance men admire and respect enough to honor with the title of "workhorse." The "Pacific"—crack steam locomotive with a 75-year service record in transcontinental commerce . . . the rugged "Jeep" of World War II . . . and the DC-3, trail blazer of the air age—all were such honored "workhorses."

And now—to match the fleeting pace of a *new era* comes an "electronic workhorse"—the IBM 650!

On-the-job today at more than 170 installations, and being installed in others at the rate of *one every working day*, the IBM 650, with its 20,000-digit magnetic drum memory, harnesses the speed of electronics to give management accurate and timely facts for *vital* decisions!

With complete versatility, this nimble "workhorse" shifts

quickly from job to job . . . from payroll to cost control . . . to research . . . production planning . . . inventory . . . sales analysis . . . almost any business paperwork problem. Whether the IBM 650 is tied into present IBM punched card equipment or functions as a separate electronic system, magnetic tapes, direct line printers and high speed core storage can be added to handle even greater volumes of data.

For 41 years, IBM has devoted its efforts to perfecting a *complete* line of machines that process business data faster, better—at less cost. For the plain facts about an IBM system for *your* business, call your local IBM representative.

 **DATA PROCESSING**

International Business
Machines Corporation
590 Madison Avenue,
New York 22, N. Y.

*Exhibit 14-22:
"Honeywell
DATAmatic;"
Business Week; May
30, 1959; p. 93;
Courtesy of
Honeywell, Inc.*

*Exhibit 14-23:
"Available now from
Philco – The Philco
transac* S-2000
Computer;" Business
Week; January 1959;
p. 83; Reprinted by
permission of Philips
Electronics North
America, Inc.*

*Exhibit 14-24: Moore
Continuous Interfold
Marginal Punched
Payroll Check; Moore
Sales News;
September 1953; p.
6; Reprinted by per-
mission of Moore
North America, Inc.
Interfolded is a copy-
righted trademark of
Moore North
America, Inc.*

Tactics to Promote Payment by Check and Early Forms of Payroll Direct Deposit

As part of a strategy to convert employees from cash to check, some companies during and even prior to this period began to offer automatic deposit of payroll funds to local banks selected by the employee. Although the process was not automatic in today's sense as this was prior to the implementation of the modern banking system and the electronic funds transfer infrastructure that is now in place, it did provide an important step in the progression toward the

next generation in pay media. During this period an employer would most likely have provided a list of employees and amounts to be deposited along with a check or authorization to debit the employer's account. The bank would then have credited each employee's account as authorized on payday.

The Norton Company of Worcester, Massachusetts cited automatic deposit privileges as one of the advantages to employees as it

announced its plans in the late fifties to convert workers from cash to check:

"Starting the week of January 9, 1960, everyone on the factory and office weekly pay roll at Worcester will be paid by check instead of in cash. The change will affect about 4,000 Norton employees. Studies conducted, both here and in companies which instituted this system some time ago, affirm that benefits derived from this innovation outweigh inconveniences. Advantages to the employee include protection against loss of money or theft, and the convenience of automatic deposit in any commercial bank of the employee's choice at his request. Advantages to the Company indicate payment by check to be more efficient, less expensive, and a means of eliminating the handling of large sums of money. In preparation for this changeover, the Company sent out an explanatory letter to those employees affected, giving reasons for the new system, and answers to questions that might arise concerning it. Of major importance to the employee is the matter of cashing facilities, as no pay roll checks can be cashed at the Company. Arrangements have been made for cashing Norton pay roll checks at the local banks. To assure prompt cashing, each employee will be furnished with an official Norton Identification Card. The commercial banks will cash checks at no charge. The savings banks will cash checks at no charge for depositors, but can not cash checks for non-depositors." (8)

Computers and State Income Taxes

The following article (titled "Fluid") appeared in *The New Yorker* just about the time that the State of New York was to implement their new state income tax program via payroll withholding. The article is being presented in its entirety (except for some minor omissions) because it provides a real sense of growing dependency that payroll organizations had on computers to support the more complex state income tax rules and also because it provides understanding of the pressures that payroll organizations have historically been subject to in the past and often continue to feel in the present when required to implement process and system changes in a very short timeframe.

"Although the majority of the state's more worldly-wise employers no doubt had a fair hunch back in January that controversy would not stay forever the withholding of state income taxes from employees' pay checks, and although they learned last month that April 1st was the anticipated day of such added reckoning, it wasn't until last Wednesday night, after the legislature had retouched and confirmed the new procedure, that the State Tax Commission was in a position to tell employers just how much to withhold, and to suggest ways of going about it. This allowed a mere twenty days for payroll offices to assimilate the new rules into their disbursing practices – twenty days, clearly, of widespread, if minor, emergency. We gave the situation until Friday to ripe. Then we went down to the 140 West Street, or Manhattan-Bronx-Westchester, office of the New York Telephone Company – which is the biggest private employer locally, paying fourteen million dollars every month to thirty-four thousand salaried personnel from this office, and is also the biggest in the new tax's jurisdiction, with a statewide payroll numbering seventy-eight thousand – and applied for intelligence from the scene of the crisis that we assumed existed. 'The situation is fluid, and it may even be that we have it in hand,' we were told by the officer assigned to deal with us – John Cuddy, a serene, stocky man with bristling reddish hair and eyebrows, pale-blue eyes, and a deep-blue suite, whose title is General Supervising Accountant in Charge of Disbursement Methods. He led us to a door

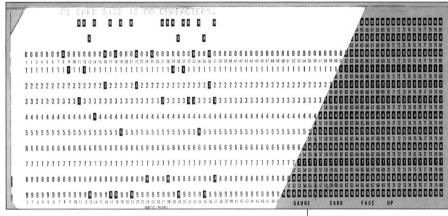

labeled '950 - Payroll Office,' and, before turning the knob, paused to say, 'What's going on at the moment is principally a series of strategy meetings of the heads of the payroll office's auditing, machine, benefit, allotment, service-record, and wage-and-tax sections. They talk things over with me, and I talk things over with my legal friends and the Tax Commission and a couple of statisticians up on the nineteenth floor. I think we'll get it all ironed out – for one thing, because we have to.' Mr. Cuddy opened the door and ushered us into a vast hall populated with fifty men and women at fifty gray metal fixtures – tables, desks, I.B.M. card-punching consoles, I.B.M. check-printing and accounting machines, and in a far corner, two I.B.M. 607 computers, each of the last being a kind of triptych, with a punch unit, resembling a covered kitchen stove, in the center, and two tall cupboard-shaped companion pieces at the sides, one for thinking electronic thoughts and the other for storing them. 'As soon as we saw this situation coming, in January, we ordered a third computer – we rent them for twenty-five thousand dollars a year each – but it won't be delivered until next month,' Mr. Cuddy said. 'Meantime, the problem is to adapt the machines we have so that they can deal with the new bite as well as with the pay-check deductions they already figure, at the rate of six

Exhibit 14-25: IBM Card Reader (used by Digital Equipment Corporation between 1957-1974 in payroll operations); author's collection; Courtesy of International Business Machines Corporation. NOTE: This Card Reader was used in the processing of the weekly payroll. Timecards were keypunched on IBM equipment (029s) as 80 column cards and processed through the payroll system. If a card rejected, this metal card reader would allow the data entry operator to locate the error and make the correction. This process was later replaced with magnetic tape technology.

Exhibit 14-26: Digital Equipment Corporation DEC-TAPE (1957 – 1985); Courtesy of Compaq Computer Corporation. NOTE: This DECTAPE was used on various systems hardware, including PDP 8s and DEC 10s. This tape, manufactured by Digital, contained the programs that were used to process the weekly payroll. This tape-based program media was later replaced with online programs.

thousand cards an hour, for four old-established taxes and fourteen varieties of voluntary allotments.' He rested an arm affectionately on a calculating cupboard and proceeded to details. 'It would be easy now, if we were faced with the job of feeding in just another standard deduction, like the flat eighteen-per-cent withholding rate provided by the federal-income-tax people for machine-operated payroll systems. However, the new state income tax gives us sixteen rates, for sixteen pay brackets, ranging form three –tenths of one per cent, for the twenty-five-to thirty-dollar-a-week bracket, to eight per cent, for the three hundred a week and over. Even that wouldn't be so tricky if it weren't for the fact that more than half our employees skip from one bracket to another from week to week – up when they have overtime, and down without overtime. Of the two formulae the Tax Commission suggests for machine-operated withholding, one struck us as altogether impracticable and the other as too expensive. The Commission allows employers to submit alternative formulae for approval, and we have one that I hope to be able to take to them next week.' We asked what the formula might be, and he answered, a trifle sheepishly, 'T equals parenthesis A plus BI close parenthesis multiplied by I, minus C, but it's a horrible thing to explain. However, it's duck soup to the computers – at least up to the point where it ceases to apply, which is on monthly executive salaries exceeding twenty-five hundred dollars. The statisticians are trying to get the bugs out of it, and I'm hoping to get the Tax Commission's O.K., and meanwhile these two gentlemen are going ahead anyhow and wiring it into fifty new control panels for the computers.' Mr. Cuddy indicated two bespectacled young men at a table, bent over what looked like a large stock of needlework frames, each two feet square, whose thousands of red, blue, green, and yellow threads had sprung loose and were now as snarled as so many platefuls of spaghetti (editorial comment - possible origin of the term spaghetti code?). Leading us over to the pair, Mr. Cuddy introduced them as John Deck and William Green, accounting supervisors who had gone to the I.B.M. school. Up close, we could see that they were plugging the ends of numberless colored strands of wire into numberless little punch board holes, guided – so, at least, they claimed – by unfathomable scrawling on elaborate charts strewn about

them. 'I don't understand exactly how it works,' said Mr. Cuddy, casting a glance warm with confidence at the respectfully silent Messrs. Deck and Green, 'but I know they'll be at it day and night and through the weekends until they get finished, which will be March 25th.' We asked how the completion date could be so exactly predicted, and Mr. Cuddy answered, 'It's easy. That's when the machines start working on the first April payroll.'" (9)

The COBOL Language Is Introduced

In 1959, COBOL computer software for business was introduced. Most early forms of payroll application software would be written in the COBOL language.

Paymasters in the Arts, Science And Literature

Throughout the 20th century, the subject of paymasters and payrolls, especially as related to payroll robberies, has appeared in radio, television and the movies. The theme first appeared in the golden days of silent movies in films such as *Ranson's Folly*. With the advent of sound flicks, paymasters and payroll robberies continued to appear in such films as *Wyoming Whirlwind* (1932), *Vengeance* (1937), *The Trusted Outlaw* (1937), and *Land of the Hunted Men* (1943). Perhaps the most famous movie along these lines was *Love Me Tender* (1956) starring Elvis Presley. The subject of paymasters and payroll would continue into future years and extend beyond the movies to include radio and television. These productions provide entertaining and sometimes informative insights into the perceptions and images of paymasters and payrolls of various periods in American History.

Open House at Crocker, Burbank & Company (1957) - A Not Uncommon Testimonial to Consistently High Levels of Payroll Performance

"Now, as to Payroll – during the 130 year history of this Company the employees have never had to worry about their pay. The Company has never failed on pay day for any reason. We are proud of this record. The time cards must be individually checked and computed. After recording approximately 25,000 transactions for each payroll, the Payroll Slips are sent to the bank by Wednesday noon, where the money is put into individual envelopes for distribution on Friday. In 1956 the Payroll amounted to millions of dollars and was distributed to more than 1,500 employees. A complete history is maintained for each employee to which numerous entries are made daily."

Douglas Crocker, President of Crocker, Burbank & Company
Invitation to Annual Open House dated May 13, 1957
Courtesy of Fitchburg Historical Society, Fitchburg, Massachusetts

Reference Sources

1. "Labor Union Policies in the U.S – Primary Pulp and Paper Industry;" Gavin, Mortimer H; United Papermakers and Paperworkers, AFL-CIO; Springfield, MA; 1950; pp. 181-182

2. "City Payroll-Income Tax Proves Its Viability;" Gregg, Ronald E.; The American City; Volume 63; January 1948; pp. 112-113, 115

3. "Cities' Hunt for New Revenue;" United States News; Volume 22; April 11, 1947; pp. 53-56

4. "Income Taxes for Cities;" United States News; Volume 20; April 1946; p. 58

5. "Profession in Pay-Offs;" Kungelmass, J. Alvin; Nation's Business; July 1948; Volume 36; p. 77

6. "Ford Ends Cash Era, Switches to Checks;" Business Week; March 11, 1950; pp.124-125

7. "Construction Company Meets Its Payroll At Far-Off Sites by Teletype System;" Business Week; Volume May-June 1957; June 29, 1957; p. 191

8. "Payment by Check to Affect 4000 on Weekly Pay Roll;" The Norton Spirit; The Norton Company, Worcester, Massachusetts; December 1959; pp. 1-2; Courtesy Collections of the Worcester (Mass.) Historical Museum

9. "Fluid;" The New Yorker; Volume 35; No 1; March 21, 1959; pp. 36-38. ©1959, 1987 by The New Yorker Magazine, Inc. All rights reserved. Reprinted by permission.

CHAPTER 15:
The Sixties – The Advancement of Computer Technology

Teletype machines help cut costly paperwork

Typing Tape Punch

Tape Reader

The Advancement of Computer Technology

While computers were born in the fifties, it was not until the latter portion of that decade that both hardware and software began to come together. Early computers in offices were crude and expensive by today's standards. But by the mid-1960s most large companies had adopted this technology to facilitate basic "back office" tasks such as storing payroll data and issuing checks. (1)

"With advances in solid-state circuit components and then with microelectronics the computer became much smaller and cheaper. Remote terminals, consisting of either a teletypewriter (Exhibit 15-1) or a keyboard and a video display began to appear, generally tapping the central processing and storage facilities of a mainframe computer. There was steady improvement in the cost-effectiveness of data-processing equipment. All of this was reflected in a remarkable expansion of the computer industry." (1)

Seeing the Possibilities

Many companies and employees could see the possibilities of leveraging the power of the computer and began to educate and conceptualize these possibilities wherever and whenever possible as illustrated in the following excerpts from this June 24, 1968 Weyerhaeuser Open House Document on its Data Processing Department:

"The Computer – Marvel of the Century. Contrary to possibly many things you have read or the jokes you have heard, and at the risk of making a brash statement, we must all admit that the computer has and will continue to revolutionize not only office practices but management functions as well. This much maligned machine is a tremendous tool in the hands of an enlightened management. We like to think we have such a management who use this tool not only to absorb the mass detail necessary in today's business, but also to assist them in making decisions. The real and necessary function of this department then is to process data – lots of it – on a 24 hour a day basis. Data such as payroll, checks, invoices, inventories, production records, sales statistics, cost and revenue reports and on and on. Our equipment has the ability to store this data, accumulate it , sort it, print it, punch it into cards, add – subtract – multiply – divide – and transmit it via telephone lines to other computers. The machinery has only one major limitation. It is limited only by the imagination or lack of it possessed by our Paper Division management team." (2)

Getting Potential Users Comfortable With Video Screens And Keyboards

It took time to get new users, including those in payroll, comfortable with the new direct link to computers that video screens and keyboards

Exhibit 15-1: "Teletype machines help cut costly paperwork;" Teletype Corporation; Business Week; September 3, 1960; p. 89; Property of AT&T Archives. Reprinted with permission of AT&T.

You are now face to face with faster computer input and data display.

brought. Burroughs, like its competitors, tailored advertisements to such potential customers by presenting these new tools in a very personal fashion as in this advertisement (Exhibit 15-2) titled "You are now face to face with faster computer input and data display" and through simple and reassuring language:

"The new Burroughs Input and Display System gives you an instant visual link to your Burroughs computer – for input and output – from any point in the country. To communicate with the computer, you simply type your message on the keyboard, which is designed much like a standard typewriter. As you type the message appears on the TV-like screen. Check it over. Correct it from the keyboard. No need to hurry; processor time is not involved until you are ready. When you are, just press a key for instantaneous transmission to the computer. The computer's message comes back to you, on the screen, the instant it's prepared. It's that simple. It's silent. It's fast. And information may be retrieved for revision and then returned to the computer just as easily. Uses? On-line keypunching. Inventory control. Bank teller inquiry. Updating or altering stored computer information. Management information

retrieval. Order entry. Hospital patient data retrieval. In fact, any application in which you can benefit from speedy conversation with your computer. Burroughs Input and Display systems are available with one or multiple monitor/keyboards per control unit. Each 9 x 12½ inch screen projects up to 25 lines of 80 positions each. A printer is available if you need permanent printed records. This new video link is just one of the many ways a Burroughs 500 system computer displays its responsiveness to your needs." (3)

In this equally effective advertisement, Burroughs (Exhibit 15-3) was now marketing and stressing hardware and software, and referencing words like third generation, and **COBOL** – "the widely accepted higher level language for business data processing."

On time – as promised: Burroughs B 2500/B 3500 third generation systems – complete with software.

Now operational.

Third generation hardware and software. That's what we promised for the two new computers we announced last spring.

We've kept this commitment. The small to medium scale B 2500 and B 3500 are now operational. Ready for deliveries.

In a series of tests at our plant in Pasadena, California, recently, they demonstrated every one of their advanced capabilities—with results that met all our expectations.

The two systems demonstrated how third generation software enables them to use part of their own computational power to allocate and organize their own work. To **automatically** match their resources to varying work loads and changing priorities through use of the Burroughs Master Control Program.

They **multiprocessed** unrelated major programs with complete freedom and ease—under totally automatic software control.

They demonstrated highly efficient operation in COBOL, the widely accepted higher level language for business data processing.

Altogether, it was an impressive demonstration not only of two third generation computers but of the idea that made them possible: the Burroughs concept of integrating hardware with software by developing **both** at the same time. Three years ago, this concept became a reality with our B 5500—the first self-operating computer. All subsequent Burroughs 500 Systems have followed this outstandingly successful lead.

If you want to see true third generation hardware and software in action—call us. Burroughs Corporation, Detroit, Michigan 48232.

Burroughs

Leveraging the Computer

Managers in many cities and corporations could see the benefits. As stated by M.J. Cook, Secretary-Treasurer of the City of Monroe, Louisiana, "The computer is the key to centralized financial control of all city costs and income. The current information we get is one of the great benefits. In business language, it gives us our inventory, cost control, accounts payable, accounts receivable and payroll information, and also tells us how much money we have in the bank. All these data are available day-to-day and/or monthly. Thus, we can exercise more businesslike control, based on current information. Because we know exactly where we stand in regard to budget – whether we are over, under, and why. Formerly, we didn't know this until 45 to 60 days after the close. By then, the horse was out of the barn." (4)

The Growing Power of the Data Processing Department

As data processing departments were created in companies, these organizations became powerful entities. Special skills and training were needed to use this developing technology and while it was becoming more affordable, it was still costly. Data processing departments leveraged their position and the situation to promote the maximum use of computers by expanding their services to a broader range of internal clients.

The net result was that data processing organizations gained greater control over business processes within companies during this period. Functions, like payroll, became heavily dependent on data processing and lost some control over the process and the product. This new relationship between data processing and the business, complicated by a whole new foreign language unfolding within the data processing world, would take many years to work itself out. This communication problem is verbalized well in a 1967 *Fortune* magazine article on the subject that summarized the problem as follows: "You know how difficult it is for people in the same field to understand each other perfectly. Here you have one man dealing with symbols and another who is not interested in symbols but wants results." (5)

Learning to use this new tool would prove to be much more difficult than many could have initially imagined, and many payroll problems would be solved and created by the use of computers during these formative years. However, business had now grasped the possibilities and could no longer live without this newest and most powerful of business tools.

Movement From FORTRAN to COBOL to Lessen the Communication Problem

The computer language FORTRAN was developed in the mid-fifties. "In the first version of FORTRAN the programmer still had to spell out specific instructions for each action of the computer; the command 'GO TO 0500,' for instance, told the computer to refer to memory location number 0500. But eventually the language underwent a number of revisions that made it more 'problem-oriented' rather than 'machine oriented,' and other languages …emerged that allowed the programmer to concentrate on his problem instead of on instructing the machine. With COBOL (Common Business Oriented Language), for instance, a programmer could write simply 'add dividends to income,' and the compiler did the rest." Most payroll-related software would be written in this language for many years to come. (5)

Computer-like Equipment Starts To Move Into the Office

While this was the era of the mainframe, smaller, more user friendly products were being developed to perform office work, like the Friden 5610 COMPUTYPER Data Processor.

"There's never been a machine at so low a price that can do as much for your business… It is the first desk-size data processor to use integrated circuits. This makes it faster, more compact, more reliable, and more versatile than any machine you can buy in its low price range. …It can handle your commission distribution, accounts payable and receivable, payroll, and reports. ….You can buy a 5610 for less than $300 a month. It can be operated by an average office girl, using your present business forms and office procedures…. There's one more thing

Exhibit 15-4 through 15-6: "Urban management needs computers;" Potthoff, E.H.; The American City; Volume 84; No. 3; March 1969; pp. 69-71; Courtesy of the City of Saginaw Michigan

First came the key-punch operation.

that makes the 5610 unique. It can be programmed in English, instead of "computerese." This means it can be re-programmed by your own staff to fit your expanding operations." (6)

Functions Like Payroll Served as Proving Grounds for Other Applications

An extract from an article titled "The Computer" appearing in the August 8, 1969 issue of *The American City* highlights the fact that high volume transaction systems, like payroll, were regularly used to cost justify initial computer investments and were among the first applications to be converted to new business computer technology:

"The bread-and-butter applications, such as payroll and utility accounting, provide the 'justification for the machine,' but other uses add 'profitability.'" (7)

Many Employers Migrated in Phases Using Service Bureaus

Many employers, after spending upwards of five years to evaluate the alternatives, chose ultimately to implement the use of computer technology in phases and with the aid of a service bureau similar to the following approach followed by the City of Saginaw, Michigan:

In 1962, after six years of recognizing the need to apply the techniques of modern technology to city government and after careful study, the City of Saginaw selected a service bureau to aid them with their first phase of the transition. Within several months, several basic applications, namely payroll, water and sewer utility billing and property tax billing, had been

converted and were operational within the service bureau. (8)

After the expiration of the initial eighteen-month contract, a new service bureau agreement was negotiated to perform expanded data processing functions using city personnel on city-leased equipment. At this time a Data Processing Division was created under Finance and staffed with a division head and two key-punch operators. (Exhibit 15-4) Initial equipment included one cardpunch, one verifier, and a lower-speed sorter. (8)

After nine months of gaining further training and experience the City had expanded operations enough to justify the establishment of a complete on-premises processing center. By the end of 1964, the necessary equipment was acquired along with the addition of a machine operator and a third key-punch operator. (8)

New applications were subsequently converted to the system. Normally a user would recognize the need and then data processing would complete an economic feasibility study with the user and other city personnel. If justified, the data processing division would then complete all development, system design, and operational work to permit implementation. (8)

By 1966, within four years of its initial phase, the City had upgraded its technology to an IBM System 360 Model 20 card computer to replace its key-punch operations (Exhibits 15-5 & 15-6) and was running over 400 computer programs including all those related to payroll such as sick leave, vacation, and personnel records. (8)

A New Profession and a Shortage of Computer Programmers

The need for programmers increased throughout the sixties and with it competition for programmers. Programmers were in demand because they produced the "software," the stuff that turns an electronic computer from an inert complex of metal parts into a versatile tool capable of performing an endless variety of jobs." (5)

At this point in the evolution of computer technology, programming was NOT a science but an art. Programming had emerged as the most expensive and most problem-plagued element of what was already a six billion dollar industry. With high wages, all kinds of people

A card computer in the new data-processing division soon followed the key-punch operation

with all kinds of experiences gravitated toward this new work. By the end of the decade, there were over 100,000 programmers and a shortage of some 50,000. (5)

Birth of Software Development Companies

With the need for software, it wasn't long before programmers and software developers began to create their own companies to support computer manufacturers and their clients by writing and installing the operational and application software needed to do all sorts of customized work. From these needs came companies like Computer Science Corporation, one of the earliest software houses.(5)

It would not be long before "off the shelf" application-specific software would be produced and sold. (5)

Other Office Tools of the Period

During this period other advancements were made by manufacturers of electronic calculators and copiers. Xerox marketed its new line of telecopiers and Kodak its Recordak Microfilm Systems (Exhibit 15-7). These new, more sophisticated tools provided everyone including those in payroll with new capabilities and options.

One for look-up. One for lockup.

Intelligent planning.
That's why there are co-pilots, understudies, spare tires, and duplicate copies. And why more and more agencies responsible for vital records protect themselves from

fire, flood, or accidental loss by making sure to have two of a kind. On microfilm.
With modern RECORDAK Microfilmers, you can expose two rolls of microfilm simultaneously. One roll is kept at hand for quick and easy reference on your RECORDAK Film Reader. The identical twin goes off premises for safekeeping.

You are covered. So are the tax payers. Plan today to call or write: Eastman Kodak Company, Business Systems Markets Division Dept. X-2, Rochester, New York 14650.
®Recordak is a registered trademark for microfilm equipment designed and produced by Kodak.

≡RECORDAK Microfilm Systems by Kodak

For more data, circle No. 449 on reply card

Traditional Solutions Continued To Provide Advantages

While the movement to computers was occurring throughout all industries, not all companies required computers to meet their current payroll needs. In fact, some employers, still reluctant to jump on the "computer bandwagon," preferred to wait instead until the technology had further advanced or until such time that it became more affordable. These employers chose more traditional products, often with immediate and positive results. For instance, in 1966 the City of Salt Lake City, Utah purchased Addressograph-Multigraph machines using more

Exhibit 15-7: "One for look-up. One for Lockup;" The American City; Volume 84; No. 2; p. 83; Reprinted courtesy of Eastman Kodak Company. KODAK is a trademark.

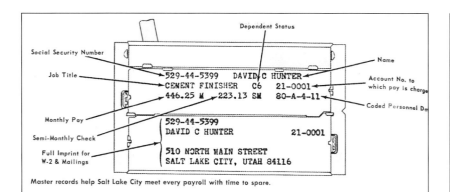

Master records help Salt Lake City meet every payroll with time to spare.

Putting Payroll on a Paying Basis

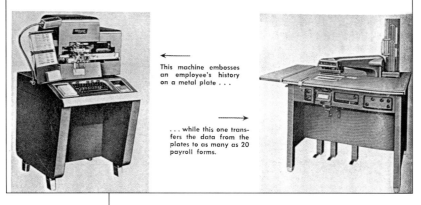

This machine embosses an employee's history on a metal plate . . .

. . . while this one transfers the data from the plates to as many as 20 payroll forms.

Exhibit 15-8: "Putting Payroll on a Paying Basis; Holley, L.E.; The American City; Volume 81; September 1966; pp. 154, 158; Courtesy of the City of Salt Lake City, Utah

traditional plate technology (Exhibit 15-8) and was able to gain many benefits through these machines including the ability to reduce its clerical staff from 36 to 3! (9)

This example highlights what has been true throughout history - that the transition from one technology to another is almost always overlapping and current technology often has advantages over new technology for some period of time.

Exhibit 15-9: Extract from Weyerhaeuser Employee Newsletter, April 1966, Volume 2, No. 8; Courtesy of Fitchburg Historical Society, Fitchburg, Massachusetts

Changes in Federal Tax Withholding Methods and the Implementation of Medicare

Company payroll organizations were now acclimated to the fact that there would be ongoing revisions to payroll systems and processes needed to support federal, state and local taxing jurisdictions. Payroll tax compliance, for many companies, was becoming a highly specialized function within the payroll department.

Exhibit 15-10: Medicare Implementation (1966); www.ssa.gov; Courtesy of Social Security Administration

In the sixties, a new graduated federal income tax withholding program was implemented, as communicated in many company newsletters like this Weyerhaeuser Newsletter (Exhibit 15-9), and the Social Security Administration announced its plans to implement Medicare (Exhibit 15-10).

BULLETIN

WITHHOLDING TAX
(Percentage Method)

Graduated withholding begins May 1, 1966. To bring withholding of income taxes from wages more in line with the ultimate tax liability of taxpayers, a new income tax law has been enacted which provides for graduated withholding on wages paid on or after May 1, 1966. Within the next few weeks new withholding certificates will be distributed to all divisional employees.

All employees are advised to complete the form as soon as possible. Otherwise under the new regulation we must treat married persons as single and withhold more tax from their pay.

Medicare Implementation, 1966

On July 1, 1966 (the start of Medicare enrollments) SSA Commissioner Bob Ball holds a press conference to announce SSA's plans for implementing Medicare.

Reference Sources

1. "The Mechanization of Office Work;" Giuliano, Vincent E.; The Mechanization of Work; W.H. Freeman and Company; San Francisco; 1982; Originally published in Scientific American, September 1982; pp. 77-78

2. Document (Open House); Weyerhaeuser; Fitchburg, MA Branch; June 24, 1968 p. 30; Courtesy of Fitchburg Historical Society, Fitchburg, MA

3. Burroughs System 500 Advertisement; Newsweek; May 15, 1967; Volume 67; p. 82

4. "The computer is the key … ;" M.J. Cook; *The American City*; Volume 84; No. 10; October 1969; pp. 127-128

5. "Help Wanted: 50,000 Programmers;" Bylinsky, Gene; *Fortune Magazine*; Volume 75; March 1967; pp. 140-143+

6. Friden Advertisement on their 5610 COMPUTYPER Data Processor; *Newsweek*; April 17, 1967; Volume 69; pp. 82-83; Used by permission of Neopost, Inc.

7. "The Computer;" *The American City*; Volume 84; No. 8; August 1969; p. 36

8. "Urban management needs computers;" Potthoff, E.H. Jr.; City Manager, Saginaw, Michigan; *The American City*; March 1969; Volume 84; No. 3; pp. 69-71

9. "Putting Payroll on a Paying Basis;" Holley, L.E., *The American City*; Volume 81; September 1966; pp. 154, 156, 158

CHAPTER 16:
The Seventies – The Arrival of Mini and Microcomputers

The seventies brought with it a proliferation of computer companies and new generations of computers called mini and microcomputers, heralded by radical changes in computer architecture. Software became a distinct product and the batch mode environment began to transition slowly toward the future model of online processing. There was, of course, a natural lag between the advancing status of technology and the actual application of that technology. Regardless, like water that naturally moves from higher to lower levels, the market began to find ways to apply the new technology and pockets of least resistance for utilizing the new technology. This was certainly true in the case of the banking community, where significant use of the new technology was occurring. All of these changes would have significant downstream impact on payroll professionals and payroll processes.

Computers and Banking

With the increasing power and portability of computers came new business possibilities and processes. In the banking world, computers presented new opportunities to financial institutions, and these opportunities, when acted on, led to many tough policy decisions. With computers, it was now easier for large commercial banks to move beyond their state-bound limitations and provide services on a regional or nationwide basis. This was of great concern to smaller financial institutions.

The First Federal Savings & Loan of Lincoln, Nebraska and other savings and loan associations around the country triggered a heated debate over the right of a financial institution to install remote computers, referred to as customer-bank communication terminals (CBCTs) in locations outside the institution's walls. This in turn precipitated an even larger debate over S&L charters and what services they could or could not offer. (1)

Terms such as Debit Cards, Direct Deposit and Electronic Funds Transfer (EFT) were introduced during this period, and it was in the 1970s that a "checkless" society was first envisioned. It would take several decades before issues of law, technology, and banking regulations would create a fertile environment that would make such a concept viable. It would take even longer for consumers, industry, and the government to fully embrace these new methods.

Because of the legal challenges and resistance by consumers (and others), major banks shifted their efforts in the second half of the seventies from consumers to corporate EFT systems. They felt that corporate EFT systems could substantially reduce the cost of check processing by U.S. banks each year while skirting the issues surrounding consumer EFT plans. In the late 1970s, 27 billion checks were being processed on an annual basis. However, this opportunity had its own set of obstacles including questions regarding funding and the role that the federal government should play in such an initiative. (2)

The Establishment of NACHA And Electronic Payroll Direct Deposit

In the early part of the decade, a number of banks had already begun to offer pre-authorized credit programs, of which the most popular was automatic payroll-deposit. The potential opportunity in this area alone was enormous. With a national labor force of some 75 million workers and with an average of 35 to 40 pay periods per year, employers were generating over three billion checks annually. This volume was costing the banking community close to $500,000,000 to process. (3)

At about the same time, the business community was also beginning to show an increasing interest in EFT. Employers were growing more dissatisfied with the high costs associated with large payrolls. Banking, clerical, and accounting costs connected with such payrolls, along with losses due to fraud, theft, and bookkeeping errors, provided additional motivation for change. (4)

Pressure for the development of efficient EFT systems also came from the government. Not only did the government have a massive payroll, but it also was issuing more than 40 million payments a year for various social programs, such as Social Security. By 1974, the U.S. Treasury, the Social Security Administration and several other government bodies (e.g., the U.S. Air Force) under Public Law 92-366 (31 U.S.C.A. 492, as amended August 7, 1972), were actively developing and acting on plans to promote EFT. (4)

As large employers and their payroll managers began to realize the financial and operational benefits of EFT, they began to educate themselves on the new capability and then to modify their systems to support automatic deposit payments. However, it was not until the eighties and into the nineties that many companies actually began to actively pursue high participation rates through employee marketing campaigns.

There were many obstacles (including concerns over errors and theft) to overcome before this could happen.

In 1974, the National Automated Clearing House Association (NACHA) was formed by the nationwide banking community for the purpose of developing an electronic banking network called the Automated Clearing House (ACH). NACHA was assigned the responsibility for setting the rules for exchange of funds between different regions of the country and was supported by 31 regional ACH associations located throughout the U.S. Each association shared the common purpose of promoting increased use of the ACH to member financial institutions (at the time numbering some 17,000 nationally), as well as to the business community and the public at large. This network would ultimately allow financial institutions, on behalf of employers, to send and receive electronic financial transactions, such as payroll credits, for deposit into employee checking and savings accounts. (5)

Since banks were not required to offer pre-authorized credit plans, it would take years before virtually all member financial institutions would have the needed computers and could participate in the process. As with the conver-

sion from cash to check, financial institutions would require time to make the transition. Some banks viewed pre-authorized payment plans as new service offerings from which the banking industry could draw short-term profits while others viewed these plans as merely methods of streamlining existing money transfer procedures with more remote gains to individual banks. (3)

In the 1970s, a payroll organization with a direct deposit program was required to deliver the pre-authorized credit information to their bank several days prior to payday to permit sufficient bank processing time. Employer software of the day was normally "hard coded" with bank information. Adding, deleting or changing bank information was a programming effort. Companies delivered employee net pay information on magnetic tapes via couriers directly to each participating bank.

While the momentum for automatic deposit of payrolls was growing, state laws on pay media were being updated to protect the worker/consumer. As a result, most states enacted laws to prohibit mandated direct deposit programs by employers by imposing the following rules 1) enrollment must be voluntary on the part of the employee 2) net pay must be fully accessible to the employee on pay day and 3) participation in direct deposit must not cost the employee any additional expense.

For these technical and legal reasons, direct deposit grew very slowly throughout the seventies. Nevertheless, many payroll organizations began during that time to support dual payment processes. In some instances, employers would permit employees to split their net pay between a check and automatic deposit as an incentive for enrollment. It is safe to say that direct deposit in these early years provided few advantages other than convenience for those few employees receptive to automatic deposit. But, it was a necessary first step in the movement to future high participation direct deposit programs.

Smaller Computers Bring Computing Power to More Users More Cheaply

It was advancements in computer technology that made all of the above possible. The movement from larger costly mainframes to less expensive smaller computers began in earnest in the seventies.

Small companies don't need big computers. They need small computers that can grow.

Big computers are fine for big companies. But when it comes to helping small companies grow bigger, nothing beats the price and performance of small interactive computer systems. And when it comes to small systems, nothing beats the price and performance of the Datasystems from Digital.

Take our new Datasystem 320 for example. It's designed to help you do a lot without a lot of effort. It can help you make short work of the long hours you spend doing your books. It can help you sell more products by giving you more information. It can keep track of your inventory. And keep tabs on your accounts. It can even tell you how well you're doing by telling you how well you've done.

In short, it gives you all the capability you need in a small business system. Including software compatibility with our larger Datasystems. And that

means you can start as small as you like and grow as big as you like, without starting over.

But that isn't all the Datasystems have going for them. Or for you. There's a network of independent application specialists who can fit our system to your business. And a network of Digital service and support specialists to give you the back-up you need when you need it.

So if you're looking for your first system, consider the Datasystems from Digital. Send

the coupon for our brochure that explains the business of buying a business system. Or call your nearest Digital sales office. Digital Equipment Corporation, Business Products Group, PK-3/M33, Parker Street, Maynard, MA 01754. European headquarters: 8, route de l'Aire, 1211 Geneva 26. Tel: 42 79 50. In Canada: Digital Equipment of Canada, Ltd.

digital

| Digital Equipment Corporation, Business Products Group, |
| PK-3/M33, Parker Street, Maynard, MA 01754. |
| I'm interested in knowing more. Please send me your brochure that |
| explains what small business systems can do for me. |
| Name_____ Title_____ |
| Company_____Phone_____ |
| Address_____ |
| City_____ State_____ Zip____ |

BW2147

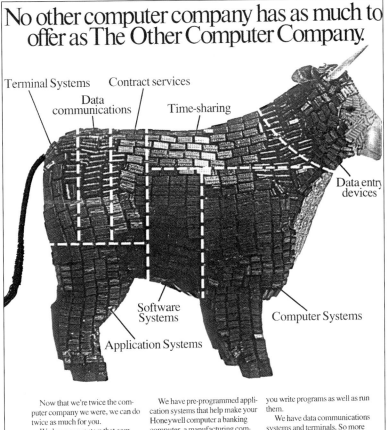

No other computer company has as much to offer as The Other Computer Company.

Terminal Systems   Contract services
Data communications   Time-sharing
Data entry devices
Software Systems   Computer Systems
Application Systems

Now that we're twice the computer company we were, we can do twice as much for you.

We have computers that compute, computers that communicate, computers that control. They can be minicomputers, little computers, medium computers, big computers. And if you can't afford a computer of your own, you can share one of ours.

We have pre-programmed application systems that help make your Honeywell computer a banking computer, a manufacturing computer, a distribution computer, a hospital computer, an education computer. Or just about any other kind of computer you happen to need.

We also have software to help

you write programs as well as run them.

We have data communications systems and terminals. So more people in more places can use your computer more effectively.

And we do everything in our power to make sure you'll be happy with your computer.

Any way you slice it, you can't ask for more than that.

The Other Computer Company: Honeywell

Honeywell Information Systems (MS 061), 200 Smith Street, Waltham, Massachusetts 02154

During this period, many new computer manufacturers came to the forefront. Competition among new minicomputer manufacturers, along with inventions like the circuit boards that permitted the storage of more memory in less space, opened the door to broader computer utilization. (6)

Minicomputer growth went from an installed base of slightly over 25,000 units to close to 100,000 units within the first three years of the decade. During those years, a minicomputer included any computer that sold for less than $20,000 and had at least 4,096 words of main memory and had a word length of 8 to 24 bits. It was this larger capacity that permitted these minicomputers to utilize languages, such as FORTRAN and COBOL, which had been previously reserved for mainframes. The minicomputer of the late sixties was a single-function "black box" that could only be programmed in complex binary code. Binary code required less storage area. However, it also required large numbers of expert programmers to code and maintain. The more sophisticated minicomputer permitted manufacturers to build smaller machines with more memory for significantly less money while providing more functionality through easier-to-use language. (6)

This sub-industry had already grown from $25 million a year in 1968 to over $250 million

in 1970, and was expected to increase at the rate of 50% to 75% annually. (7)

By 1971 there were over 75 manufacturers producing small computers, of which Digital Equipment Corporation (Exhibit 16-1) was the leader. Others included Honeywell Information Systems (Exhibit 16-2), Hewlett-Packard (Exhibit 16-3), NCR (Exhibit 16-4), and Data General Corporation (Exhibit 16-5). IBM soon entered the market as well (Exhibit 16-6). (7) All of the computer manufacturers of the day were communicating a similar message - "our new computers can do more for you for less."

Intel Introduces "the Computer On a Chip" and Microcomputer Processing

Rapid product obsolescence was characteristic of the industry from its very beginning. With the introduction of new semiconductor integrated

161

Exhibit 16-3: "This HP computer advance automates financial reporting for $21,700;" Business Week; March 21, 1977; p. 96; Reprinted by permission of Hewlett-Packard Corporation

Exhibit 16-4: "Meet the newest NCR mini-computer system;" Business Week; February 28, 1977; p. 85; Courtesy of the NCR Corporate Archives at the Montgomery County Historical Society, Dayton, Ohio

circuits, computer technology took a big leap forward. A microcomputer using the new chip could process more data faster and more accurately than ever before, forcing mini-computers to become even cheaper while threatening mainframes and time sharing products and services. (8)

In less than 30 years, computer technology had progressed from the 30 ton monster, built by the University of Pennsylvania and running on 18,000 vacuum tubes, to the microcomputer processor using circuitry placed on miniature silicon chips. (9) This 1979 IBM advertisement captures the historical evolution of computer technology nicely from the late fifties through the end of the seventies (Exhibit 16-7).

New Computers Offer Stiff Competition

By 1975 both IBM and Digital Equipment Corporation announced new products in the low-priced end of the market. First, IBM announced its lowest priced IBM business machine ever and shortly thereafter, Digital Equipment Corporation announced the world's lowest priced fully programmable computer system. These new products now provided in-house solutions not previously available and offered new competition to time-sharing services, programmable calculators, computer terminals, and accounting machines, as well as to other small business computers. (10)

Computer Fraud in the Mid 1970s

The computer era brought with it a down side in the form of increased occurrences of process fraud. Early computer programs did not always have the controls needed to prevent fraud, as illustrated in the following example:

"In May of 1972, the borough of Brooklyn reported a fraud in the payroll of its Board of Education. The District Attorney charged that a ring of swindlers had submitted, to the computer center, fraudulent payroll reports that included hours worked by teachers no longer employed by the city. The computer system processed the reports in a normal manner, apparently because the system was not programmed to note employee severance. Reportedly, discovery of the manipulation occurred when the computer rejected a card because the name on it was misspelled. When the correct spelling was being checked, it was found that the teacher was no longer employed by the Board of Education."

Users' Guide to Computer Crime by Stephen W. Leibholz & Louis D. Wilson
Chilton Book Company, Radnor, Pennsylvania – 1974; pp. 20-21

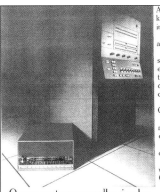

Anyone who knows anything about computers knows they have to be big, complicated and incredibly expensive.

An idea propagated by big, complicated and incredibly expensive computer companies.

In fact, there are full-fledged computers small enough to fit inside a coat closet. Simple enough to put in the hands of anyone who needs them. And inexpensive enough to get some jobs done for as much as 50% less than big, complicated computers.

Who's buying them? Industry. Research. Government. Education. Commerce.

Enough forward-thinking companies to make Data General one of the fastest growing outfits in America today.

Let us show you what we can do with your computer problems.

We don't know exactly what our answer will be. But it won't be big. Or complicated. Or incredibly expensive.

DataGeneral

The computer company you can understand has a brochure you can understand. Write:

Our computers are smaller, simpler, and much less expensive. That's why many companies don't buy them.

From IBM, more technological advances.

The Beginning of the Shift From Data Center to Office and Hardware to Software

This new technology - faster, cheaper, and easier to use - precipitated the beginning of a movement from the data center to the office and from centralized to distributed data processing (Exhibit 16-8). The framework was now in place for the software market to produce application-specific and off-the-shelf software. These products were in development by the mid-1970s and were well established by the end of the decade. In the meantime, however, the average in-house payroll organization continued to use large centralized computers with keypunched data. (11)

"Keeping our prices current was a problem until we got this small IBM computer."

A small computer can make a big difference. IBM

The Early Years of the Payroll Software Industry

In the mid 1960s, large corporations were recruiting college graduates with physics and mathematics majors to work on new third generation business machines that IBM called 360 computers. At that time there were no programmers trained on the 360s and business technology was not yet a part of any college curriculum.

I was hired in 1966 by International Harvester and assigned to work on developing a payroll/labor system for their new IBM 360. In those days payroll was a back office operation and was viewed as a "dreaded necessity." There was no strategic component to the work. It was purely a tactical operation with lots of logistical challenges. I spent my first six months at an IBM training center to learn about computers and a language called COBOL. At this time hardware and software were not viewed as separate and distinct products and only in the late sixties would these two components be unbundled. It was this unbundling that, in part, triggered the subsequent birth of the software industry.

Following my experiences at International Harvester, I was hired by Management Science America as a consultant and was appointed to a project team working on a new payroll system for the Sunbeam Corporation. One payroll system project followed another. Each new payroll system was developed "from scratch." In 1971, when Management Science America entered into bankruptcy, the Receiver, in an attempt to save the company, suggested that MSA should focus on products rather than consulting services as we built products for payroll, personnel, fixed asset, general ledger, etc., for the market. This suggestion put MSA in the young application packaged software industry! By the early 1970s Computer Science Corporation on the west coast and Information Science Corporation in the east were major players in the payroll software industry.

In the early 1970s I met a "whiz bang" independent contractor/programmer named Jim Pierce while working on a consulting project at Henry Ford Hospital. It wasn't long before we jointly decided to embark on our own payroll/human resource application enterprise, and in 1974 we created Cyborg Systems, Inc. Our first client was the Reflector Hardware Corporation. They were upgrading their second generation IBM 1400 to the third generation IBM 360 and hired us to develop and implement a new payroll system, with the understanding that the system developed would become the property of Cyborg and would be resold to other clients. To give you an idea of how young the industry was back then, Reflector's requirements for the payroll were handed to us on a single page!

Michael Blair, Chairman and CEO of Cyborg Systems, Inc.

Contingency Planning and the Impact of Weather on Payrolls

Payroll professionals, like U.S. Postal Service mail carriers, are expected to deliver their products and services on time regardless of adverse weather conditions or other unplanned obstacles. With the advent of computers and the ability to support larger geographic areas, contingency planning has become an increasingly important component of payroll work.

Over the years, payroll employees have had to overcome hurricanes, floods, earthquakes and a myriad of other natural and man-made catastrophes. In the northern climates, winter snow storms have often presented special challenges for payroll organizations, like the "New England Blizzard of '78." While the following efforts may seem to be far beyond the call of duty, such actions by payroll professionals, in the face of adversity, are not that unusual.

Computers Couldn't Beat the Holiday Payroll Blues

For many payroll employees, with or without computers, the year-end reporting period during the 1970s was often very stressful. There was little time for holiday celebrations as remembered in this article (Exhibit 16-9) titled "A Blue Christmas"

appearing in the November, 1987 *Payroll Exchange* by James C. Maumus, CPP - especially for any individual moving into a new payroll managerial position around the end of the calendar year.

On the "receiving end" the taxpayer in this 1978 photo titled "Income Tax at the 6th and Arch Street Building" catches the mood of some citizens during the tax filing period (Exhibit 16-10).

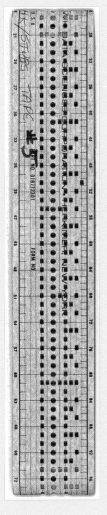

Exhibit 16-10: "Income Tax at the 6th and Arch St. Building;" Philadelphia Inquirer; April 18, 1978; Reprinted by permission of the Philadelphia Inquirer & Photographer William F. Steinmetz

Exhibit 16-11: Digital Equipment Corporation LP10 Printer Carriage Control Tape; Courtesy of Compaq Computer Corporation

Exhibit 16-9: "A Blue Christmas – The Realities of Holiday Time in the Payroll Department; Maumus, James C.; Payroll Exchange, American Payroll Association; Volume 11; No. 10; November 1987; p. 16; Reprinted by permission of James C. Maumus, CPP

A Blue Christmas

MY HORRENDOUS HOLIDAYS

– by James C. Maumus, CPP
McDermott, Inc.
New Orleans, La.

As Christmas descended on the university that December in 1970, the season marked many firsts for me: my first Christmas at the university as payroll supervisor, my first payroll quarter, and my first six weeks on the job. The many daily surprises of doing this involved payroll of faculty contracts with durations of a semester, nine, ten or twelve months, administrative salaried exempt and nonexempt personnel, hourly employees, and hourly work-study students had finally begun to diminish. Little did I know the surprises still in store for me.

The university celebrated the holidays in a big way and practically closed down when the students went on holiday break in mid-December. During this momentary lull, I decided to look ahead to quarter end and to January when W-2's would be issued. I knew this to be a treacherous time and contemplated getting a head start by determining how big (or hopefully small) this job would be.

I ran totals of the earnings and withholdings for the first three quarters of the year from the quarterly returns which had already been submitted. Then I compared them to a printout of the year-to-date accumulations from the computer. They weren't hundreds, but thousands of dollars off! Thinking I had made some miscalculation, I redid the figures. Again, the same massive inconsistencies appeared.

I then ran the totals quarter by quarter. None of them balanced, they weren't even close! The university had an in-house program at the time, so my first step was to talk to the programmer. She confirmed that I was using the right figures from the computer. I knew that the quarterly report figures were the ones submitted, so I knew then that something was terribly wrong.

My predecessor in the payroll department had been an accountant with a master's degree in accounting. Even though I had heard that he was an argumentative sort, someone who had debated with people about anything and everything including the spelling of their own names, I expected that things would have been in some order. Instead, things were indeed a mess when I took over, and I could not fathom how anyone with his credentials could have left the last three quarters so grossly out of balance, if, indeed, he had balanced them at all.

"They weren't hundreds, but thousands of dollars off."

After investigating the matter thoroughly, I discovered that the quarters for at least that year had not been balanced, and had been plugged. My predecessor had obviously not concerned himself with the accuracy of his reporting but only with the timeliness of it to avoid penalties. I began to review the first quarter to determine what caused the errors. I soon discovered that my predecessor had no real comprehension of how the computer system worked and, as a result, he had erroneously handled all of the entries for adjustments, voided checks and manually prepared checks.

For various reasons, all unknown to me, there had been a huge number of these adjustments each quarter and it became painfully apparent that the only way to balance the year was to completely reconstruct it. This meant taking every bi-weekly payroll and manually reconstructing the quarter-to-date and year-to-date accumulators, employee by employee, all 1,200 of them!

Since there was little time during regular working hours to accomplish this task, I began to work unpaid overtime cramped in a little office crowded with printouts and balance sheets. Since I was the entire payroll department, I sought help from my bride of a little over a year, who was then expecting our first child. I pressed her into service (with her permission) and we began to spend our evenings and weekends huddled over computer sheets, payroll rosters, check requests, ledgers and quarterly reports.

By mid-January I realized that we would be unable to complete the monumental task in time for the January 31 deadline. I convinced my superior that we faced a critical situation and he finally agreed to bring in two payroll clerks from a temporary agency to work with me in this tedious task. Our computer programmer was pressed into service as a data entry operator to keypunch the corrections directly from the worksheets. We worked seven days a week, 12 hours a day. Just under the wire, early on the morning of the 31st, the final runs were made, and the W-2's rolled through the printer and were in the employees' hands at last!

This was definitely the most horrendous experience in my 17 years of payroll, a virtual baptism of fire, which gave me the opportunity to investigate every detail of a payroll system and impressed upon me for life the need for internal controls as well as accuracy and accountability in payroll processing. May you all be spared such an experience.

Reference Sources

1. "An electronic tremor shakes the bankers;" Business Week; March 10, 1975; pp. 26-27

2. "Electronic banking aims at business;" Business Week; January 24, 1977; p. 77

3. Electronic Money; Richardson, Dennis W.; The Massachusetts Institute of Technology; Cambridge, MA; 1970

4. The Cashless Society: EFTS at the Crossroads; Bequai, August; John Wiley & Sons; New York; 1980; p. 15

5. "Payroll Direct Deposit – An Employee Benefit and Convenience;" Good, John F.; Payroll Exchange; December 1985; Volume 9; No. 12; pp. 4-5

6. "New memories boost minicomputer capacity;" Business Week; July 7, 1973; pp. 72-73

7. "The big-time beckons minicomputers;" Business Week; January 31, 1971; pp. 32, 33+

8. "Microcomputers aim at a huge new market;" Business Week; May 12, 1973; pp. 180-181

9. "Here Comes the Second Computer Revolution;" Fortune; Volume 92; November 1975; pp. 134-9

10. "A minicomputer tempest;" Business Week; January 27, 1975; pp. 79 & 82

11. "At last, major roles for minicomputers;" Harvard Business Review; Volume 53; May-June 1975; pp. 148-156

CHAPTER 17:
The Eighties – Payroll Comes of Age

The Payroll Environment of the Early Eighties

The payroll profession as depicted in this book and as illustrated here (Exhibit 17-1) had evolved over thousands of years. However, for many reasons, it can be argued that the U.S. payroll profession first came of age during the 1980s.

Technology was advancing at a record pace, with computer hardware becoming faster, more powerful and less expensive. During the eighties, computers also began to move from the data center to the office and home. The industry was driving more toward standardization of products. Software was moving to the forefront, with application-specific products in full force and software, in general, becoming more "user-friendly."

Both federal and state governments and the banking community were leveraging these technological advancements to implement their own agendas, which in turn required employers to comply with new, more complex payroll tax, legal, and banking regulations and processes. These changes, while sometimes mutually beneficial, required payroll organizations across the country to acquire and apply new technology.

In the midst of all this, or perhaps in response to it, the payroll profession was being re-defined and solidified under a newly created professional association - the American Payroll Association.

There was no doubt that the pace of business was quickening and the payroll environment was becoming more complex and moving at what appeared to be an ever faster pace. At the beginning of the decade, many payroll organizations were in a constant "react" mode, operating on outdated in-house solutions while striving to understand and implement (often in parallel) new complex regulatory changes. For many, the 1980s were filled with too much work, too much change, and too little time.

QUOTATION OF THE PERIOD:

"Firemen and payroll employees have much in common as they are always fighting fires."
Anonymous

However, throughout the eighties, the payroll community began to mature and take more command and control over the events shaping it. In the end, the profession would be significantly changed and the process substantially improved.

The American Payroll Association Is Created

In the 1970s, AMR International, Inc., a publishing and seminar company, held a payroll conference in Chicago. It was one of the first of its kind. More than 300 people attended the conference, thereby confirming a need for this type of educational forum. AMR International

PAYROLL EXCHANGE
THE PUBLICATION OF HUMAN RESOURCES COMPENSATION
Volume 12 No. 8   October 1988
THE EVOLUTION OF PAYROLL
EXHIBIT

PREHISTORIC PAYROLL
EGYPTIAN PAYROLL
TURN-OF-THE-CENTURY PAYROLL
(SOB!) WILL UPPER MANAGEMENT EVER TAKE MY PROFESSION SERIOUSLY?!
PAYROLL CLERK
MODERN PAYROLL PROFESSIONALS

Growth and Change Within the Payroll Profession

Exhibit 17-1: "The Evolution of Payroll;" Artist: Soderberg, Thomas J.; Payroll Exchange; American Payroll Association; New York, N.Y.; Volume 12, No. 8; October 1988; p. front cover

then acquired a newsletter dedicated to the subject of payroll (*Payroll Exchange*) and over the following years developed a subscriber base of several thousand individuals. In 1981, *Payroll Exchange* conducted a survey of its subscribers that confirmed subscriber interest in forming an association. (1)

Out of these early initiatives, the American Payroll Institute, Inc. was chartered as a non-profit educational and professional organization, and its membership arm, the American Payroll Association (APA), was formed shortly thereafter, acquiring all prior rights to the Association and to *Payroll Exchange.* Subscribers automatically became honorary members of the American Payroll Association. (1)

Donald W. Sharper (Exhibit 17-2), formerly of AMR International, officially founded the American Payroll Association on January 2, 1982 with headquarters in New York City. (1)

Payroll Exchange, which became the membership publication of the American Payroll Association, provided a communications link to otherwise isolated and self-taught payroll personnel throughout the country and served as the Association's primary educational tool in the early years. From those humble beginnings, the APA continuously grew in both membership and services offered. Expanded services included local chapters, training and educational programs, annual membership congresses (Exhibit 17-3), publications, and Washington, D.C. representation on matters pertaining to government affairs.

Exhibit 17-2: Donald W. Sharper, (early 1980s); Founder of the American Payroll Association; Courtesy of the American Payroll Association, New York, NY

Exhibit 17-3: Attendees at first American Payroll Association Congress, San Antonio, Texas; Payroll Exchange; Volume 7, No. 10; October 1983; p. 11

Fred O'Boyle and the Rest of the Story – History Leading Up To the Birth of APA

The following article from the February 1988 issue of Payroll Exchange is being included in its entirety because of the historical perspectives that it offers on activities leading up to the creation of the newsletter *Payroll Exchange* and the founding of the American Payroll Association. (Exhibit 17-4)

Payroll Survey of the Early Eighties

In 1981, AMR conducted a survey of its early *Payroll Exchange* subscriber base. Payroll managers responsible for paying some 900,000 employees responded to the survey. Summarized below, the survey provided the first glimpse of the payroll organization of the early eighties. (2)

Regarding payroll structure, 92% of the respondents were processing their payrolls on computers, with the majority using in-house systems, while 25% were using service bureaus and 8% bank services. 46% of all respondents were paying multiple companies and an even larger portion were supporting multiple pay frequencies, although 80% of all companies were paying at least some employees on a weekly basis. (2)

In the area of organizational structure, 86% of all payrolls were centralized at the corporate level; 40% supported employee populations in excess of 1,000; and 75% of all payroll organizations defined themselves as full service payroll units, meaning that their responsibilities extended beyond timecard processing and payment issuance to include duties related to payroll taxes, benefits, and accounting. (2)

Exhibit 17-4: "Payroll Exchange – The Beginning;" O'Boyle, Fred; Payroll Exchange; Volume 12; No. 2; February 1988; pp. 7-8

Payroll Exchange - The Beginning

- by Fred O'Boyle, CPP
Dun & Bradstreet
New York, NY

During the Second Opening Session of the 1987 Congress in Orlando, Florida, I had the privilege of representing the Education Committee on the dais. It was during this time that Donald Sharper took the opportunity to announce the ten-year anniversary of Payroll Exchange and to introduce me as "a pioneer in payroll", perhaps deserving to be called "Mr. Payroll". Regardless, the point of the introduction was that the founder of the newsletter-Payroll Exchange was Fred O'Boyle, CPP.

Following that opening session introduction and throughout the rest of the conference, I was approached by a number of people inquiring into the reasons, ideas and mechanics of the newsletter. These questions culminated in a formal request from the Association to write this article answering the prime question of what prompted me to undertake this endeavor.

Perhaps the best answer to this question is found in the paragraphs of my "get acquainted" column reprinted below. This article appeared in the very first issue , Volume 1, Number 1, in July, 1977.

"Hello! This seems to be the most universal way of getting acquainted. As I sit here trying to conquer space - the white space of blank paper - I can't help but succumb to the emotions and ideas of years past when I first encountered the idea of giving payroll management a voice. That moment is still pretty clear in my mind; yet it happened about a dozen years ago in discussion with a few associates who shared this feeling.

Our concern was real! Payroll was already rapidly moving out of the rather simple shell it endured in for so long and we felt that those of us dedicated to the prompt, accurate payment of employees had not only a right but a duty to be heard. After all, Accountants, Personnel Managers, Wage and Salary Specialists, Controllers, Tax Managers, and a variety of other professional groups had their voice - yes, even Secretaries. Why not Payroll?

Well, years passed and those few associates and I went our separate ways...and still no voice. It was not that the idea was forgotten, it just became inactive rising to the surface a few times during the years only to be "put on the back burner" for a while each time it

"Payroll was already rapidly moving out of the rather simple shell it endured in... (we) not only had a right but a duty to be heard."

appeared. No organization would materialize and no voice emerged!

Finally, about three years ago, I began to pursue the idea with an intense desire to establish some communication between payroll colleagues. But how? For two years I researched ways of trying to frame and organize an approach. The idea of a newletter was formed but that really was only a one-way street - how were we going to get an expression of views and opinions? That was the key - to give payroll a voice.

Hours were spent on trying to think this one out. Lying in bed - in the shower - commuting - traveling - sitting in airports - on planes - anytime I could reasonably devote to just thinking and planning, my attention would turn to developing that voice!

Now it's here! And it enshrines itself in the name of the newsletter - PAYROLL EXCHANGE. The newsletter as a vehicle and the "exchange" aspect to give voice to that vast world of payroll.

Give me the opportunity to show you how the voice can grow!"

As noted in the reprinted words of eleven years ago, the idea of some vehicle to serve payroll was conceived some ten to twelve years earlier, or as early as 1965. Also evident is that the final drive toward my goal began some three years before the first issue materialized. As I think back over the years, I believe the final impetus came from this question, posed by my Corporate Controller at the time. That question went something like this, "Fred, who besides yourself makes these decisions? Is there anyone you know in other companies to ask how they treat a problem?"

Sparked with this question, I began the three-year stretch which ended in July, 1977. I began sifting through the perceived needs at the time. This list of needs included these major issues:

1. Need for more prompt notice, response and opinion on tax and payroll related changes. Tax services were good but often contained so much information that most managers were too busy to read everything, thus giving rise to a need to educate.

2. A need to exchange ideas.

After all the research and thought, the

general format was developed to include timely articles on specific topics relative to payroll, a check list of tax related changes as reported in the various services so that managers could review only that legislation which concerned their specific related jurisdictions, and an exchange column (hence the newsletter name) designed to bring issues and opinions together for general reporting.

A target date was finally established and I undertook the research and planning of those specific articles to be included in the first issue. As with all of the first eighteen issues, I did all the research and writing literally off my dining room table while my wife, Marilyn, did all of the typing and assisted in the actual layout work. Remember, this was in the days preceding PC's, word processing and all those great software packages of today which make this type of work so much easier.

Our target date of July, 1977, saw the first issue finally emerge with such articles

as: Early Instructions an Annual Reporting (Social Security); individual articles on how the newsletter would handle matters affecting Manual Payroll Systems, Computer Payroll Packages, and Service Bureaus; a call for newsclippings and local legislation dealing with payroll; the first Check Your Service column; Editor's Check which was basically an editorial feature each month which in this first issue stated our purpose (the bulk of this first editorial reprinted earlier in this article); and, of course, the first Exchange column which in this issue was a description of its purpose and a call for support.

Following this first issue, we published from home seventeen more issues through December, 1978. In mid-1978 I became associated with AMR (Advanced Management Research). AMR assumed marketing and production of Payroll Exchange in January, 1979. This association, wherein I continued to do all research and writing, eventually evolved into the first Payroll Management Conference taking place in

Chicago in November, 1979. This, too, I organized. I recruited the faculty and exhibitors, many of whom stayed with these conferences and eventually the Congress.

Due to philosophical differences, I parted company with AMR in March of 1980. AMR retained the newsletter-Payroll Exchange and continued the Payroll Management Conferences. Next came the American Payroll Association based on the subscription listings and the rest, as they say, "is history".

Little did I realize that that history would bring together such a great group of people who have worked so hard in developing a real organization which has, in its own way, sown and nurtured those same seeds of interest that I entertained for so many years. The payroll voice I sought so long ago has arrived and it's a pleasure to be a part of it.

Mr. Fred O'Boyle, CPP, is a contributing editor to the Payroll Exchange

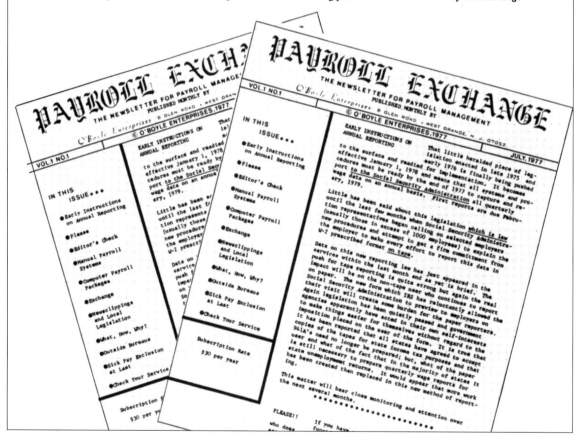

Technology Enables Centralization of Payroll Operations

As reflected in the above survey, many companies, newly enabled by technology, began to understand the advantages of centralizing payroll operations. While not a new concept, computer technology along with a vast array of new business devices (many using embedded microprocessor chips) enabled many companies for the first time to act on these opportunities. Remote sites could now be serviced via telephone lines and remote terminals to submit time data, access pay information, and print paychecks. Direct deposit and overnight air courier services made it feasible for companies located on the east coast to pay west coast employees or vice versa, while gaining the benefits derived from centralized operations. The implementation of company networks and e-mail systems, along with the adoption of voice mail and interactive voice response (IVR) systems that came on line during the eighties, further enhanced the feasibility of centralized payroll operations while at the same time creating new issues and concerns regarding payroll data ownership, access, and security.

Social Security and FLSA Celebrate Their 50th Anniversaries

SOCIAL SECURITY
PARTNERSHIP WITH TOMORROW
50
ANNIVERSARY

Since its passage in 1935, the Social Security Act has probably been changed more often than any other piece of social legislation, having been expanded and/or amended on multiple occasions throughout the years to provide new and different types of coverage beyond its original provisions. Throughout these 50 years (Exhibit 17-5), payroll and payroll professionals have truly acted as partners with the Social Security Administration. As of 1985, payroll collected employer and employee social security taxes amounting to more than $200 billion annu-

ally. On a monthly basis, the SSA was issuing over $15 billion to more than 36 million benefit recipients. (3)

In addition, in 1988, the Fair Labor Standards Act (Exhibit 17-6) celebrated its 50th anniversary.

> **50TH ANNIVERSARY CELEBRATION**
> **FAIR LABOR STANDARDS ACT**
> **1938-1988**

Social, Regulatory, and Tax Changes Push Payroll Forward

While the 1930s and 1940s were important decades for regulatory, social, and tax change, the 1970s and 1980s were perhaps equally significant. Not since these early periods had so much legislation been enacted in the form of so many new and revised social programs, new and revised regulatory laws, and new and revised tax statutes. These new and revised programs and laws brought with them changes for everyone - both employees and employers. Before the end of the decade, there would be many new withholding, payment and reporting rules for employers and their payroll organizations to follow. Uppermost among these changes was the Tax Reform Act of 1986.

The Tax Reform Act of 1986

The 1986 Tax Reform Act introduced sweeping changes to both corporate and individual tax structures, especially as related to compensation and benefit programs. Revisions would impact health and group-term life insurance plans, individual retirement accounts, cafeteria plans, 401(k) and thrift/savings plans, and much more. These programs would face new and tougher nondiscrimination rules as well to ensure that employees at all compensation levels would be able to benefit from them The reforms had a major impact on payroll and human resource administration organizations. Under the Tax Reform Act, every employee would need to resubmit a new Form W-4, *Employee's Withholding Allowance Certificate*, and most forms used in the tax withholding, payment, and reporting process at both the federal and state levels would have to be revised. (4)

Exhibit 17-6: "50th Anniversary Celebration Fair Labor Standards Act 1938-1988;" Payroll Exchange; Volume 12, No. 6; June 1988; p. front cover

Exhibit 17-5: Social Security Celebrates its 50th; Illustration from "Social Security – Partnership with Tomorrow;" Payroll Exchange; Volume 9; No. 6; June 1985; p. 3

Flexible Compensation and Benefit Programs Take Root

Flexible compensation plans were originally developed in the 1960s, but did not gain much recognition until the latter half of the seventies. In the late seventies, after large corporations had begun to implement flexible benefit programs, Congress passed legislation to establish choice-related benefit plans through the enactment of Section 125 of the Internal Revenue Code. (5)

During the eighties, an increasing number of companies began to move toward "cafeteria benefits" by providing a broader selection of flexible benefits tailored to individual employee needs. Under such programs, employers could offer their employees new taxable and non-taxable benefit options, including a Section 401(k) Cash or Deferred Arrangement. Under the 401(k) program, employees could contribute and defer portions of their income to a retirement savings plan and have these deferrals treated as pre-tax dollars. Employers could also contribute to employee 401(k) plans by matching some or all of an employee's contribution.

Because such programs were designed to encourage long term savings, short term access to these funds was limited, although loans could be taken out against 401(k) balances and than repaid. While exempt from federal income tax, these pre-tax contributions to deferred income plans were quickly made subject to Social Security, Medicare, and Federal Unemployment taxes. To further complicate matters, some states and local taxing jurisdictions required 401(k) deferrals to be reported as fully taxable and subject to state income tax withholding. By 1988, approximately 45% of all companies were offering 401(k) plans and another 31% were planning to adopt such programs (Exhibit 17-7).

The impact on the payroll community is captured in an article titled "Deferred Compensation and Cafeteria Plans – Their Effect on the Payroll Profession" appearing in the September 1986 issue of *Payroll Exchange.*

"The implementation of these plans has produced a multitude of difficulties that payroll managers must contend with:"

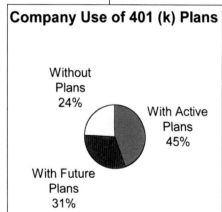

Company Use of 401 (k) Plans

Without Plans 24%

With Active Plans 45%

With Future Plans 31%

Exhibit 17-7: Data for Chart: Company Usage of 401(k) Plans from "Cafeteria Plans;" Levy, Joel F.; Coopers & Lybrand; Payroll Exchange; Volume 12, No. 5; May 1988; p. 6

- Personnel departments charged with the plan administration generally do not have the training to answer tax related questions.

- Accountants not familiar with payroll required laborious payroll training to facilitate a smooth flow of accounting entries and expedite plan reporting requirements to government regulatory agencies.

- Management Information Services (MIS) departments and service bureaus experienced difficulties in programming 401(k) and cafeteria plans which resulted in an inordinate number of errors. These errors created tremendous stress on payroll departments. The resulting domino effect caused incorrect quarterly reports and W-2 forms at year- end." (6)

However, the author goes on to itemize some of the positive benefits that these changes have had on the payroll community:

- "Personnel departments across the country are now working together with payroll people and recognizing the importance of their functions, as well as beginning to use the payroll department's tax knowledge.

- MIS people and service bureaus have developed a greater respect and understanding of payroll operations and have learned not to make any system selections without first consulting with a payroll professional. (6)

In short, although the implementation of these plans initiated headaches for many, the recognition brought to the payroll profession has proven to be outstanding." The author, however, quickly points out that additional headaches (and recognition) are likely to follow as legislation on these types of programs is enacted over the coming years. (6)

Child Support Enforcement Through Mandatory Payroll Withholding

Child support withholding laws had been on the books since 1975 when Congress passed major legislation to establish the Federal/State Child Support Enforcement Program. However, financially abandoned children continued to be a problem. In 1984, Congress enacted stronger legislation that required employers to deduct child support payments from wages upon notice from authorized officials (previously left to the discretion of the court). Employers not complying with authorized orders became liable for such payments. The provision also permitted states to withhold child support from sources of income other than wages. States subsequently passed laws implementing these changes. (7)

"Experience across the nation shows that income withholding is the most effective tool for enforcing child support obligations. It taps the parents' income at its source and becomes a regular deducted item along with other deductions, such as income taxes or Social Security. With regular wage deductions for child support, the children are assured of getting their support payments on time, and in the correct amount. A stable pattern is established over a long period of time. The General Accounting Office, in an October 1983/1984 report to Congress, stated that in its review of 532 cases where wage withholding was used, 74% of the support due was collected, as opposed to 45% for cases where this technique was not used." (7)

While the payroll community was actively supportive, these changes resulted in increased payroll workloads across the country. State specific rules and formulas for withholding, disbursing, and reporting child support payments varied and added to the complexity of the process. Vendors soon began to develop software products to help employers administer these types of programs, and many payroll organizations worked with their respective accounts payable organizations to automate the voucher check request process.

Sick Pay Taxation Rules Change

Effective January 1, 1982, the first six months of sick pay became subject to FICA taxes and employees, employers, and all third parties making payments to workers on the employer's behalf were now liable for the payment of such taxes. Penalties and interest charges for under-withholding were waived for the first six months in response to the uproar over the short notice given to employers and their payroll organizations. (8)

Use of Federal Supplemental Flat Tax Rate Allowed

During this period, the flat 20% withholding rate was introduced to employees, replacing the standard withholding method for "supplemental" payments. (9)

The Beginning of Magnetic Media Reporting

During the early eighties, larger payroll organizations began to file Form 941, *Employer's Quarterly Federal Tax Return*, via magnetic tape rather than paper. (2) Soon, magnetic media reporting of Form W-2 would become compulsory for large employers at both the federal level and in many states.

On the issue of magnetic media reporting, the Acting Commissioner of the Social Security Administration, Martha A. McSteen, had the following to say in addressing the payroll community on the occasion of the SSA's 50th anniversary: "I'd like to tell you that we in Social Security appreciate much that you have done in the area of magnetic media reporting. You are the key to the future of our magnetic tape reporting. We have had a major drive in this past year, and .... 2,500 large employers have agreed to report on magnetic media. This makes a great deal of difference to us. We can post the record much more rapidly, we can compute the benefit much more accurately and completely, up to the time of the filing, and I'm sure that those of you who report on magnetic media now recognize the advantage in your own organization." (3)

Year-End Reporting Can Be a Full-Time Job

Beginning in the eighties, the process of year-end reporting had become a much more significant effort for many companies than it had been in prior years. As a result, senior people with highly specialized payroll tax knowledge and skills were being assigned by more companies to this critical process. "Year-end" tax reporting often extended over a six-month period, from initial preparations beginning in late Fall through W-2 issuance in January and final close out activities in late Spring.

In 1985, the payroll tax experts at Manpower may have broken W-2 volume records. In that year, Manpower, Inc., the world's largest temporary help service, filed 460,348 W-2 forms with the Internal Revenue Service (Exhibit 17-8) and sent a cable to the "Guinness Book of World Records" seeking recognition for this feat. The mass filing and employee W-2 mailing, believed to be the largest of its kind by a private employer in history, was accomplished on the firm's IBM master computer at its world headquarters in Milwaukee, Wisconsin. It took just 120 hours of processing, printing and packaging time. (10)

Exhibit 17-8: W-2 Form Photo/Manpower, Inc. Press Release; "Manpower Seeks Guinness Record for Employee W-2 Count in 1985;" February 1986; Reprinted by permission of Manpower, Inc.

The IRS "Audit"

The practice of government audits of employer records had been around for a long time before the eighties. Over the years, however, the number of federal, state, and local taxing jurisdictions and regulatory bodies had increased to keep

Exhibit 17-9: NACHA Direct Deposit Promotion "SAVE MONEY. ELIMINATE PAYCHECKS;" National Automated Clearing House Association; Payroll Exchange; Volume 14, No. 4; April 1989; p. 7; Courtesy of NACHA – The Electronic Payments Association

pace with the ever more complex body of compensation, benefit, and tax rules. Keeping records and providing data in response to Department of Labor, IRS, and state and local audits were time consuming tasks filled with anxiety for those being audited. Audits were normally conducted for past periods, and retrieving records from old systems and processes that were no longer in place was often very difficult or impossible. Often, those resources responsible for prior periods were no longer employed by the company being audited. All of these factors added to the fear and trepidation that payroll personnel felt when notified of the imminent arrival of "an auditor," especially one from the IRS.

As government reporting requirements increased, more and more payroll information was being placed on Computer Output Microfiche (COM) to facilitate storage and retrieval of government required data. (11)

Banking Update

The 1980s also brought significant changes in the banking arena. By the beginning of the decade, NACHA had established standardized formats for banks and employers to utilize, and magnetic tapes generated by employers, service bureaus, and banks were now moving more and more payroll dollars through the ACH network via direct deposit. (11) During this period, many companies began to realize operational savings and improved operational performance through direct deposit. The eighties represented a significant advancement toward higher levels of direct deposit participation as NACHA (Exhibit 17-9) and payroll organizations jointly began to promote direct deposit use.

Other banking improvements introduced during the eighties, such as the Account Reconciliation Program (ARP) and Check Truncation Program, not only improved banking operations, but also had an important impact on company payroll operations. Through ARP, banks were able to provide company payroll operations with automated check reconciliation data, thereby reducing the headaches associated with the reconciliation of issued and outstanding checks. Check Truncation eliminated the need for the banking community to physically move checks from the cashing bank to the issuing bank. (12)

Many companies and their payroll organizations and supporting programming staffs were stretched during this period to keep up with these banking changes, which also required employer computer and process changes. For example, to take full advantage of efficient direct deposit processing, employers needed to consolidate direct deposit data for all banks and employees onto one magnetic tape instead of separate tapes for each receiving bank; organize the data into the NACHA prescribed format; and include data not previously required like Transit Routing Numbers to identify each employee's receiving bank along with the employee's bank account type code (checking, savings, etc.) and the employee's bank account number. (13)

During the eighties, Automated Teller Machines (ATMs) were also introduced and consumer acceptance and utilization of these new banking machines grew throughout the decade. ATMs had a positive impact on worker acceptance of payroll direct deposit. (12)

Ending the "100 Years War" With Human Resources

While admittedly at least a partial overstatement of the long-term relationship problems between payroll and human resources, this subject received considerable attention during the 1980s as social, regulatory and tax changes impacting both groups forced a closer working relationship (Exhibit 17-10) between these two traditionally separate organizations.

Vendors Begin to Offer Integrated Payroll and Human Resources Software

In addition to those software companies already in existence (such as Cyborg Systems, Integral Systems, MSA, McCormack & Dodge, PDS, and Tesseract) many new software compa-

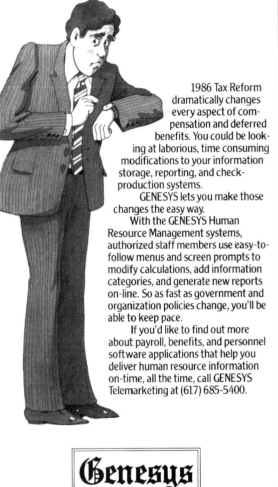

Facing 1986 Tax Reform, Can You Change Compensation and Benefits Programs in Time?

1986 Tax Reform dramatically changes every aspect of compensation and deferred benefits. You could be looking at laborious, time consuming modifications to your information storage, reporting, and check-production systems.

GENESYS lets you make those changes the easy way.

With the GENESYS Human Resource Management systems, authorized staff members use easy-to-follow menus and screen prompts to modify calculations, add information categories, and generate new reports on-line. So as fast as government and organization policies change, you'll be able to keep pace.

If you'd like to find out more about payroll, benefits, and personnel software applications that help you deliver human resource information on-time, all the time, call GENESYS Telemarketing at (617) 685-5400.

Genesys
SOFTWARE SYSTEMS, INC.

20 Ballard Way
Lawrence, MA 01843
(617) 685-5400

Exhibit 17-10: Illustration: "Bridging the Gap;" Artist: Thomas J. Soderberg; Payroll Exchange; Volume 12, No. 8; September 1988; p. front cover

Exhibit 17-11: "Facing 1986 Tax Reform, Can You Change Compensation and Benefits Programs in Time?;" Payroll Exchange; Volume 10. No. 11; December 1986; p. 24; Reprinted by permission of Genesys Software Systems, Inc.

nies like Genesys (Exhibit 17-11) emerged during the 80s.

Software companies, like Tesseract (Exhibit 17-12), marketed software products exclusively to companies with IBM-based mainframes, while a growing number of vendors like Cyborg Systems (Exhibit 17-13) were selling products that could operate on mainframes from different manufacturers. Most software vendors had incorporated "on-line," and "real-time" features in their products and in their advertisements. In recognition of the growing and overlapping relationship between payroll and human resources, software vendors began to emphasize both their payroll and personnel software product offerings.

Since such products rarely met the complete needs of a large complex company, software providers had to work with their clients to customize the software. Conversions or upgrades to new software often required upwards of six to nine months and sometimes longer to implement.

Many companies were still producing their payrolls with software developed in-house during the sixties and seventies. In the eighties, some of these companies began to see the potential cost advantages of purchasing an outside package to gain the benefits of new software architecture.

One such company was the Ford Motor Company. According to Jim Beckett, Ford's Payroll Manager, Ford embarked in 1983 on a three-year project to replace its existing systems with a fully operational on-line Human Resources Information Management System (Payroll/Personnel) using Integral Systems Incorporated (ISI) software. When completed, payroll processing for some 200,000 active and retired employees would continue to be performed centrally, but all wage-related input would be entered at the local (plant) level. (14)

Hewlett-Packard, a computer hardware manufacturer, entered the software market during this period with their payroll product called HPPAY

(Exhibit 17-14); and other software providers who previously had not offered a payroll application product began producing and marketing payroll software products.

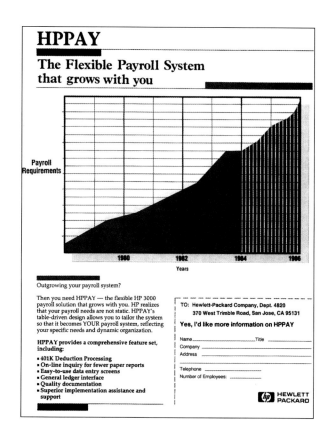

Exhibit 17-15: " The ADP Friendly Takeover – We'll Take Over Your Payroll Headaches;" Payroll Exchange; Volume 11, No. 8; September 1987; p. 9; Reprinted by permission of ADP, Inc.

Exhibit 17-16: "Why Carry the Burden of Payroll Tax Filing Alone?;" Payroll Exchange; Volume 14, No. 10; November 1989; p. outside back cover; Reprinted by permission of ADP, Inc.

Growth of the Service Bureau Industry

By 1987, ADP was close to 40 years old and had more than 150,000 clients (Exhibit 17-15). The service bureau, an entity created in the post-World War II economic boom, had now grown into a multi-billion dollar industry and had expanded its services beyond payroll preparation and accounting to include employment tax reporting, human resources reporting, management and union information reporting, and cost accounting. Slowly, the payroll service bureau industry was beginning to transition into an employment service industry. (11) In addition to early service providers, like ADP, Inc. (Exhibit 17-16), many other such companies were now in existence, with some of them specializing in payroll tax administration products and services (Exhibits 17-17 through 17-19) to assist clients with the growing complexities of federal, state, and local tax reporting and payment.

The Birth of the Modern Time And Attendance Industry

Kronos Incorporated was founded in 1977, by its current CEO and Chairman, Mark S. Ain, who is credited with first merging microchip technol-

ogy with the mechanical time clock, and thereby creating the first intelligent device that could capture, record and add employee hours. The application of microchip technology to traditional time and attendance products not only

Exhibit 17-17: "Payroll Pressure? – For Less Taxing Payroll Preparation, Contact Control Data Business Centers;" Payroll Exchange; Volume 10, No. 5; May 1986; Reprinted by permission of Ceridian Corporation

Modern Time Solution

KRONOS® Timekeeping Systems help you schedule, track and control labor hours *automatically...* from punch-in to paycheck.

Think of the benefits. *Direct* bottom-line benefits. Improved labor management control. Reduced overtime or premium time. Elimination of costly human errors. Increased personnel productivity. Full, custom integration with your current computer systems by the recognized leader in electronic time accounting. If you're in the market, check us out.

Call Toll Free
1-800-225-1561

Time Accounting Systems by **KRONOS**
Because every minute counts.

© 1989 KRONOS, Inc. 62 Fourth Avenue, Waltham, MA 02154
National Sales and Service

enabled the automation of time collection, but also led to the modernization of the time and attendance industry.

From this point forward, time and attendance systems would move away from stand-alone data collection and time accounting systems to frontline workforce devices enabling management to better, plan, schedule, and measure employee work-related data as illustrated by these advertisements from Kronos (Exhibit 17-20) and Simplex (Exhibit 17-21).

Views and Perspectives on Payrolls of the Eighties

Greater Emphasis on Information Impacts the Work of Payroll

In the eighties, payroll managers and their systems were beginning to be viewed more as informational resources (out of business need) than merely as transaction processing managers and systems. Finance, Tax, Human Resource, and Business Managers were now looking for current and historical analytical information regarding worker compensation for a myriad of purposes. Unfortunately, systems of the period were largely designed as transaction processing

systems. Accessing, retrieving, and manipulating payroll-related data was a time consuming and labor intensive function. This need for Decision Oriented Systems and information had a beneficial impact on the role of payroll as it gave many payroll professionals the opportunity to have direct contact with senior members of their organization. Payroll managers began to perceive themselves as "business partners" and be perceived by others as valuable business professionals for the first time in many companies. (15) This need for information also stimulated interest in shared payroll-human resource data

Managing payroll shouldn't keep you from managing people.

It doesn't with the new Atlas System from Simplex. Atlas is a software-based time and attendance recorder that ties into your personal computer. It collects, compiles, and totals employee hours automatically, and puts staff activity reports at your fingertips. You spend your time analyzing the data, not gathering it. You are able to make timely management decisions based on up-to-the-minute employee information.

With the Atlas System, time recording is more efficient. Accuracy is greatly improved. The result is consistent enforcement of your pay policies. And significant cost-cutting along the way.

For more information and a product demonstration, consult the White or Yellow Pages for your local Simplex office. Simplex Time Recorder Co., Gardner, Massachusetts 01441, TEL. (508) 632-2500.

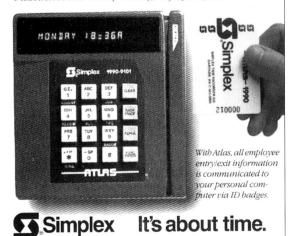

With Atlas, all employee entry/exit information is communicated to your personal computer via ID badges.

bases and integrated systems. Donald M. Bowles, in his article titled "People Systems Now" appearing in the October 1988 issue of *Payroll Exchange*, called for a more aggressive move toward shared information systems, citing it as the only plausible solution to meet the increasing demand for more data and information.

New Payroll Project-Related Roles Created

With larger, more automated payrolls and from experiences gained from the sixties and seventies in "how not to install new automated systems," many new payroll roles were created. Some individuals became managers, analysts or project leaders responsible for the implementation of payroll software and for ongoing revisions, changes, modifications, and enhancements to that software. Structured project management processes and large test files were used more often than in the past to control development and to test new software prior to implementation. (16)

Payroll Roles Become More Technical

One perspective on payroll in the eighties is presented here by Kit Mathews, Personnel Accounting Manager and Assistant Vice President for the Wells Fargo Bank who headed a staff of 32 responsible for the payment of 20,000 interstate employees. The organization was responsible for human resources and payroll processing, key input, general ledger balancing, tax reporting, and payments on a company-wide basis.

"Payroll has become a highly technical field in the past ten years. Dealing with complex tax regulations requires a good working knowledge of both Federal and state tax laws, as well as an ability to interpret these laws in individual cases where any errors could result in substantial penalties to the company. This is especially true for large multi-state companies dealing with many local taxes."

"In the past, training of entry level Payroll employees was straight-forward and took a minimum amount of time. Now, with the sophisticated laws and systems used in the payroll field, training is ongoing and complex. One of the most valuable assets to any Payroll Manager is having knowledgeable and reliable Data Processing support, because Payroll breakdowns are critical and usually occur in the middle of the night."

"Over the past few years, management has had to examine its thinking regarding the Payroll Department. This is especially true in regards to priorities of systems commitment and cost

Exhibit 17-21: "Simplex - It's About Time;" Payroll Exchange; Volume 14, No. 3; March 1989; p. 14; Reprinted by permission of Simplex Corporation

Exhibit 17-22: "Payroll People Speak Out;" Payroll Exchange; Volume 10; No. 5; May 1986; p. 19

enhancements. Many companies have had to reevaluate payroll positions since what was once a clerical-level position is now regarded as highly technical."

"To many people, Payroll is a thankless job, despite personal rewards. Employees rarely consider complimenting anyone in Payroll for getting them an accurate and timely paycheck. However, if anything is incorrect, it's always the Payroll Department's fault. Rarely do employees consider how much of the information is submitted by and dependent on other departments. If employees could only see the many extra things being done to insure that their pay is proper, they might understand the Payroll Manager better."

"The factor of major importance to the Payroll Manager is the Payroll staff. I have been fortunate to have had the pleasure of working with many fine dedicated Payroll technicians. The Payroll Department must work as a team at all times. The processing of Payroll cannot be left to a later date due to someone who is on vacation or ill. This may require the entire unit to pitch in and help each other. Many areas can have impact on an individual Payroll and may require last minute overtime for checks to be received on time. Again a dedicated and cooperative staff is essential." (17)

Payroll Managers Speak Out on The Challenges of the Eighties

The challenges that payroll managers and organizations faced in the eighties focused largely on keeping pace with regulatory changes. These feelings are fairly represented by the comments of the following three payroll professionals from Indiana, Missouri, and North Carolina as captured in the May 1986 issue of *Payroll Exchange*. (Exhibit 17-22)

On the Lighter Side – Through The Eyes of Payroll Managers With a Sense of Humor

Humor has played an important role in the payroll profession. Many successful payroll employees over the years have developed a keen sense of humor that has enabled them and others to deal with the pressure and stress of the job. Following are two examples.

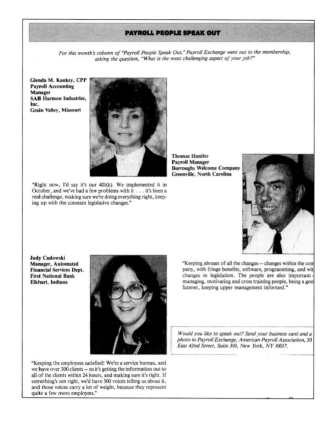

PAYROLL PEOPLE SPEAK OUT

For this month's column of "Payroll People Speak Out," Payroll Exchange went out to the membership, asking the question, "What is the most challenging aspect of your job?"

Glenda M. Kankey, CPP
Payroll Accounting
Manager
SAB Harmon Industries, Inc.
Grain Valley, Missouri

"Right now, I'd say it's our 401(k). We implemented it in October, and we've had a few problems with it . . . it's been a real challenge, making sure we're doing everything right, keeping up with the constant legislative changes."

Thomas Hanifer
Payroll Manager
Burroughs Welcome Company
Greenville, North Carolina

"Keeping abreast of all the changes — changes within the company, with fringe benefits, software, programming, and with changes in legislation. The people are also important - managing, motivating and cross training people, being a good listener, keeping upper management informed."

Judy Cudowski
Manager, Automated
Financial Services Dept.
First National Bank
Elkhart, Indiana

Would you like to speak out? Send your business card and a photo to Payroll Exchange, American Payroll Association, 50 East 42nd Street, Suite 301, New York, NY 10017.

"Keeping the employees satisfied! We're a service bureau, and we have over 300 clients — so it's getting the information out to all of the clients within 24 hours, and making sure it's right. If something's not right, we'd have 300 voices telling us about it, and those voices carry a lot of weight, because they represent quite a few more employees."

Sam McLaughlin and "A Computer With a Mind of Its Own"

Automated payrolls of the 1980s helped to make payroll work possible, but not necessarily easy! Technology made it feasible to pay more employees with fewer resources. At the same time this new technology added complexity. Sometimes, it would even seem to the payroll manager of the day that the "computer had a personality and mind of its own." (18)

Howard Freedman and "The Many Hats a Payroll Professional Wears in a Day"

Howard Freedman, CPP has often helped the payroll profession put things in proper perspective through the use of humor. In an article appearing in the October 1987 issue of Payroll Exchange, Howard presents a view of contemporary payroll processes and personnel. While humorous, there is much truth in "The Many Hats a Payroll Professional Wears in a Day." In one 24-hour period, Howard presents the payroll professional as thinker, service representative, analyst, banker, psychologist, diplomat, fireman, writer, interpreter, lawyer, CPA, media-

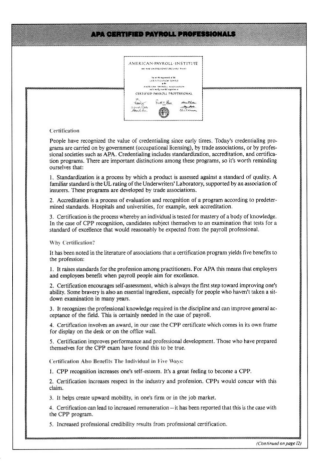

Exhibit 17-23: "APA Certified Payroll Professionals;" Payroll Exchange; Volume 11, No. 6; June 1987; p. 11

Exhibit 17-24: "APA Certified Payroll Professionals;" Payroll Exchange; Volume 11, No. 6; June 1987; p. 12

tor, labor relations specialist, compensation specialist, philanthropist, accountant, industrial engineer, creative thinker, psychiatrist, surgeon, anesthesiologist, professor, auditor, rubbish collector, parolee, dreamer and folk hero, and finally as an insomniac who, at 2:00 a.m. the following morning, has trouble sleeping after reading that last tax bulletin!" (19)

End of a Decade – and Payroll Comes of Age

By the end of the decade, the payroll profession, in general, had made significant progress. This advancement can be attributed to a number of factors.

The business world had become more complex than it was 10 years earlier and new requirements demanded change. As a result, employers began to recognize the importance of the payroll function and to value and respect those responsible for payroll. This led to companies upgrading payroll job classifications and making investments in payroll/human resources and supporting technology.

Computer hardware and software products and services also advanced significantly and enabled employers and their payroll business and technical staffs to respond better to external forces within shorter timeframes. These new tools triggered changes in both the pay process and in the profession.

Added to the above, the formation of the American Payroll Association brought standards

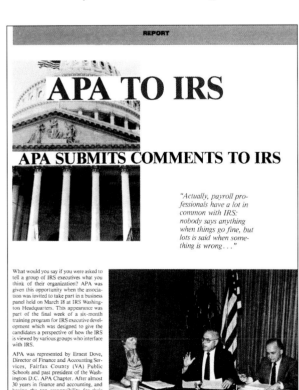

Ellen Murphy, Ernest Dove, Charles T. Rau of MCI Telecommunications.

Exhibit 17-25: "APA to IRS – APA Submits Comments to IRS;" Payroll Exchange; Volume 11, No. 5; May 1987; pp. 6-7

183

Exhibit 17-26: "Government/Public Sector Conference: A Huge Success in Washington;" Payroll Exchange; Volume 11, No. 10; November 1987; p. 7

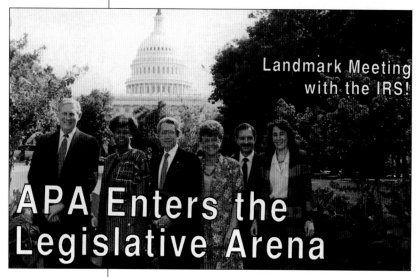

Exhibit 17-27: "APA Enters the Legislative Arena;" Payroll Exchange; Volume 12, No. 11; November 1988; p. 5

Exhibit 17-28: "Letter from the White House;" Payroll Exchange; Volume 11, No. 7; July/August 1987; p. 4

jects and less on reactive themes. Attention was being given to how to manage and influence change, how to anticipate and plan, how to communicate and resolve conflict, how to improve operational performance and customer service, etc.

In addition, much more attention was being given to training, education and career planning than ever before in the history of the payroll profession. Within less than 10 years, the American Payroll Association had implemented a professional certification program (Exhibit 17-23) that was helping hundreds of payroll employees to learn and grow in their profession (Exhibit 17-24). In February 1985 the first examination was administered in 56 cities throughout the U.S. Over 469 payroll employees passed the examination to become the first Certified Payroll Professionals in the U.S.

In addition, instead of merely responding to external forces, as had largely been the case in the past, payroll professionals, with the support and leadership of the Association, were now beginning to meet with government agencies such as the IRS (Exhibits 17-25 and 17-26) to share and exchange ideas. It was not long afterwards that those in government began to solicit input from members of the payroll community, seeking their advice on key issues of the day. By the end of the decade, the American Payroll Association had officially entered the legislative arena by expanding beyond its initial educational charter. (Exhibit 17-27).

The growing importance of the payroll industry was given high level recognition when President Ronald Reagan wrote the following letter to payroll professionals on March 10, 1987 (Exhibit 17-28) on the occasion of the American Payroll Association's Fifth Annual Congress.

As further confirmation of the growing recognition being given to the payroll industry, resolutions were submitted by Congressman Bill Green and Senator Daniel Moynihan to the House of Representatives and Senate, respectively, during the month of September 1989 proposing that January 31, 1990 be declared "National Payroll Practitioner Appreciation Day." (20)

Yes, payroll had indeed come a long way in a relatively short time period.

and consistency while providing communications, education and focus on the key issues of the day. By the end of the eighties, the payroll profession had developed a collective feeling of confidence.

This growing confidence was reflected in the themes and subjects covered in APA trade publications and association meetings of the late eighties, which focused more on proactive sub-

---

THE WHITE HOUSE

WASHINGTON

March 10, 1987

It gives me great pleasure to extend warm greetings to the members of the American Payroll Association as you gather from across our Nation for your Fifth Annual Congress.

The American Payroll Association plays a vital role in helping to make sure we enjoy a healthy economy and prosperous society. A key to our commitment to sustained economic growth and greater opportunity for all Americans is carrying out fair and equitable tax reform that will provide incentives for employment, savings, investment and innovation. I know that your daily involvement with tax issues, and your vital efforts to educate and oversee compliance with new regulations, will help bring that about. Thanks to the efforts of honest and hard working Americans, our Republic continues to reap the benefits of a revitalized free enterprise system that makes our prosperity possible.

Nancy joins me in sending all of you our best wishes for a memorable occasion. God bless you.

Ronald Reagan

Reference Sources

1. "Spotlight on Donald W. Sharper;" Maddux, Dan, Associate Editor; Payroll Exchange; APA; New York; March 1984; Volume 8; No.3; pp. 11-14

2. "Annual Payroll Management Subscriber Survey: Phase II Summary;" Payroll Exchange; AMR; New York; January, 1982; Volume 6, No. 1; p. 1-4

3. "Social Security – Partnership with Tomorrow;" Extract of Speech delivered by Acting Commissioner, SSA, McSteen, Martha; Payroll Exchange; APA; New York; June 1985; Volume 9; Number 6; pp. 3-4

4. "Payroll Points – Federal Facts;" Westphal, Teresa; Payroll Exchange; APA; New York; January 1987; Volume 11; No. 1; pp. 6-7

5. "Flexible Compensation Plans Offer Menu of Benefits for Today's Workforce;" Wujcik; Tim; Payroll Exchange; April 1988; Volume 12; No.4; pp. 10-11

6. "Deferred Compensation and Cafeteria Plans - Their Effect on the Payroll Profession;" Payroll Exchange; Glus, George; September 1986; Volume 11; No. 8; p. 9

7. "The Child Support Enforcement Program;" Extract from speech delivered by Deputy Director, Office of Child Support Enforcement, U.S. Department of Health and Human Services; Payroll Exchange; APA; New York; July/August 1986; Volume 10; No. 7; pp. 10-11

8. "FICA Taxes on Sick Pay: Business in an Uproar;" Payroll Exchange; APA; New York; March 1982; Volume 6; No. 3; p. 1

9. "Flat 20% Withholding Rate Allowed for Supplemental Portion of Combined Wage Payment;" Neumark, Avery E.; Payroll Exchange; APA; New York; May 1983; Volume 7; No.5; p. 2

10. "Manpower Seeks Guinness Record for Employee W-2 Count;" Manpower, Inc. Press Release; Office of the President; February 1986

11. "Future Shock – The Evolution of the New Employment Service Industry;" Payroll Exchange; APA, New York; February 1982; Volume 6; No. 2; pp. 1-2

12. "Payroll-Banking Integration: The Birth of Employment Services;" Payroll Exchange; APA; New York; March 1982; Volume 6; No.3; pp. 2-4

13. "Automatic Deposit of Payroll Checks;" Dilgard, Robert C.; Payroll Exchange; APA; New York; October 1982; Volume 6; No. 10; p. 2

14. "Spotlight on Jim Beckett;" Payroll Exchange; APA; New York; January 1983; Volume 7; No. 1; p. 5

15. "Building Decision-Oriented Management Systems;" Payroll Exchange; APA; New York; April 1982; Volume 6; No. 4; pp. 2-4

16. "Bill Sentnor: A Payroll Manager is First and Foremost a Politician;" Payroll Exchange; APA; New York; October 1982; Volume 6; No. 10; p. 3

17. "Spotlight on Kit Mathews;" Payroll Exchange; APA; New York; November 1982; Volume 6; No. 11; pp. 3-4

18. "Spotlight on Sam McLaughlin; Computer with a Mind of Its Own;" Payroll Exchange; APA ; New York; July 1983; Volume 7; No. 7; p. 5

19. "The Many Hats a Payroll Professional Wears in a Day;" Freedman, Howard; Payroll Exchange; October 1987; Volume 11, No. 9; pp. 10-12

20. "Announcing National Payroll Practitioner Appreciation Day!;" Payroll Exchange; APA; New York; December 1989; Volume 14; No. 11; p. 12

CHAPTER 18:
The Nineties — Leaping Toward the New Millennium

The Payroll Environment of the Nineties

The last decade of the twentieth century was truly an exciting one. The demand for change was great. The pace of change was rapid. The state of technology was often beyond the ability of users to comprehend and apply. The pressure to do more with less permeated "the air" of almost every business and much of what was happening in corporations and in government was impacting payroll. Payroll professionals, consistent with their performance track record throughout history, jumped in and faced the challenges head on. Some failed. Most succeeded. Some excelled. By the end of the decade, the payroll profession was stronger than ever and payroll practitioners had earned their "stripes" many times over.

Major Trends and Issues of the 1990s

Focus on Total Quality Management

Total Quality Management (TQM) was a driving force during the nineties and included, among other things, benchmarking activities and best practice studies and seminars. Through these efforts many companies and their payroll organizations, for the first time, were able to step outside of their existing four walls and learn from others better ways of performing payroll.

Qualitative and quantitative (especially cost) comparisons represented a big portion of this work. A number of consulting firms like A.T. Kearney, The Hackett Group, and Gunn Partners provided important leadership during this period and, along with the American Payroll Association, helped companies to fully understand their challenges and their opportunities.

Businesses Begin to Look at End-To-End Processes

Some very important insights were obtained from benchmarking, best practices, continuous improvement, and process re-engineering. Most importantly, these efforts identified the need for companies to look beyond individual functions and to see the greater opportunities made available by looking at the entire end-to-end process. For the first time, many companies began to fully understand that Payroll and Human Resources were not separate functions but instead were parts of a single larger employee-related process that extended from point of hire to point of retirement. As a result of this realization, integrated employee-related process planning became a major theme of the 1990s.

Downsizing and Its Cousin "Rightsizing"

Much of the interest in Total Quality Management methodologies (and end-to-end processes) in the 1990s was rooted in the desire (and need) to reduce costs to maintain a competitive edge. Companies with problems in growing revenue were extremely focused on reducing operating costs during this period. Large organizations and costly processes (such as those often associated with payroll, benefits, and human resource administration) became prime candidates for headcount reductions.

Cost reduction was a major focus in the 1990s. Reduction in headcount was the strategy and TQM was often used (or misused) as the tool to achieve the objective.

As it turned out, companies that were truly interested in improving the process obtained increased efficiencies and lower headcount as a by-product. Those that used TQM only as a means for reducing headcount often ended up with more operational problems than they started with.

Shared Service Centers Seen by Many as THE Solution

In response to all of the above, companies began to move aggressively to consolidate, standardize and upgrade their systems, and in the process, many began to adopt the shared service center concept as a more cost effective method for delivering financial and non-financial services to their internal business clients. Such organizations became expertise centers and were chartered with the delivery of high quality, low cost products and services to their internal business clients. Focus on customers increased with a greater emphasis on performance metrics, customer satisfaction, cost of product, and client service level agreements.

Service bureaus began to offer expanded services to support this concept as well and some companies elected to use third-party providers to deliver employee-related services to their business clients.

Haunted by the Past – The Y2K Problem

For all of their technological sophistication, the 1990s provided an important lesson about dependencies on the past. As companies prepared for the new millennium, a warning voice was raised regarding what would later be called the "Y2K" problem (Exhibit 18-1). By the end of the decade, billions of dollars would have to be spent by governments, businesses, and consumers alike around the world to correct outdated software that prohibited the use of dates beyond 1999. Companies that could not move all of their systems to new Y2K compliant solutions fast enough were compelled to retrofit their existing programs. Those that could afford to bring systems into compliance would still carry the knowledge of their dependence on other computer systems around the world. Some predicted massive global failures. Others were more optimistic. The race was on and time was running out. While initial results were encouraging and the

Exhibit 18-1: Y2K Image: "APA Works to Ease Y2K Crunch for Payroll;" PVN, American Payroll Association; Volume 5, Issue 6; December 1998; p. 2

money seems well spent, historians will evaluate the final outcome.

While the Y2K problem is fairly simple to state, it has been complex and costly to repair. "The problem – computer software which recognizes years only by the last two digits – is widespread and difficult to fix because datelines are buried throughout interlocking software systems, applications, and programs. Any computerized tasks requiring date-dependent computations or comparisons, such as computing interest, determining length of service or calculating retirement benefits can be affected by the Year 2000 problem. The problem involves not only plan record keeping systems, but also such systems as employer payrolls that interface with plans and other systems essential to plan operations." (1)

A Continuous Stream of Acquisitions and Mergers

Throughout the nineties, there was a steady increase in the number of business acquisitions and mergers. This phenomenon occurred in all industries and often created both problems and opportunities for the payroll, human resource, and benefits-related personnel of the predecessor and successor. Workloads often shifted and administrative processes within both companies were often consolidated and moved from one location to another. These monumental events were often seen as ideal times to re-engineer processes and upgrade antiquated systems, thereby adding to the pressure of the acquisition or merger. As a result, many payroll organizations and personnel were displaced. At the same time, an equal number inherited larger and more complex workloads and were stretched to keep pace with existing processes while understanding and absorbing the new work in the time frames required.

Movement Away From Paper

Government Lends Support for Electronic Filing and Reporting

During the 1990s, real progress was made in methods of reporting in both the private and public sectors. At the federal level, the IRS took the first step toward replacing the paper W-4

Form by permitting employees to change certain data on the form electronically. (2)

"Employers have been able to file wage reports electronically using SSA's Online Wage Reporting Bulletin Board Service (OWRBBS) for several years using the diskette TIB-4 format. Electronic filers have steadily increased. In Tax Year 1997, over 2.2 million electronic Form W-2s were submitted, more than a 30% increase over the prior year. In 1999, SSA began to phase in the implementation of its new Magnetic Media Reporting and Electronic Filing record formats. By the year 2001 all employers will be required to use these new formats." (3)

By 1996, payroll professionals could also receive tax help from the IRS via their new World Wide Web homepage. Users could access tax forms and publications and receive individual and company taxpayer assistance online. (4)

Employers and Employees Embrace Direct Deposit

By late 1998, based on independent surveys conducted by both NACHA (Exhibit 18-2) and the APA, direct deposit had became the number one method of payment. According to APA findings, 81% of those paid semimonthly, 71% of employees paid monthly, 58% of those paid biweekly, and 25% of those paid weekly were paid via direct deposit.

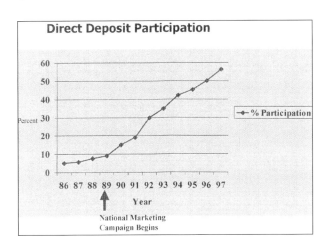

This shift in payment method not only helped improve the accuracy and timeliness of pay delivery but also enabled employers to offer their employees more services. For example, technology now permitted employers to allocate employee net pay (based on employee instructions) to multiple bank accounts (checking, sav-

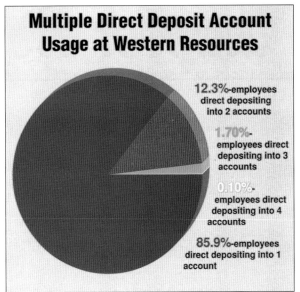

ings, etc.) as illustrated in this Western Resources graph (Exhibit 18-3).

Electronic Pay Statements Begin To Replace Paper

Given the higher direct deposit participation levels, a number of companies began to capitalize on this transition to electronic pay delivery by replacing paper pay deposit statements with electronic notifications via internally developed solutions. Companies with large populations, such as IBM, Mobil Oil, and Texas Instruments, were among the first high profile companies to act on this opportunity. The elimination of paper not only helped to reduce the cost of the payroll, but also provided employees with higher levels of service.

Expanding Beyond Domestic Boundaries

Banking Community Moves to Support Cross-Border Payments

The Cross-Border Council of the National Automated Clearing House Association (NACHA) approved the first set of Cross-Border Payment Rules in December 1995, thereby providing a legal, technical, and operational framework for the exchange of electronic business-to-individual credit payments between Canada and the United States. Under these Rules, employers could begin to send ACH payments, such as those related to payroll direct deposit, between the two countries. (5)

Exhibit 18-3: Western Resources Direct Deposit Graph; "Targeted Campaigns + Payroll Enthusiasm = Increased Direct Deposit at Western Resources;" Tom Tucker; PAYTECH, American Payroll Association; New York, NY; Volume 5, Issue 1; January/February 1996; pp. 48-49; Courtesy of Western Resources

Exhibit 18-2: "Graph of Direct Deposit Historical Participation Rates;" 1999; Courtesy of NACHA – The Electronic Payments Association

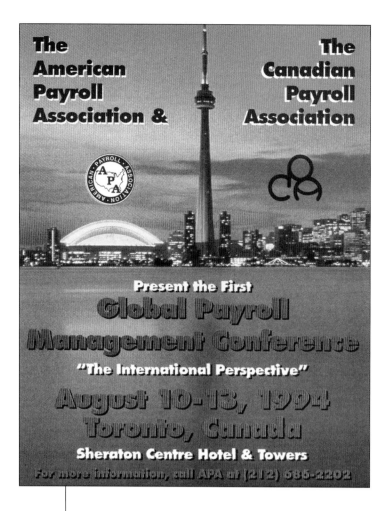

The
American
Payroll
Association &

The
Canadian
Payroll
Association

Present the First

Global Payroll
Management Conference

"The International Perspective"

August 10-13, 1994
Toronto, Canada

Sheraton Centre Hotel & Towers

For more information, call APA at (212) 686-2202

Exhibit 18-4: "Global Payroll Management Conference;" PVN; Volume 2, Issue 3; June 1994; p. 8

Exhibit 18-5: Image extract from "ADP introduces control over payroll that's ready when you are!"; PAYTECH; Volume 2, Issue 1; January/February 1993; p. 5; Reprinted in edited form by permission of ADP, Inc.

190

Professional Employer Organizations (PEOs) Arrive

"Launched in the 1970s, PEOs were created to help companies manage complex human resource matters – medical benefits, workers' compensation claims, payroll, etc. In an arrangement commonly known as 'employee leasing,' the PEO puts a client company's employees onto its own payroll, becoming their administrative employer and assuming an array of human resource functions. The client company remains the worksite employer, responsible for overseeing employees' day-to-day activities and 'care and custody' issues." The process seems to work best for companies with fewer than 500 employees, and while PEO volumes continued to grow in the nineties, larger companies still preferred more traditional solutions. (6)

Technological Wonders to Behold!

While the 1980s brought many technological advances, it was in retrospect only a prelude to those that would follow in the 1990s. The final decade before the new millennium brought with it a proliferation of powerful off-the-shelf desktop computers with a dazzling array of supporting hardware and software. Users could now view standardized monitor screens complete with color and sound. They could more easily execute commands either by striking a single key on a keyboard (Exhibit 18-5) or by using a graphical user interface (GUI), and with the aid of a "mouse" point and click on an icon (picture). Software companies provided a multitude of programs that could run on personal and laptop Local Area Network (LAN) PCs using

Employers Begin to Adopt Global Payroll Models

With the globalization of business in full swing and with a general movement toward the shared service center concept, U.S. companies with workers in multiple countries began to seriously look beyond country-based service models to regional and world-wide service models. Armed with more robust hardware, integrated employee-related software and improved banking capabilities, many international companies began to formally investigate and act on plans to deliver integrated payroll, human resource, and benefit administration services from consolidated locations. In recognition of this trend and to assist payroll professionals faced with expanding responsibilities, the American Payroll Association and The Canadian Payroll Association held the first Global Payroll Management Conference in Toronto, Canada in August 1994 (Exhibit 18-4).

client/server technology that could connect a variety of front-end tools, hardware platforms, networks, and databases into a single integrated set of applications.

Most importantly, users within a company or around the world could now communicate easily with each other, share data, and access information in ways never before possible. Company intranets and the Internet (in the form of e-mail and the World Wide Web) quickly opened up new possibilities for conducting business. New industries and processes were created to enable companies to utilize and leverage these new capabilities.

Seemingly overnight, that which seemed impossible only a few years earlier was now not only possible but also essential to the survival of many businesses. Not since the movement of work from farm to factory had such profound changes occurred. Every aspect of business would be impacted directly or indirectly by these fundamental changes. Some companies began to operate as "virtual corporations" with work teams, telecommuting, and computer networks eliminating all vestiges of the traditional organization that no longer added value to the customer. (7).

An Avalanche of Vendor Payroll-Related Products and Services

Vendors quickly applied this emerging technology and responded with new and updated products and services to solve and meet the unique problems and needs of the 1990s (Exhibit 18-6).

Payroll Software Advances to a New Level

Software vendors, who in the past were selling payroll or human resource specific software designed for mainframes (often limited to specific hardware environments), were now developing and marketing integrated human resource-payroll-benefit-time and attendance packages that could function in a number of operating environments. PeopleSoft was one of the first companies (in 1989) to offer a client/server application. By the end of the decade, with the availability of more powerful servers, virtually all companies were offering products and services for use in the client-server environment. Existing and new soft-

ware vendors emphasized the flexibility of their products to accommodate both growth and change. Software was now being built around user controlled and rules-based tables to eliminate needless programming and support rapid change across the enterprise. Shared data bases and on-line, real time products helped to eliminate redundant data entry and storage while providing rapid access to more accurate and timely information by authorized individuals through user-customized screens. Traditional programming languages (such as COBOL) were being replaced with new languages. A sampling of vendor software products of the 90s (Exhibits 18-7 through 18-14) gives evidence of the growing sophistication of software and the payroll function in general.

Specialized Payroll Software Products Assist the Payroll Professional

During the 1990s, many began to view payroll as not one function but a collection of many sub-functions and processes. As a result, specialized software products, beyond those already in place, were introduced, such as year-end tax reporting software to produce W-2c's as well as W-2s (Exhibit 18-15), tax administration products (Exhibit 18-16), penalty avoidance software (Exhibit 18-17), and wage attachment products, as well as tax withholding, payment and reporting tools (Exhibit 18-18).

Disk (Exhibit 18-19), CD-ROM (Exhibit 18-20) and Document Image Processing technology facilitated the storage and retrieval of payroll information, records, and forms. Seemingly overnight, paper reference manuals were replaced with electronic guides along with decision-making tools that enabled users to find

Exhibit 18-6: Image of Trends in Payroll Technology from "Kicking the Paper Habit in the Payroll Department;" Becker, Sandy; PVN; Volume 6, Issue 1; February 1998; p. 6:

answers to complex payroll-related problems and questions rapidly.

Pressure-seal forms, (Exhibit 18-21) along with magnetic ink character recognition (MICR) and desktop laser printers, made it much easier to produce out-of-cycle payments, and many new products were introduced throughout the 1990s to tap this market.

Time and Attendance Solutions Characterize Technology of the Nineties

Perhaps no area better characterizes the state of technology during the last decade of the twentieth century than that of the time and attendance industry. The industry quickly recognized that no one front-end solution would be sufficient to meet the diverse needs of its clients. Time and attendance systems of the 1990s, therefore, utilized all of the latest technologies to provide businesses with an endless variety of tools to reduce the time and cost of capturing and processing worker time.

Data entry devices as illustrated (Exhibits 18-22 through 18-27) ranged from stationary electronic time clocks using bar-coded employee identification cards, to hand-held keyboard devices, to interactive voice response (IVR) systems, to Web-based tools, and even to biometrics, such as devices using employee hand dimensions (Exhibit 18-28).

Time and attendance tools of the 1990s were no longer designed as "stand-alone" systems that depended on file transfer capabilities to a payroll system or service provider. Instead, time and attendance systems were smart systems with front-end validations and calculation capabilities installed locally, with responsibility for data entry and editing residing with local management. Centralized payroll organizations maintained overall accountability for database integrity and overall administration of the entire system. (8)

Time and attendance systems had become more open in that more and more of these tools could not only accept input from a variety of front-end devices but could also interface with other standard computer applications (such as Microsoft Office). A good application also possessed the ability to download employee attendance data to local spreadsheets or databases for purposes of consolidation and analysis.

Movement in these products had also been away from proprietary networked environments to single user, network, and client-server versions that could support future changes in operating systems platforms without requiring changes on the part of the end user. (9)

Partnerships and Alliances Abound

Since no one vendor or service provider was expert in all of these emerging technologies, the trend during this period was toward partnerships and alliances. Under these new relationships, vendors were able to broaden and strengthen their product offerings and therefore increase their market potential.

Focus on Employee Self-Service (ESS) Tools

During the 1990s, a combination of business and technical forces and enablers resulted in the creation of a new process model in which the employee would play a key role. Under the Employee Self-Service model, employees were given much greater ownership of the maintenance and updating of their personal data, including everything from home address changes, to benefit choices, to banking options. Previously, these types of changes were dependent on the completion of forms and the review, approval, and data entry of information on these forms by others including payroll, human resources and benefits personnel. Two key tools made this shift in ownership and improvement in process possible.

Using IVR Technology to Reduce Labor and Costs and Improve Customer Service

As a supplement to PC-based self-service tools, many companies turned to the use of Interactive Voice Response systems as a way of improving payroll and human resource-related services.

One of the first companies to employ this technology within payroll was Digital Equipment Corporation. Designed as an Employee Self-Service tool, Digital's "PAYEEphone" permitted its employees to enroll, change, or stop direct deposit as well as access current week pay information twenty-four hours a day. Following its initial introduction in 1992, it proved so successful that the service was later expanded to provide additional services. Other companies soon followed. (10)

Companies such as the TALX Corporation have applied interactive voice response systems to develop services (Exhibit 18-29) that unburden payroll and human resource organizations from the time consuming task of providing employment and salary verification information to third parties (such as lenders, perspective employers, government agencies, etc.). Through touch tone telephones and now through the Internet, authorized requesters can obtain data quickly while protecting the security of the employer and the privacy of the employee.

Tapping the Internet and the Intranet

Technology allowed companies to achieve the "do more with less" paradigm. The Internet (e-mail and the Web) made it possible for companies to reduce costs and improve employee service. The Web became a great source of reference information for payroll professionals and provided a great communication vehicle for discussing problems and getting information. Intranets provided a secure intra-company network based on the same technology used in the Internet. They utilized a Web browser to connect PCs to servers, thus permitting employees to review, transmit, and share information that was once paper-based. Forms were obtained by employees and completed electronically, from work or home. Benefit enrollment, direct deposit, and personal profile data could all be submitted and approved electronically, saving enormous amounts of time and money for everyone while speeding up the process. "With the Intranet, the employee did not have to spend valuable time at work calling various departments. Also, printing and distribution costs for forms were eliminated, duplicate data entry was eliminated, the cycle time was shortened, and personnel time was saved." Because getting up a corporate Intranet was more expensive, many vendors modified their products to enable their clients to use these tools on the Internet to perform similar types of functions.

Kiosks or employee service centers were also used to provide similar services to those employees without direct access to a personal computer. (11)

Competition Between In-house And Service Bureau Solutions Increases

While newer technologies made payroll easier and less expensive to perform in-house, new compensation, benefit and tax laws added complexity to the function. These conflicting forces provided fertile ground on which both software companies and service providers could promote their solutions (Exhibits 18-30 through 18-33). As a result, many companies re-evaluated their approaches to employee process-related services during the 1990s with some choosing one direction and others a different one. Outsourcing clearly made some inroads during the nineties, especially in areas of benefits administration and ancillary services such as payroll tax administration and employee verification services.

Ceridian – A Payroll Service Provider with a Link to the Past

Ceridian Employer Services was created in 1992. However, its roots go back to 1932 and the IBM Service Bureau Company. Like a number of other present day enterprises, Ceridian was not created from scratch, but rather evolved over an extended period of time. In 1957, the Control Data Corporation, a company that would become a leader in scientific computing, was founded. Through acquisitions, the company moved into the data services arena in the late fifties and then into computer-based services in the late sixties. Through a 1968 settlement of an antitrust suit with IBM, Control Data acquired IBM's Service Bureau Company, one of the earliest service bureau businesses in the United States. This portion of the business was to become a forerunner of the contemporary Ceridian Employer Services, a business unit within the modern day Ceridian Corporation.

Courtesy of the Ceridian Corporation

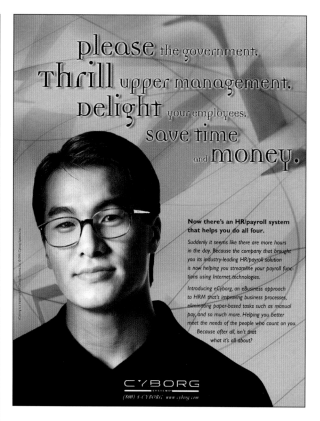

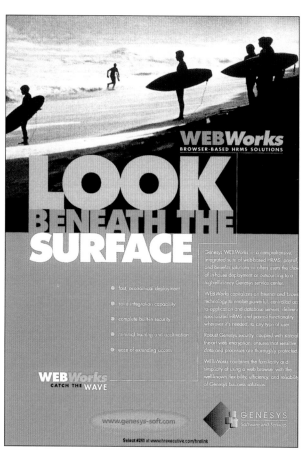

Exhibit 18-11: "When it comes to controlling and managing PAYROLL/PERSONNEL/BENEFITS costs....;" PVN; Volume 1, Issue 1; October 1993; p. 3; Reprinted by permission of PDS

Exhibit 18-12: "Client/server business applications – there's a big difference between talking about it and delivering it. PeopleSoft delivers;" PAYTECH; Volume 2, Issue 2; March/April 1993; p.11; Reprinted by permission of PeopleSoft

Exhibit 18-13: "SAP makes Human Resources as easy as humanly possible;" PAYTECH; Volume 6, Issue 6; November/December 1997; Reprinted by permission of SAP

Exhibit 18-14: "One of these employees is likely to quit. Do you know which one?" PAYTECH; Volume 8, Issue 5; September/October 1999; p. 3; Reprinted by permission of Ultimate Software Group

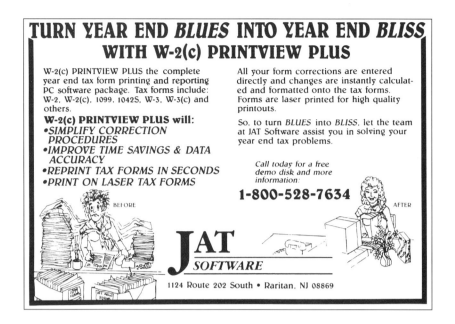

Exhibit 18-18: "Hot New Releases for 1996;" PVN; Volume 4, Issue 1; February 1996; p. back cover; Reprinted by permission of FLS Corporation

Exhibit 18-19: "Meet your new Payroll Assistant;" PVN; Volume 2, Issue 5; October 1994; p. back cover; NOTE: Product advertised no longer offered. Telephone number listed no longer valid; Reprinted by permission of CCH for historical purposes only.

Exhibit 18-20: "Introducing BNA's Payroll Library on CD;" PVN; Volume 2; Issue 3; June 1994; p. 11; Reprinted by permission of the Bureau of National Affairs, Incorporated

Exhibit 18-21: Pressure Seal Pay Check Form (1996), Reprinted by permission of Moore North America, Inc.

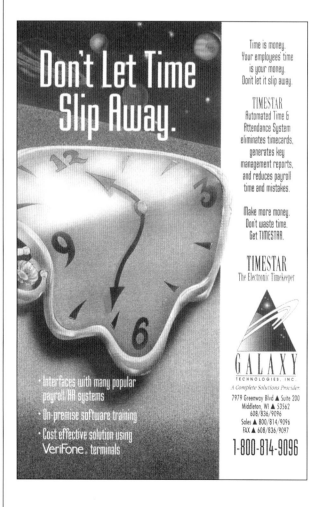

Exhibit 18-26: "It Punches, Bytes And Kicks Out Payroll;" PAYTECH; Volume 5, Issue 2; March/April 1996; p. 11; Reprinted by permission of Lathem Time

Exhibit 18-27: "You Couldn't Be Happier;" PAYTECH; Volume 8, Issue 2; March/April 1999; p. 47; Reprinted by permission of Simplex

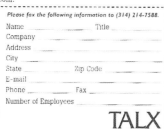

Exhibit 18-29: "Payroll Managers Who Use The Work Number® to Automate Employment Verifications Have One Less Ball to Juggle...;" PAYTECH; APA, New York; Volume 7, Issue 3; May/June 1998; p. 25; Reprinted by permission of the TALX Corporation

Exhibit 18-28: "Use It ... Or Lose It!" PAYTECH; Volume 5, Issue 1; January/February 1996; p. 23; Reprinted by permission of Recognition Systems, Inc.

The History of Payroll in the U.S.

Exhibit 18-30: "This year, one out of three companies who tackle their own payroll taxes will get hit with a penalty;" PAYTECH; Volume 5, Issue 1; July/August 1996; p. 5; Reprinted by permission of ADP, Inc.

Exhibit 18-31: "Looking For A Better Way To Be In Two Places At Once?" PVN; Volume 2, Issue 2; April 1994; p. back cover; Reprinted by permission of Ceridian

Exhibit 18-32: "Your Business Is Not About Payroll Taxes – Ours Is;" PAYTECH; Volume 5, Issue 4; July/August 1996; p. inside back cover; Reprinted by permission of ProBusiness Services, Inc.

Exhibit 18-33: "The Evolution of Payroll Processing;" PVN; Volume 3, Issue 4; August 1995; p. back cover; Reprinted by permission of The Ultimate Software Group

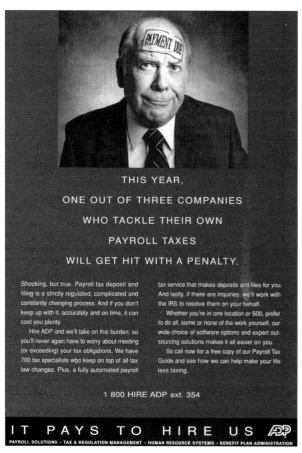

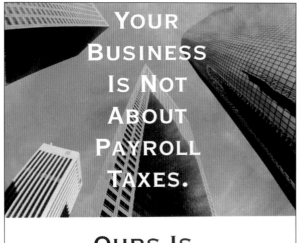

200

New Management Approaches – Self-Directed Teams

Given the growing complexity of the payroll function and the increasing demands placed upon it, many payroll organizations began in the early '90s to move away from the traditional organizational structure consisting of manager, supervisors, and employees. In its place, new organizational structures, often referred to as self-directed teams, were being designed, tested, and implemented in many payroll organizations.

Within the new organizational structure, the number of supervisory levels were reduced or eliminated. With the elimination of these middle positions, managers delegated more of the work and more of the authority for the work to payroll employees. Payroll employees began to develop and assume highly specialized payroll skills and as a team began to share greater accountability for total payroll performance. Managers, in turn, began to focus more on providing guidance and direction to team members. Many managers began to view themselves as team leaders and mentors versus managers. Experimentation with new organizational structures permitted payroll organizations to reduce headcount and cost while providing more growth opportunities for payroll employees. Overall, self-directed teams and variations of this approach have helped to keep pace with the realities of the new workplace.

The Arrival of the Payroll Telecommuter

By the end of the 20th century, millions of Americans had become telecommuters, working out of their homes. In order to attract and retain needed skill sets, some payroll organizations began to pilot this new concept as well. Enabled by new technologies that provided greater access to information, these organizations learned that payroll accounting, administration, and even customer service functions could be effectively performed by telecommuters.

Profile of a Typical Payroll Organization of the Nineties

The Digital Equipment Corporation payroll organization was typical of many company payroll organizations of the period. Throughout the nineties it had supported a series of changes, including multiple divestitures and acquisitions along with major revisions to its compensation and benefit programs. With an increasing company focus on doing more with less, heavy emphasis was placed on total quality management and process reengineering initiatives. Payroll began to operate as part of a shared service center. Headcount and cost of product became important metrics. Payroll for Canadian operations was transferred to the U.S. and renewed interest was given to alternative payroll solutions including outsourcing and third-party software products to replace its reliable but inflexible in-house software. With a growing focus on global versus national competition, the company purchased SAP for its financial operations and PeopleSoft for its human resource administration needs. By early 1998 the Digital Equipment Corporation payroll organization was beginning to prepare for the implementation of an integrated human resource and payroll software environment. By mid-1998, plans were interrupted when the company was acquired by the Compaq Computer Corporation. In subsequent months, Compaq decided to outsource payroll. This transition would ultimately extend over two years. Throughout this entire period, the Digital payroll team and its technical support resources (Exhibit 18-34), like so many other payroll organizations of the period, performed their jobs well and continued to deliver timely and accurate services to clients, in spite of

Exhibit 18-34: Photo of Digital Equipment Payroll Team, Compaq Computer Corporation – left to right (row 1) Anna Lipofsky, Maureen Margraf, Ken Bourgeois, Kathy Catineau (row 2) Maria Cashmon, Carmen Vargas, Judy Ortiz, Gail Rogers, Hae Hart (row 3) Kathy Quigley, Deborah Gomez, Claire McLellan, Jim Visconti, and Dan Tripp

Exhibit 18-35: " After
10 Years with APA, at
the Age of 31, Daniel
J. Maddux Becomes
Executive Director;"
Payroll Exchange;
Volume 17, No. 6,
June 1992; p. front
cover

Exhibit 18-36: "Carol
Franket, CPP APA's
First President-Elect;"
Payroll Exchange;
Volume 15, No. 8;
September 1990; p.
front cover

the fact that many of their jobs would be eliminated at the end of the transition.

American Payroll Association Contributes to Payroll Progress

The growth occurring in the payroll industry
during this final decade of the century and the
millennium can be seen in the activities and the
accomplishments of the payroll industry's professional association under the direction of the
Association's Executive Director, Daniel J.
Maddux (Exhibit 18-35).

At the same time that Dan Maddux became
Executive Director of APA, PAYTECH Magazine
became the APA's official membership publication, succeeding *Payroll Exchange.* PAYTECH
was joined in October 1993 by *Payroll Views &
News.* To accommodate the expanding needs of
its more sophisticated membership, in 1999 APA
folded *PVN* into a new publication, *APA's
Employer Practices,* a quarterly journal providing
the latest in accounts payable, benefits and systems information, and introduced PAYBACK,
APA's first audio magazine on CD-ROM.

First President-Elect – Carol Franket, CPP

On May 2, 1990, the first payroll professional
was elected to the position of president-elect of
the APA. Carol Franket, CPP (Exhibit 18-36),
Director of Payroll Operations for the Edward J.
DeBartolo Corporation, was elected to succeed
the Founder and President, Donald W. Sharper,
beginning in 1991. Each year following Ms.
Franket's term, a new payroll professional has
been elected to lead the Association. Those
serving as president to date have included: Don
Soula of Texaco (1992), Lisbeth Green, CPP of
Intel (1993), Michael Jones of NYNEX (1994),
Mary Lou Koch-Hanners, CPP of Abbott
Laboratories (1995), Mary Jo Maley, CPP of
Vicorp (1996), Walter Shubert, CPP of Sony
Corporation (1997), Sue Darring, CPP of CSC
Pinnacle (1998), Maureen Reed, CPP, CGBA of
County of Loudoun, Virginia (1999), and Corey
Lehr, CPP of the University of Cincinnati (2000).

Emphasis on Education and Training

Development and training of payroll professionals (Exhibit 18-37) was a high priority
throughout the decade.

Exhibit 18-37: Illustration "Training & Development;" Payroll Exchange; Volume 15, No. 10; November 1990; p. front cover

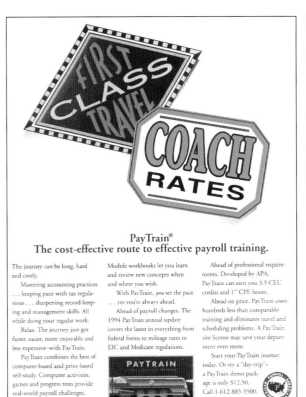

Exhibit 18-38: "First Class Travel, Coach Rates – PayTrain™"; PVN; Volume 2, Issue 2; April 1994; p. 5

The Certified Payroll Professional (CPP) Examination was accepted by the American Council on Education's (ACE) Credit by Examination program. This recognition permitted those passing the examination to receive up to 12 college-level credits from accepting institutions of higher learning. (12) By May 1998, the APA, in alliance with the American Association of Community Colleges, was offering the Payroll Professional Learning Series to college-level students on a national scale including three courses – Primary Payroll Skills, Essential Payroll Skills, and Advanced Payroll Skills. (13)

In addition to a series of educational publications and courses now available to payroll employees, including *The Payroll Source®, Payroll Currently, The Payroll Manager's Guide to Successful Direct Deposit, The Guide to Global Payroll Management, Preparing for Year-End, Foundations of Payroll Practice,* and *Effective Payroll Administration and Management,* APA introduced a new computer-based self-study program called "PayTrain®" (Exhibit 18-38) to facilitate the training and development of payroll employees across the country. In 1995, APA opened The Payroll Learning Center in San Antonio, Texas, with two classrooms containing individual computerized workstations and the latest in training technology, enabling APA to provide a comprehensive, hands-on learning experience.

In 1997, it also activated the APA Web site (www.americanpayroll.org) to provide payroll professionals with online resources never before possible including up-to-the minute information on legislative and regulatory issues, interactive Q&A forums, searchable APA membership directories, payroll-specific vendor information, and live discussions and teleconferencing capabilities. (14)

Influencing Legislative Outcomes

In 1993, Carolyn Kelley, APA's Director of Education, Government and Public Affairs, was appointed to serve as the first chair of the IRS Information Reporting Program Advisory Committee (IRPAC). She served on IRPAC for three years, and APA has had a representative on IRPAC since then.

By 1993, APA membership had increased to over 10,000 members and payroll organizations throughout the U.S. were collecting in excess of $300 billion (Exhibit 18-39) from salary and wage payments, giving the APA greater influence on Capitol Hill. By 1999, membership exceeded 18,000, and payroll professionals were collecting more than $1.2 trillion for the U.S. Treasury.

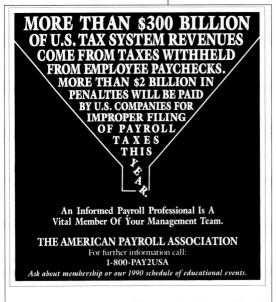

Exhibit 18-39: "Payroll Professional Publicity Campaign;" Payroll Exchange; Volume 15, No 2; February 1990; p. 27

In 1994, APA Member Nora Daly, CPP was appointed Chair of the prestigious IRS Commissioner's Advisory group (CAG), the first person from the field of payroll management to chair the CAG. At the time, Daly was a Senior Analyst for Payroll Taxes at Pacific Bell. (15)

During this decade, the APA and its members became effective change-agents and worked as partners with Congress, the IRS, the SSA, and various other government agencies and committees, as well as organizations within the banking community to identify and resolve many payroll-related issues as illustrated by the following:

- It addressed payroll-related problems associated with the proposed Omnibus Budget Reconciliation Act of 1993 related to educational assistance programs, reporting service payments, and health benefit reporting. (16) Work in this area brought national press coverage appearing in both the *New York Times* and the *Wall Street Journal.* (17)

- It participated in the design of the North American Free Trade Agreement Implementation Act (NAFTA) as it related to mandated electronic funds transfer for the collection of federal depository taxes. (18)

- It testified on multiple occasions before Congress on complex administrative issues surrounding health care reform (19) and won a legislative victory on health benefit reporting rules. (20)

- It worked with IRS' Office of Tax Forms & Publications by presenting recommendations to improve forms and instructions. (21)

- It testified before the National Commission on Restructuring the Internal Revenue Service to sensitize lawmakers on the impact of law changes on business systems. (22)

- It appeared before the House Ways and Means Subcommittee on Human Resources to recommend actions that would accomplish welfare goals regarding the collection of child support from delinquent parents while making it easier for employers to comply (23) and worked aggressively toward a single collection point within each state via EFT/EDI. (24)

- It participated in federal and state initiatives on the Simplified Tax and Wage Reporting System (STAWRS) as part of Vice President Gore's National Performance Review and received support from the White House for its efforts. (25 & 26)

- It joined forces with major federal and state government agencies to form a proactive work group to address issues related to child support payments.

- It conducted a payroll survey on pre-note procedures and presented findings and recommendations to make the process optional to a NACHA subcommittee. Optional pre-notification was later approved by NACHA and became effective on September 20, 1996 based, in part, on the efforts of payroll professionals. (27)

- It published an updated inventory of state pay media laws and launched a collaborative effort with NACHA to influence changes in state laws to permit employers greater latitude in utilizing direct deposit. (28 - 30)

In the National Limelight

During the last decade of the millennium, members of the payroll industry were placed in the forefront of national attention on a number of occasions.

In-flight Video Tells Public About Payroll

During 1993, APA ran a series of 90-second films promoting payroll and the American Payroll Association on American Airlines' long distance domestic and international flights as part of a 30-minute video magazine called Minding Your Business. In total, 8,000 flights carried the clip, which was viewed by one million business travelers.

*Exhibit 18-40:
Illustration for
"National Payroll
Week;" PVN; Volume
4, Issue 4; August
1996; pp. 7-9*

Using Television to Educate Taxpayers on W-2s

In 1997, between December 15 and January 31, APA appeared on television sets across the nation helping to explain Form W-2 and the early part of the tax reporting process to some 400,000 viewers. (31) Again in 1998 the American Payroll Association reached over 800,000 viewers in disseminating W-2 information on local channels across the country. (32)

APA's Dan Maddux Founds Annual National Payroll Week

As part of his continuing efforts to emphasize the positive results of the U.S. tax withholding system and to promote the payroll profession, APA's Executive Director, Dan Maddux, designated the week of September 16-20, 1996 as the first National Payroll Week (Exhibit 18-40). This high profile event included a full-page insert in *USA Today* (33) plus the support of President Clinton and the White House (Exhibit 18-41). Since 1996, National Payroll Week has become an established and highly recognized and celebrated event to commemorate workers in America and those payroll professionals who

serve employees, employers and the government.

At the End of the Millennium

By the end of the decade, the payroll profession had made great strides. Payroll professionals were better educated and more equipped than ever to do their jobs. Successful payroll managers and employees were better compensated than ever and were in great demand. Never before had payroll professionals been faced with such complex and fast moving change as in the nineties. Never before had they demonstrated such leadership and such competency. Never before had they been so needed.

Thanks to the opportunities and challenges afforded to payroll in the nineties, images and impressions have been changed. Management and government agencies alike have gained a fresh, new appreciation of the importance of payroll and the complexity of the function. Payroll professionals can be rightly proud of their individual and collective accomplishments during this last decade of the twentieth century!

*Exhibit 18-41:
Message from
President Clinton;
PAYTECH; Volume 6,
Issue 1;
January/February
1997; p. front cover*

Reference Sources

1. "DOL Urges Employer Preparation for Y2K Issues;" Payroll Views & News; APA, New York; October 1998; Volume 6; Issue 5; p. 4

2. "IRS Issues Temporary Regs Allowing Limited Electronic Form W-4 Implementation;" Payroll Views & News; APA; New York; February 1995; Volume 3; Issue 1; p. 1

3. "Electronic Wage Reporting – Now More than Ever;" Payroll Views & News; APA; New York; October 1998; Volume 6; Issue 5; pp. 1-2

4. "Access the IRS by Computer;" PAYTECH; APA; New York; Volume 5; Issue 2; p. 15

5. "Cross-Border Rules Approved by Council;" Payroll Views & News; APA; New York; December 1995; Volume 3; Issue 6; p. 5

6. "Employee Leasing Offers Additional Benefits for Employers;" Payroll Views & News; APA; New York; October 1996; Volume 4; Issue 5; p. 14

7. "The Virtual Corporation is Coming;" Moore; Tanna L.; Payroll Views & News; APA; New York; April 1995; Volume 3; Issue 2; pp. 1 & 5

8. "Time and Attendance: A Complete Staff Solution;" Holland, Randall; Payroll Views & News; APA; New York; June 1997; Volume 5; Issue 3; pp. 6-7

9. "Current Trends in Employee Attendance Systems;" Barrington, Mary E.; Payroll Views & News; APA; New York; June 1997; Volume 5; Issue 3; pp. 6-7

10. "Voice Response Technology Can Improve Your Direct Deposit Program;" Haug, Leonard A.; PAYTECH; APA; New York; March /April 1993; Volume 2; Issue 2; pp. 48-49

11. "Cut Your Costs and Time by Using the Internet;" Clements, Tom; Payroll Views & News; APA; New York; October 1997; Volume 5; Issue 5; pp. 10-11

12. "CPPs Now Eligible for College Credit;" Payroll Views & News; APA; New York; August 1996; Volume 4; Issue 4; p. 3

13. "APA Takes Payroll to the College Level;" Payroll Views & News; APA; New York; April 1998; Volume 6; Issue 2; p. 11

14. "Conferencing the Online Way;" PAYTECH; APA; New York; January/February 1996; Volume 5; Issue 1; pp. 10-11

15. "Nora Daly Appointed CAG Chair;" Payroll Views & News; APA; New York; April 1994; Volume 2; Issue 2; p. 5

16. "APA Receives Coverage in National Newspapers;" PAYTECH; APA; New York; November/December 1993; Volume 2; Issue 6; p. 8

17. "APA Impacts President's Tax Bill;" Payroll Views & News; APA; New York; October 1993; Volume 1; Issue 1; p. 1

18. "NAFTA to Require Electronic Deposits;" Payroll Views & News; APA; New York; February 1994; Volume 2; Issue 1; p. 1

19. "APA Testifies for Second Time Before Congress on Health Care;" Payroll Views & News; APA; New York; April 1994; Volume 2; Issue 2; p. 1

20. "Legislative Win for Payroll;" Payroll Views & News; APA; New York; December, 1994; Volume 2; Issue 6; p. 1

21. "APA Meets with IRS Tax Forms & Publications for the Fifth Time;" Payroll Views & News; APA; New York; June 1994; Volume 2, Issue 3; p. 1

22. "APA Testifies on IRS Restructuring;" Payroll Views & News; APA; New York; June 1997; Volume 5; Issue 3; p. 1

23. "Association Urges Lawmakers to Make Reforms Payroll-Friendly;" Payroll Views & News; APA; New York; April 1995; Volume 3; Issue 2; p. 1

24. "OCSE Eases Child Support With Centralized Processing;" Callahan, Carol; Payroll Views & News; APA; New York; December 1998; Volume 6; Issue 6

25. "STAWRS Project Moves Forward to Ease Payroll Reporting Burden;" Payroll Views & News; APA; New York; June 1995; Volume 3; Issue 3; p. 1

26. "APA Gets Nod From White House for Association's STAWRS Efforts;" Payroll Views & News; APA; New York; August, 1995; Volume 3; Issue 4; p. 1

27. "Pre-notification Becomes Optional;" Markus, Carinda; PAYTECH; APA; New York; September/October 1996; Volume 5; Issue 5; pp. 48-49

28. "APA Launches Direct Deposit Campaign;" Payroll Views & News; APA; New York; December 1996; Volume 4; Issue 6; p. 6

29. "APA, NACHA Work to Promote Direct Deposit;" Payroll Views & News; APA; New York; February 1997; Volume 5; Issue 1; p. 7

30. "APA Member Achieves Direct Deposit Success in UT;" Payroll Views & News; APA; New York; August 1998; Volume 6; Issue 4; p. 3

31. "APA Explains Form W-2 on Television;" Payroll Views & News; APA; New York; April 1997; Volume 5; Issue 2; p. 1

32. "APA Reaches Public on Importance of W-2;" Payroll Views & News; APA; New York; April 1998; Volume 6; Issue 2; p. 1

33. "APA Boosts National Payroll Week;" Payroll Views & News; APA; New York; June 1996; Volume 4; Issue 3; pp. 1 & 11

CHAPTER 19:
Looking Back With Pride and Moving Ahead With Confidence

Looking Back With Pride

The payroll process and the payroll profession have certainly come a long way since ancient times. Some would say that the job has become much easier. For one thing, payroll employees no longer have to maintain pay records on stone or clay tablets! (Exhibit 19-1) They also don't have to worry about handling cash and being robbed or murdered on payday. So from these perspectives, the job is certainly both easier and safer than it has ever been in the past.

However, the work has also changed dramatically. The contemporary payroll professional has a much more complicated job than that of his predecessors - the scribe, the clerk, the book-keeper, and the accountant of the past.

The focus of the job has shifted from adding hours or pieces of work completed and calculating and disbursing pay to something much more

. . . and YOU thought hammering out the payroll was hard!

robust. Today's payroll professional is a hybrid individual – part technical expert, part tax expert, part compensation and benefits expert, part financial expert, part banking expert, and part communications expert. The job is less clerical and more professional. No longer viewed as a "back room" employee, the payroll professional of the late 20th century has earned her or his position as a true business partner within the organizational hierarchy of every U.S. company.

The tools of the trade have certainly changed. The rate of change in the pay process and the profession has been most notable over the last century. Just one hundred years ago, most payrolls were still maintained by hand. By the end of the twentieth century, hard copy ledger books and writing utensils have been replaced with desktop computers and software programs of awesome power. These new tools have enabled the payroll professional to process a transaction, make an out-of-cycle payment, create an accounting entry, correct an error, or even produce an entire payroll in a fraction of the time it took in the past. Tools in use by the end of the twentieth century could not have even been conceptualized a hundred years earlier. Even now, the movement toward new generation Web-based products and services that will enable the worker of the 21st century to become almost totally self sufficient in matters pertaining to human resources and payroll administration exceeds comprehension for many — and yet this reality is just around the corner.

However, only through the combined accomplishments of the past have the payrolls of the present and the future been made possible. Contemporary payroll professionals owe much to past generations for their struggles, failures, and successes.

As illustrated in this book, the history of payroll is a dynamic one that is closely linked and intertwined with American history and the evolution of business and technology.

There is much that can be learned from a study of the history of American payroll, and it

Exhibit 19-1: Illustration from American Payroll Association Birthday Cards Sent to Members. Copyright 1993

209

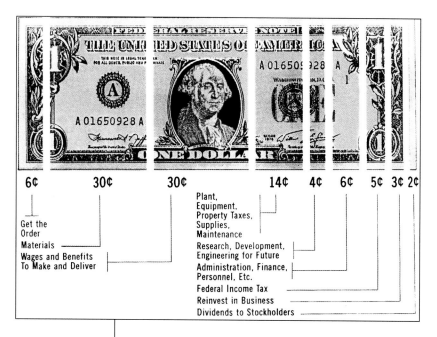

6¢ 30¢ 30¢ 14¢ 4¢ 6¢ 5¢ 3¢ 2¢

Get the
Order

Materials
Wages and Benefits
To Make and Deliver

Plant,
Equipment,
Property Taxes,
Supplies,
Maintenance

Research, Development,
Engineering for Future

Administration, Finance,
Personnel, Etc.

Federal Income Tax

Reinvest in Business

Dividends to Stockholders

Exhibit 19-2: Allocation of spending by a company in the 1970's; The Norton Spirit; April 1975; Volume 61, No. 8; p. 4; Courtesy of Collections of Worcester Historical Society, Worcester, Massachusetts

Exhibit 19-3: Political Cartoon with Paymaster in Background; U.S. News and World Report; July 5, 1999; p. 8; Reprinted by permission of artist, Richard Thompson

is the author's hope that readers of this book will not only take great pride in the history of the profession and the process, but will be encouraged to pursue further studies that can help prepare the way and the profession for the new millennium.

Moving Ahead With Confidence

Any prediction for the future is beyond the scope of this book and would likely be wrong. It is, however, highly probable that wages and other forms of compensation will continue to represent a sizable portion of every dollar spent by companies as it has in the past (Exhibit 19-2) and that this probability will likely translate into job security for most payroll professionals.

However, the only real certainty is continued change. That the nature of work will continue to change is beyond doubt. The definition of compensation and the formula by which it is calculated will most certainly continue to change. Benefits will change. Tax withholding, payment, and reporting requirements and processes will change. How, when, and where payroll work is performed in the future will also change as businesses change and technology advances. Traditional pay cycles may, as some predict, be replaced with a flow of continuous pay issued to workers as work is completed.

However, no matter what comes, the payroll industry and its members have never been better prepared for the future than they are now. As long as payroll professionals remain flexible and continue to develop the new skills that will be needed for the future and strive to be part of the solution rather than part of the problem, payroll professionals (or whatever they are called in the future) will do fine.

Remember the power of a positive attitude! Anything is possible. Who knows, the payroll professional in the coming century may even finally escape from the outdated image of the paymaster as that "person behind the caged bars or window" (Exhibit 19-3). Oh well, as history has taught us, not all change happens quickly.

Among all this uncertainty, one thing is absolutely sure – accurate and timely delivery of pay (regardless of how advanced the technology becomes) will continue to be a key measurement of success.

Somehow, payroll professionals will never escape the fact that they will only be as good as their most recent pay cycle. Some things will never change! But then again, payroll professionals love the pressure!

Index

Abbott Laboratories 202
Accounting, ancient origins and evolution . . . 1
Acquisitions and mergers 56, 188
Across the Plains in 1864 With Additional
   Paymaster Samuel C. Staples 53, 54
Adams, John G. 46, 47
Adding machines, early 69
Addressing machines, importance of 99
Addressograph & Addressograph-
   Multigraph . . . . 68, 69, 82 - 84, 95, 156
ADP, Inc. 139, 140, 179, 200
AFL-CIO 138, 142
African-
   Americans . . . 40, 41, 46, 51, 53, 62, 63, 137
Ain, Mark S. 179
Alabama & Chattanooga Railroad 55
Alvord, Benjamin 49
Amalgamated Metals Company 102
American Accounting Association 61
American Arithmometer 68, 69
American Bankers Association 112, 113
American Council on Education (ACE) 203
American Electric Railway Association . 112, 113
American Payroll Association
   birth and early years . . . . 169 - 172
   establishment of National
      Payroll Week 205, 206
   focus on education 184, 202, 203
   growth and expansion 183, 184
   legislative successes 203, 204
   roster of current and past presidents . . . 202
American Sales Book Company 131
American Telephone and Telegraph
   Company 82, 100, 124, 128, 151
American Tobacco Company 56
American Woolen Company 100
Americanisms
   eagle screams 55
   ghost walks 34, 110, 198
   paymaster's car 54
Andrews, Timothy P. 38
Apprenticeship Indentures 13, 14
Apthorp, Charles 7
Aristides 1
Arithmograph 69
Arlington Mills 123, 125
Armored cars and
   services 89, 101, 102, 110, 111, 114
Armored Service Corporation 110
Armour Company 124
Army paymaster general office
   amended 23
   established 17
Army paymaster generals 17, 20, 24, 38

Army paymaster's manual from Civil War . . . 37
Arnold's Ready Reckoner 29
Arts, literature and science,
   paymasters in 17, 23, 26, 27, 39, 40,
      41, 50, 52, 53, 75 - 79, 98, 127, 128, 148
A.T. Kearney 187
Athenian Disbursements Tablet 1
Atlantic & Pacific Railroad 55
Audits, IRS 176
Austin, Texas 133
Baldwin Locomotive 67, 122, 123
Baltimore & Ohio Railroad 55
Baltimore, Maryland 111, 120
Bandit "Proof" pay-car 89
Banking 24, 26, 61, 90, 112, 113, 159,
                  160, 176, 189
Barter bookkeeping system 13
Bartlett, Josiah 19
Bartlett-Snow 125
Becket, Jim 178
Bell Telephone 109
Bendix 145
Blair, Michael 164
Block, H&R 128
Bookkeepers 29, 68, 84, 86, 98, 99
Bookkeeping, double entry, origin of 5
Bookman, Hazel Gibson 137
Boott Cotton Mills 32
Boss as paymaster 84, 87
Boston Manufacturing Company 31
Bowery Savings Bank 124
Braddock, Edward 7
Brainerd, Francis G 75
Brice, Benjamin W. 38, 49
Bridgeport, Connecticut 133
Brink's Express Company 110, 111, 114
British Army, paymaster generals and pay
   processes of 5, 6, 7
Brown, W.E. 53
Bundy Time Recorder Company 61
Bureau of Internal Revenue 126
Bureau of National Affairs (BNA) 197
Burke, Sir Edmund 6
Burroughs 68, 69, 84, 86, 133, 143, 152
Business Guide or Guide to Safe Methods of . . .
   Business 59
Business Software, Inc (BSI) 180
Caesar, Julius 2
Calculating machines 85, 95
Calcumeter 69
Cambria Steel 67
Canadian Payroll Association, The 190
Carbon paper 61
Card reader 147

Card sorters 108, 134, 154

Casement, Dan and Jack 5

Cash payrolls 73, 89, 111

Cavalry, U.S. paymasters and pay
    processes . . . . 49 - 53

CCH, Incorporated 197

CD-ROM technology 191, 197

Central & Southern Pacific Railroad 55

Central Pacific Railroad 53, 54

Centralization, of payroll
    operations 18, 87, 133, 170, 173

Ceridian 193

Certified Payroll Professional (CPP) . . . 184, 203

Chaldean-Babylonian Empire 1

Check cashing and protection
    devices 88, 90, 96, 102

Check versus cash, as pay method . 77, 87 - 90,
          102, 103, 112, 113, 139, 140, 141, 146

Chicago Ornamental Iron Company 110

Chicago Rapid Transit Company 110

Chicago Surface Railway Lines 89

Child support, evolution and payroll role . . 174

Citizens Union National Bank of
    Louisville, Kentucky 112

City and municipal payrolls 85, 86, 87, 88,
               137, 138, 142, 153, 156

Civil War, paymasters and pay
    processes of . . . . 37 - 47

Client/server technology 190, 191

Clinton, President William 205, 206

COBOL 148, 152, 153, 191

Coca Cola 120

Colonial and pre-revolutionary America,
    industries and pay processes of . . 13, 14, 15

Columbia University 114

Columbus, Ohio 139

Commissioner's Advisory Group (CAG) 204

Compaq Computer Corporation 201

Comptometers 68, 84

Computer Science Corporation 164

Computers . . . . . 144, 145, 147, 148, 151 - 155

Connecticut 139

Continental army, paymasters and
    pay processes of . . . . 17 - 20

Continental Congress 17

Continental Notes 19

Contingencies, payroll readiness for . . 164, 165

Control Data Business Centers 179

Control Data Corporation 193

Cook, M.J. 153

Copley, John Singleton 17

Corn Exchange Bank 88

Corporation, birth of British 11

Country pay 13

County of Loudon, Virginia 202

Crocker, Burbank & Company 68, 149

Crompton & Knowles Loom Works 72

Cross Border Council and payments 189

CSC Pinnacle 202

Custer, Elizabeth B. 49, 50

Cyborg Systems, Inc. 164, 177, 178

Daly, Nora 204

Darring, Sue 202

Dashiell, Jeremiah Yellott 25, 26

Data General 161, 163

Data processing departments, early 153

De Bree, John 47

Deductions, payroll 2, 7, 9, 37, 47, 51, 55,
          81, 82, 100, 124, 125, 132, 138

Defense Bonds, payroll deduction
    plans during WWII 124, 125

Deltek Systems 198

Denniston & Denniston, Inc. 198

Detroit, Michigan 139

Dewitt, Larry 120

Digital Equipment Corporation . . 147, 161, 162,
                165, 192, 201

Disk technology 191, 196, 197

Dodge, Francis S. 52, 62

Downing, John R. 112

Downsizing, of the 90s 187

Du Pont 81, 82, 83

Eaton, J.H. 37

Edison Company 74

Edison, Thomas 70

Edward J. DeBartolo Corporation 202

Eighties (1980s), issues, challenges,
    technology, payroll comes of age . . 169-184

Electric accounting machines . . . 130, 137, 141,
                143, 144

Electronic filing 188, 189

Electronic pay statements 189

Electronic payroll direct deposit . 159, 160, 189

Elliott Addressing Machine 129

Employee number card, early example of . .7 2

Employee Self-Service, direction
    of the 90s 192

Employee stock purchase plans, early 100

Ensign Company 95

Essex Company 58

Esso Refinery 123

Estrada, Jose 26

Etymology of pay-related words 2, 5

European and British heritage . . . . 5 - 11

Everett Mills 75

Factory gate and gate-keepers 32

Factory system, birth of large corporations . . 56

Fair Labor Standards Act . . . 108, 121, 122, 173

Fargo, William G. 110

Fay-Sholes 68

Federal pay-as-you-go income tax
    plan . . . . 126 -128

Federal Reserve System, establishment of . . . 67

Felt & Tarrant 68, 82, 84

Fesler & Evans 9 0

F.H. McGraw & CO 43

First Federal Savings & Loan of Lincoln, Nebraska 159

Flexible compensation and benefits take root 174

Florsheim Shoe Company 110

FLS 197

Ford, Henry 74, 97, 98

Ford Motor Company 74, 97, 98, 34, 140, 141, 178

Form 1040, first use 79

Form W-2 . . . . 189, 191

Form W-4 . . . . 126, 173, 188

Forms and forms processing equipment 130, 132, 133, 146 192, 197

Forrest, Douglas French 44

Fox, Henry 6

Fox, Steven 6

Franket, Carol 202

Franklin Mills 58

Fraud 77, 78, 90, 161

Friden 144, 153, 154

Fringe benefits, growing impact in the 80s . 138

Galaxy Technologies, Inc. 198

Gallup, David L. 55

Galloway, Lee 93

General Electric 124

GENESYS Software Systems, Inc. 177, 194

Girl Paymaster, WWII 123

Gleason, A.H. & Company 89

Global payrolls, first Global Payroll Management Conference 190

Gooding, James Henry 46

Goodman, Richard French 40, 41

Goodyear Rubber Company 56

Graduated income tax, implementation . . . 156

Graphical User Interface (GUI) 190

Gray Institute Association 112

Great Depression, paymasters and pay processes of . . . . 107 - 114

Greek and Roman pay practices 1, 2

Green, Bill 184

Green, Lisbeth, CPP 202

Gross and net off-reckonings, British 7

Gunn Partners 187

Hackett Group, The 187

Hall-Welter Company 96

Hambleton, Samuel 24

Hanford, California 55

Hanford, James Madison 55

Hart, Schaffner & Marx 77, 110

Hayes Wage Computing Tables 59

Heald Corporation 86

Health and Safety, late 19th century 58

Held Electric Accounting Company 135

Held, Harold W. 135

Henderschott, F.C. 74, 75

Henry Ford Hospital 164

Hewlett-Packard 161, 162, 178

H.J. Heinz Company 57

Hollerith, Herman 108

Homer, Winslow 40, 58

Honeywell 145, 146, 161

Hope Factory 33

Hughes Aircraft Employees Federal Credit Union 50

Hults, Ellsworth H. 41, 42

Human Resources function, origin and evolution 73, 74, 103

Humor, payroll-related 8, 90, 111, 127, 134, 182, 183, 209

Hutton, William Rich 26, 27

Illinois Chamber of Commerce . . 112, 113, 114

I. Miller & Sons 138

Income tax
British origins 10, 11
Civil War 37, 38
progressive tax of 1913 67

Income tax withholding and reporting 79, 83, 86, 100, 101, 126, 128, 139, 147, 148, 156, 175, 188

Independence Bureau 83

Indiana 139

Industrial revolution
American 31, 56
British 8, 9

Infinium 194

Information Science Corporation 164

Integral Systems 177, 178

Integrated payroll and human resource solutions 177, 180, 187

Intel Corporation 161, 202

Interactive Voice Response (IVR) technology 192, 193

Internal Revenue Service Information Reporting Program Advisory Committee (IRPAC) . . 203

International Association of Government Labor Officials 122

International Business Machines (IBM) 70, 133, 140, 144, 145, 147,148, 154, 162, 163, 164, 189, 193

International Dial Recorder 96

International Harvester 112, 124, 164

International Money Machine Company . 95, 97

International Payroll Machine 95, 97

International Resistance Company 144

International Time Recorder Company 68, 70, 82, 96

Internet 193

Intranet 193

James Boys, The 52

JAT Software 196

J. D. Edwards 194

Jones & Laughlin 67

Jones, Michael 202

Keeler, William F. . . . . 37, 42 - 44

Keen, W. Ralph 139, 140

Kelley, Carolyn 203
Kellogg Company 77, 107
King, Joseph T. 39
Koch-Hanners, Mary Lou 202
Kodak 155
Kraft Cheese 124
Kronos, Incorporated 179, 180, 198
Larned, Benjamin 38
Lathem 199
Lawrence Textile Mills 75
Lee, Robert E. 45
Lehr, Corey, CPP 202
Lewis, Meriwether 23
Leyendecker, J.C. 76, 77
Liberty Loans 82
Lincoln, Abraham 46
Littleton, A.C. 1
Local income tax, first cities to
    implement 138, 139
Local Area Network (LAN) 191
Love, John 25
Lubbick, Donald 126
Lumber industry, 19th century pay
    processes 57
Lund, Adelaide 78
Luttenberg, Henry 140
Lynch, John R. 62, 63
MacAdam, G.M. 87
Maddux, Daniel J. 202, 205
Magnetic media reporting 175, 189
Maley, Mary Jo, CPP 202
Management Science America (MSA) . 164, 177
Mann, Major James 44
Manpower, Inc. 176
Marchant Calculating Machines 82, 138
Massachusetts Electric Railway (ERA) 107
Mass production, early British forms 9
Mathews, Kit 181
Maumus, James C., CPP 165, 166
Maximum work hours 57, 58, 75
McConnell, H.H. 50
McCormack & Dodge 177
McLaughlin, Sam 182
McSteen, Martha A. 175
Meat Packing industry, paymasters and
    pay processes of "Packingtown" 77
Medicare, implementation of 156
Meilicke Calculators 82, 85
Merrimack Utility Company 120
Metropolitan Life 112, 124
Microcomputers, history of 161
Midland Die & Engraving Company 135
Military pay escorts 18, 25, 49, 51, 52
Mill bell, early time keeping device 31
Minicomputers, history of 161
Minimum wage
    beginning of U.S. debate on 107, 108
    British origins 10

Mobil Oil 189
Moley, Raymond C. 114
Money, origin of 2
Monroe Calculating Machine Company, ... 95
Monroe, Louisiana 153
Moore North America, Inc. . 130 - 133, 143, 144,
                                        146, 197
Moore, Samuel 131
Morrison-Knudsen Company 142
Morse and Walsh 68
Moynihan, Daniel 184
National Association of Corporate Training . 74
National Automated Clearing House
    Association (NACHA) . . . 159, 160, 176, 177,
                                        189, 204
National Cash Register
    (NCR) 138, 141, 142, 161, 162
National Commission on Law Observance
    and Enforcement 110
National Crime Commission 113, 114
National Payroll Week, founding of . . . 205, 206
New Deal 117, 120
New Jersey 101, 114
New York City . . . . 87 - 89, 111, 144, 145
New York State 101
New York Telephone, implementation
    of state income tax 147, 148
New York University 74
Nineties (1990s) themes, trends, technology,
    payroll environments of . . . . 187 - 206
Norfolk, Virginia 137, 138
North American Free Trade Agreement . . . 204
Norton 144, 210
NYNEX 202
O'Boyle, Fred 170, 171
Old West and expanding territories,
    paymasters and pay processes of . . . 23 - 27
Organizational structures and charts
    payroll 57, 70, 93
Overtime, Civil War dispute over 45
Pacific Bell 204
Pacific Mills 75
Pacioli 5
Packingtown 77
Paine, Thomas 10
Palfrey, William . . . . 17 - 20
Parmenter, Frederick A. 109
Payday at the Works, British 11
Pay envelopes 75, 97, 98
Pay frequency laws 57, 122
Pay lines, offices, and windows 67, 76, 77, 82,
                            83, 104, 107, 123, 125, 140
Pay message, national debate
    on proper use 120, 121
Paying the Bounties, Walt Whitman 39
Paymaster, British origin and evolution of . . . 5
Paymaster diaries, ... 24, 42, 44, 53
Paymasters, images of . 41, 42, 50, 76, 104, 210

Paymasters, Inc. 139
Payroll and Human Resources,
    historical relationships 177
Payroll and the 21st century . . . . 209 - 210
Payroll clerks   1, 6, 7, 11, 16, 23, 37 - 40, 41, 42,
            44, 45, 47, 51, 71 - 73, 78, 93, 134
Payroll, early process flow diagram of 94
Payroll robberies   19, 25, 49, 51, 52, 89, 90, 109,
                                    110, 161
Payteller, the 85
PDS 177
Pennsylvania Railroad 112
PeopleSoft 191, 195, 201
Personal income tax filing deadline
    change (1940s) 128
Philadelphia Chamber of Commerce 122
Philadelphia, Pennsylvania 139
Philco 145, 146
Phillips-Jones Corporation 142
Pierce, John 20
Polybius 2
Porter-Cable Machine Company 82, 85
Post-Civil War, paymasters and pay
    processes . . . . 49 - 63
Post-World War I, paymasters and pay
    processes . . . . 93 - 104
Post-World War II, paymasters and pay
    processes . . . . 137 - 149
Pre-Civil War, paymasters and pay
    processes . . . . 29 - 34
Pre-World War I, paymasters and pay
    processes . . . . 67 - 79
Printer carriage control tape, sample
    and use of 165
ProBusiness Services, Inc. 200
Professional Employer
    Organizations (PEO) 190
Programmers, as a new profession . . . 154, 155
Promontory, Utah 54
Railroads, paymasters and pay
    processes . . . . 53 - 57, 78, 79, 141 - 143
Reagan, President Ronald 184
Recognition Systems, Inc. 199
Record keeping, payroll forms &
    processes   1, 2, 15, 18, 31, 33, 38, 39, 42 -44,
        47, 51, 54, 58, 59, 68, 71 - 73, 89, 96, 103,
            118 -120, 122, 123, 129 - 131, 133 - 135,
155 Reed, Maureen, CPP, CGBA   202
Reflector Hardware Corporation 164
Remington, Frederic S. 52
Remington Rand Corporation . . . 132, 133, 144
Remote check printing, early 143, 144
Renatus, Flavius Vegetius 1
Republican National Committee 120
Revere, Paul and Son 15
Richardson, Dorothy 78
Rigby, Richard 6
Riggs National Bank 124

Robinson, George Foster 44, 45
Rochester, New York 132, 133
Rockwell, Norman 128
Roman army pay practices 1
Romboli, Mark 165
Roosevelt, Franklin Delano 117, 121
Royal McBee 145
Royal Weaving Mills 67
Rudkis, Jurgis 77
Ruml, Beardsley 126
Sacco, Nicola 109
Saginaw, Michigan 153, 154
Saint Louis, Missouri 139
Salt Lake City, Utah 155, 156
SAP 195, 201
Saugus Iron Works 13
Savage Arms Company 90
Savings, early payroll deduction programs . 100
Scientific management 70, 93, 94
Scoville Manufacturing 70
Scrip 33
Self-Directed Teams 201
Semple, James A. 47
Service Bureau industry, history and
    implementation of . . .135, 137, 139, 140, 154,
                                    188, 193, 200
Seward, Secretary of State 44, 45
Seventies (1970s), payroll implications
    of mini and microcomputer
    technology . . . . 159 - 166
Shared service centers 188
Sharper, Donald W. 170, 171
Shubert, Walter, CPP 202
Sick pay taxation 175
Simplex 56, 60, 61, 70, 181, 199
Sinclair, Upton 77, 78
Sixties (1960s), payroll participation in
    early computer utilization . . . . 151 - 156
Slater & Morrill Shoe Company 109
Smith, Adam 9
Social Security Act
    design and implementation . . 118 - 121, 131
    path NOT taken 118
    signing 117
Software industry
    birth 155
    early years 164
    shift from hardware to software 163
Software products
    of the 80s . . . . 177 - 182
    of the 90s 190, 191, 196, 197
Soldier pay records, WWII 123, 124
Somerville, Massachusetts 142
Sony Corporation 202
Soula, Don 202
South Bend Watch Company 71
Southern Railway System . . . . 141 - 143
Spanish-American War, paymasters of 61, 62, 63

Spermaceti "Manufactury" 15
Standard Oil Company 56
Standard Oil of New Jersey 124
Stanton, T.H. 53
Staples, Samuel C. 53
State income tax withholding . . . 139, 147, 148
Sternau, Howard E. 139
Stromberg Electric Company 96
Sunbeam Corporation 164
Sun Oil Company 142
Supervisor and manager, British origin of . . . 9
Supplemental flat tax rate 175
Sutler 25, 37, 40, 49, 50
Swift, John 45
Tabulating machines 69, 70, 108, 133
TALX Corporation 193, 199
Tape, DECTAPE, sample and use of 147
Taub, Henry 140, 141
Taub, Joseph 140
Taylor, Frederick W. 70
Tax Reform Act of 1986 173
Telecommuters 201
Teletypewriters, early use in remote
    check printing 143, 151
Termination laws
    British origins 10
    early forms 103
Tesseract 177, 178
Texas Instruments Inc. 189
Textile industry, pay processes of early 31
Textile strikes of the early 20th century 75
Thirty-hour workweek, experimentation
    during Great Depression 107
Time and attendance industry
    birth and evolution of . 58 - 61, 68, 70, 71, 96,
                                            122, 123
    of the 80s 179, 180, 181
    of the 90s . . . . 192, 198 - 199
TimeValue 196
Todd (Protectograph) Company . . 96, 129, 133
Toledo, Ohio 138
Total Quality Management 187
Towson, Nathan 24
Twentieth Century, early, paymasters
    and pay processes of 71, 72
Typewriters, ... 61
Ultimate Software 195, 200
Unemployment program, recognition
    of need for 73
Union Pacific Railroad 54
United Auto Workers 141
United Shoe Machinery Company 56
United States Distribution Corporation 110
United States Mail, use of for army pay
    delivery 53
United States Rubber Company 94, 124
United States Steel 56, 112
University of Cincinnati 200

USS Monitor 42, 43
Uxbridge Mills 103
Valley Forge "Red Tape" 19
Vanzetti, Bartolomeo 109
Vertex Systems, Inc. 180
Vicorp 202
Video screens and keyboards, early
    forms 151, 152
Virginia Company 13
Wage tables and tools, early manual . . . 29, 59
Walling, L. Melcafe 122
War bonds and sureties,
    paymaster 17, 23, 39, 41
Warrant men, British 8
Warren, James 17
Watkins, Edward G. . . . . 59 - 61
Waud, A. R. 40, 41
Wedgwood, Josiah 9
Welch Foods 178
Welfare programs
    British origins of 10
    "Welfare Consciousness" 57, 73
Wells Fargo 26
Wells, Henry 110
Western Electric 110
Western Resources 189
Western Union 108
Westinghouse Electric 56, 103, 104
Weyerhaeuser 151
Whaling industry, pay processes of 29, 30
Wham, Joseph W. 51
Whitbread, Samuel 10
Whitehurst, John 60
Whitman, Walt 38, 39
Wilson, Lillian 123
Wisconsin 107
Women in payroll   13, 47, 57, 61, 67, 70, 71, 82,
                                            123, 137
Workman's Compensation, beginnings of . . 93
World War I, paymasters and pay
    processes . . . . 81 - 90
Wright, Richard R. 63
Xerox 145, 155
Yawman & Erbe Manufacturing
    Company 95, 97
Year 2000 (Y2K) challenge 188
Year-end wage and tax reporting
    A Blue Christmas 165, 166
    full-time job 175
    impact on taxpayers 127, 128, 176
Youngstown Sheet & Tube Company 104
Zeck, Van 125
Zogbaum, Rufus F. 51, 52